Anthony Edwards

Edward's Cork Remembrancer

Tablet of memory

Anthony Edwards

Edward's Cork Remembrancer
Tablet of memory

ISBN/EAN: 9783743407862

Manufactured in Europe, USA, Canada, Australia, Japa

Cover: Foto ©ninafisch / pixelio.de

Manufactured and distributed by brebook publishing software (www.brebook.com)

Anthony Edwards

Edward's Cork Remembrancer

Cork Remembrancer;

OR,

TABLET OF MEMORY.

ENUMERATING

EVERY REMARKABLE CIRCUMSTANCE

THAT HAS HAPPENED IN THE

CITY AND COUNTY OF CORK,

AND IN THE KINGDOM AT LARGE.

INCLUDING ALL THE

MEMORABLE EVENTS IN GREAT BRITAIN;

WITH AN ACCOUNT OF ALL THE

BATTLES BY SEA AND LAND

IN THE PRESENT CENTURY.

ALSO, THE REMARKABLE

EARTHQUAKES, FAMINES, INUNDATIONS, STORMS, FROSTS, FIRES,

AND ALL OTHER ACCIDENTS OF MOMENT,

IN

EVERY QUARTER OF THE GLOBE,

FROM THE EARLIEST PERIOD, TO THE YEAR 1792.

BY ANTHONY EDWARDS,

PRINTER, BOOKSELLER AND STATIONER, CASTLE-STREET, CORK.

1792.

TO THE PUBLIC.

SINCE the publication of the *firſt* CORK-REMEMBRANCER, ſo many applications have been made for that very uſeful work, as to induce the preſent Editor to take up the matter, in which he has been countenanced by a moſt reſpectable and numerous liſt of Subſcribers; in gratitude for which, he has extended his plan much beyond his original intentions. Every event of material conſequence, that has happened, not only in theſe Kingdoms, but in every quarter of the Globe, he has with great labour, endeavoured to collect. Many inaccuracies will be found; but he ſincerely hopes none of material moment will appear: if ſuch ſhould be diſcovered, the very complex nature of the work, he hopes, will plead his excuſe with his numerous friends; for which, as alſo for the many favours he has received, he muſt ever remain with the greateſt gratitude.

THE PUBLIC's MOST OBEDIENT

HUMBLE SERVANT,

THE EDITOR.

A. Edwards, Bookfeller, Stationer, and Printer, oppofite the Merchants New Coffee-Houfe, No. 6, Caftle-ftreet, intends publifhing by Subfcription,

THE NEW CORK DIRECTORY:

In which the Chriftian and Sirnames, place of refidence, and occupation of every inhabitant of the City of Cork, of any note, will be alphabetically arranged; to which will be added,

The Bounds of the City Suburbs and Liberties thereof. Regulations refpecting Coaches, Chaifes, and Chairs to hire;—Buying and felling Coals, and the carriage thereof; —Weigh-Houfes, and Pawn-Brokers;—Ships and Boats coming to the Quay;—Cleaning the Streets, encumbering them with rubbifh, or projected Buildings;—Driving Cars or Carts;—Breaking Lamps; Watchmen;—Combination among Workmen;—Market Jurors and their authority;—Building Parapet Walls to the Quays; —Corn Trade and Bakers. Alfo,

A complete lift of the Freemen of the City of Cork, as they are called over on the Pannel;—Lifts of the Phyficians, Surgeons, and Attornies. Alfo, Commiffioners for taking Affidavits in the different Courts. A lift of the Bye Pofts from Cork, and the Days and Hours each go out and come in at. A Docket of the various Tolls and Cuftoms paid in the City and Liberties of Cork, by which the Country Gentleman and Farmer may know when and how they are impofed upon. Charitable Inftitutions in the City, the proper Objects to be admitted, and the Rules neceffary for their conforming to, the knowledge of which may prevent many from with-holding their charitable aid. A Schedule of the price of each piece of ftamped Paper or Parchment, for any particular purpofe; with many other ufeful Pieces of Information.

  Price to Subfcribers - - 2s. 8d.h.
  To Non-Subfcribers - - 3s. 3d.

☞ Some of the above Lifts being fubject to errors, by Deaths, Removals, Partnerfhips, &c. to render the firft attempt of this work perfect as poffible, the Editor will thankfully receive, and diligently attend to any information he may get in writing (previous to the firft of May, 1792) at No. 6, Caftle-ftreet, Cork, where a Book is opened for the purpofe of entering Subfcribers names, as alfo authentic information.

A CHRONOLOGICAL TABLE

OF

REMARKABLE EVENTS, DISCOVERIES, AND INVENTIONS,

FROM THE CREATION TO THE YEAR 1791.

BEFORE CHRIST.

4008 THE creation of the World, and Adam and Eve.
4007 The birth of Cain, the first who was born of a woman.
3017 Enoch, for his piety, is translated to heaven.
2352 The old world is destroyed by a deluge, which continued 377 days.
2247 The tower of Babel is built about this time by Noah's posterity, upon which God miraculously confounds their language, and thus disperses them into different nations.
2207 About this time, Noah is, with great probability, supposed to have parted from his rebellious offspring, and to have led a colony of some of the more tractable into the east, and there either he or one of his successors to have founded the ancient Chinese monarchy.
2234 The celestial observations are begun at Babylon, the city which first gave birth to learning and the sciences.

2188 Misraim,

2188 Misraim, the son of Ham, founds the kingdom of Egypt, which lasted 1663 years, down to the conquest of Cambyses, in 525 before Christ.

2059 Ninus, the son of Belus, founds the kingdom of Assyria, which lasted above 1000 years, and out of its ruins were formed the Assyrians of Babylon, those of Nineveh, and the kingdom of the Medes.

1985 The covenant of God made with Abram, when he leaves Haran to go into Canaan, which begins the 430 years of sojourning.

1961 The cities of Sodom and Gomorra are destroyed for their wickedness by fire from heaven.

1856 The kingdom of Argos, in Greece, begins under Inachus.

1822 Memnon, the Egyptian, invents the letters.

1715 Prometheus first struck fire from flints.

1635 Joseph dies in Egypt.

1574 Aaron born in Egypt, 1490, appointed by God first high-priest of the Israelites.

1571 Moses, brother to Aaron, born in Egypt, and adopted by Pharaoh's daughter, who educates him in all the learning of the Egyptians.

1556 Cecrops brings a colony of Saites from Egypt, into Attica, and begins the kingdom of Athens in Greece.

1555 Moses performs a number of miracles in Egypt, and departs from that kingdom, together with 600,000 Israelites, besides children, which completed the 430 years of sojourning: they miraculously pass through the Red Sea, and come to the desart of Sinai, where Moses receives from God, and delivers to the people, the Ten Commandments, and the other laws, and sets up the tabernacle, and in it the ark of the covenant.

1546 Scamander comes from Crete into Phrygia, and begins the kingdom of Troy.

1515 The Israelites after sojourning in the Wilderness forty years, are led under Joshua into the land of Canaan, where they fix themselves, after having subdued the natives; and the period of the sabbatical year commences.

EVENTS. 3

1503 The Deluge of Deucalion.
1496 The council of Amphictions established at Thermopylæ.
1493 Cadmus carried the Phenician letters into Greece, and built the Citadel of Thebes.
1490 Sparta built by Lacedemon.
1485 The first ship that appeared in Greece was brought from Egypt by Danaus, who arrived at Rhodes, and brought with him his fifty daughters.
1480 Troy built by Dardanus.
1452 The Pentateuch, or five first books of Moses, are written in the land of Moab, where he died the year following, aged 110.
1406 Iron is found in Greece, from the accidental burning of the woods.
1344 The kingdom of Mycenæ begins.
1326 The Isthmian games instituted at Corinth.
1325 The Egyptian canicular year began July 20th.
1307 The Olympic games instituted by Pelops.
1300 The Lupercalia instituted.
1294 The first colony came from Italy into Sicily.
1264 The second colony came from Italy into Sicily.
1252 The city of Tyre built.
1243 A colony of Arcadians conducted by Evander into Italy.
1233 Carthage founded by the Tyrians.
1225 The Argonautic expedition.
1204 The rape of Helen by Paris, which gave rise to the Trojan war, ending with the destruction of the city in 1184.
1176 Salamis in Cyprus built by Teucer.
1152 Ascanius builds Alba Longa.
1130 The kingdom of Sicyon ended.
1124 Thebes built by the Bœotians.
1115 The mariner's compass known in China.
1104 The expedition of the Heraclidæ into Peloponnesus; the migration of the Dorians thither; and the end of the kingdom of Mycenæ.
1102 The kingdom of Sparta commenced.
1070 The kingdom of Athens ended.

A 2　　　　1051 David

1051 David befieged and took Jerufalem.
1044 Migration of the Ionian colonies.
1008 The Temple is folemnly dedicated by Solomon.
 996 Solomon prepared a fleet on the Red Sea to fend to Ophir.
 986 Samos and Utica in Africa built.
 979 The kingdom of Ifrael divided.
 974 Jerufalem taken and plundered by Shifhak king of Egypt.
 911 The prophet Elijah flourifhed.
 894 Money firft made of gold and filver at Argos.
 884 Olympic games reftored by Iphitus and Lycurgus.
 873 The art of fculpture in marble found out.
 869 Scales and meafures invented by Phidon.
 864 The city of Carthage, in Africa, enlarged by queen Dido.
 821 Nineveh taken by Arbaces.
 814 The kingdom of Macedon begins.
 801 The city of Capua in Campania built.
 799 The kingdom of Lydia began.
 786 The fhips called *Triremes*, invented by the Corinthians.
 779 The race of kings in Corinth ended.
 776 The era of the Olympiads began.
 760 The Ephori eftablifhed at Sparta.
 758 Syracufe built by Archias of Corinth.
 754 The government of Athens changed.
 753 Era of the building of Rome in Italy by Romulus, firft king of the Romans.
 747 The era of Nabonaffar commenced on the 26th of February, the firft day of Thoth.
 746 The government of Corinth changed into a republic.
 743 The firft war between the Meffenians and Spartans.
 724 Mycenæ reduced by the Spartans.
 723 A colony of the Meffenians fettled at Rhegium in Italy.
 720 Samaria taken after three years fiege, and the kingdom

EVENTS. 5

kingdom of Ifrael finifhed by Salmanazer king of Affyria, who carries the ten tribes into captivity. The firft eclipfe of the moon on record.
713 Gela in Sicily built.
703 Corcyra, now Corfu, founded by the Corinthians.
702 Ecbatan in Media built by Deioces.
685 The fecond Meffenian war under Ariftomenes.
670 Byzantium (now Conftantinople) built by a colony of Athenians.
666 The city of Alba deftroyed.
648 Cyrene in Africa founded.
634 Cyaxares befieges Nineveh, but is obliged to raife the fiege by an incurfion of the Scythians, who remained mafters of Afia for 28 years.
624 Draco publifhed his inhuman laws at Athens.
610 Pharaoh Necho attempted to make a canal from the Nile to the Red Sea, but was not able to accomplifh it.
607 By order of the fame monarch, fome Phenicians failed from the Red Sea, round Africa, and returned by the Mediterranean.
606 The firft captivity of the Jews by Nebuchadnezzar. Nineveh deftroyed by Cyaxares.
600 Thales, of Miletus, travels into Egypt, confults the priefts of Memphis, acquires the knowledge of geometry, aftronomy, and philofophy; returns to Greece, calculates eclipfes, gives general notions of the univerfe, and maintains that an only Supreme Intelligence regulates all its motions.
Maps, globes, and the figns of the zodiac, invented by Anaximander, the fcholar of Thales.
598 Jehoiakin, king of Judah, is carried away captive, by Nebuchadnezzar, to Babylon.
594 Solon made Archon at Athens.
591 The Pythian games inftituted in Greece, and tragedy firft acted.
588 The firft irruption of the Gauls into Italy.
586 The city of Jerufalem taken, after a fiege of 18 months.
582 The laft captivity of the Jews by Nebuchadnezzar.

581 The Isthmian games restored.
580 Money first coined at Rome.
571 Tyre taken by Nebuchadnezzar after a siege of 13 years.
566 The first census at Rome, when the number of citizens was found to be 84,000.
562 The first comedy at Athens acted upon a moveable scaffold.
559 Cyrus the first king of Persia.
538 The kingdom of Babylon finished; that city being taken by Cyrus, who, in 536, gives an edict for the return of the Jews.
534 The foundation of the temple laid by the Jews.
526 Learning is greatly encouraged at Athens, and a public library first founded.
520 The second edict to rebuild Jerusalem.
515 The second temple at Jerusalem is finished under Darius.
510 Hippias banished from Athens.
509 Tarquin, the seventh and last king of the Romans, is expelled, and Rome is governed by two consuls, and other republican magistrates, till the battle of Pharsalia, being a space of 461 years.
508 The first alliance between the Romans and Carthaginians.
507 The second census at Rome, 130,000 citizens.
504 Sardis taken and burnt by the Athenians, which gave occasion to the Persian invasion of Greece.
498 The first dictator appointed at Rome.
497 The Saturnalia instituted at Rome. The number of citizens 150,700.
493 Tribunes created at Rome; or, in 488.
490 The battle of Marathon, September 28th.
486 Æschylus, the Greek poet, first gains the prize of tragedy.
483 Questors created at Rome.
481 Xerxes, king of Persia, begins his expedition against Greece.
480 The defence of Thermopylæ by Leonidas, and the sea-fight at Salamis.

The

476 The number of Roman citizens reduced to 103,000.
469 The third Messenian war.
466 The number of Roman citizens increased to 124,214.
458 Ezra is sent from Babylon to Jerusalem, with the captive Jews and the vessels of gold and silver, &c. being seventy weeks of years, or 490 years before the crucifixion of our Saviour.
456 The Ludi Seculares first celebrated at Rome.
454 The Romans send to Athens for Solon's laws.
451 The Decemvirs created at Rome, and the laws of the twelve tables compiled and ratified.
449 The Decemvirs banished.
445 Military tribunes, with consular power, created at Rome.
443 Censors created at Rome.
441 The battering ram invented by Artemones.
432 The Metonic cycle began July 15th.
431 The Peloponnesian war began, and lasted 27 years.
430 The history of the Old Testament finishes about this time.
A plague over the known world.
Malachi, the last of the prophets.
405 The Athenians entirely defeated by Lysander, which occasions the loss of the city, and ruin of the Athenian power.
401 The retreat of the 10,000 Greeks under Xenophon: the 30 tyrants expelled from Athens, and democratic government restored.
400 Socrates, the founder of moral philosophy among the Greeks, believes the immortality of the soul, a state of rewards and punishments; for which, and other sublime doctrines, he is put to death by the Athenians, who soon after repent, and erect to his memory a statue of brass.
399 The feast of Lectisternium instituted. Catapultæ invented by Dionysius.
394 The Corinthian war begun.

Rome

390 Rome burnt by the Gauls.
387 The peace of Antalcidas between the Greeks and Persians.
The number of Roman citizens amounted to 152,583.
384 Dionysius begins the Punic war.
379 The Bœotian war commences.
377 A general conspiracy of the Greek states against the Lacedemonians.
373 A great earthquake in Peloponnesus.
371 The Lacedemonians defeated by Epaminondas at Leuctra.
367 Prætors established in Rome: the Licinian law passed.
363 Epaminondas killed at the battle of Mantinea.
359 The obliquity of the ecliptic observed to be 23° 49′ 10″.
358 The Social war began.
357 Dionysius expelled from Syracuse.
A transit of the moon over Mars observed.
356 The sacred war begun in Greece.
Birth of Alexander the Great.
343 Dionysius II. expelled from Syracuse.
Commencement of the Syracusian era.
338 Philip of Macedon gains the battle of Chæronæa, and thus attains the sovereignty of Greece.
335 Thebes taken and rased by Alexander the Great.
334 The Persians defeated at Granicus, May 22d.
333 They are again defeated at Issus in Cilicia, Oct.
332 Alexander takes Tyre and marches to Jerusalem.
331 Alexandria built.
Darius entirely defeated at Arbela.
330 Alexander takes Babylon, and the principal cities of the Persian empire.
The Calippi period commences.
328 Alexander passes Mount Caucasus, and marches into India.
327 He defeats Porus, an Indian prince, and founds several cities.

The

326 The famous sedition of Corcyra.
324 His family exterminated, and his dominions parted by his officers.
323 Alexander the Great dies at Babylon.
315 Rhodes almost destroyed by an inundation.
311 The Appian way, aqueducts, &c. constructed at Rome.
308 The cities of Greece recovered their liberties for a short time.
307 Antioch, Seleucia, Laodicea, and other cities, founded by Seleucus.
301 Antigonus defeated and killed at Ipsus.
299 The first barbers came from Sicily to Rome.
294 The number of effective men in Rome amounts to 270,000.
293 The first sun-dial erected at Rome by Papirius Cursor.
285 Dionysius of Alexandria, began his astronomical era on Monday June 26, being the first who found the exact solar year to consist of 365 days 5 hours and 49 minutes.
The watch-tower of Pharos at Alexandria built.
Ptolemy Philadelphus, king of Egypt, employs 72 interpreters to translate the Old Testament into the Greek languages, which is called the *Septuagint*.
284 The foundations of the Achæan republic laid.
283 The college and library founded at Alexandria.
282 The Tarentine war begins.
280 Pyrrhus invades Italy.
269 A census at Rome: the number of citizens 278,222.
269 The first coining of silver at Rome.
265 The number of Roman citizens augmented to 292,124.
264 The first Punic war begins, and continues 23 years. The chronology of the Arundelian marbles composed.
262 A transit of Mercury over the Bull's horn; the planet being in 23° of ♉, and the sun in 29° 30'.
260 Provincial Questors established at Rome.

The

The Romans first concern themselves in naval affairs, and defeat the Carthaginians at sea.
255 Regulus, the Roman Conful, defeated and taken prisoner by the Carthaginians under Xantippus.
252 A cenfus at Rome: the number of citizens 297,897.
247 Another cenfus: the number of citizens 251,212.
246 The records of China deftroyed.
241 Conclufion of the firft Punic war.
240 Comedies firft acted at Rome.
237 Hamilcar, the Carthaginian, caufes his fon Hannibal, at nine years old, to fwear eternal enmity to the Romans.
236 The Tartars expelled from China.
235 Rome at peace with other nations. The temple of Janus fhut.
231 Corfica and Sardina fubdued by the Romans. The firft divorce at Rome.
230 The obliquity of the ecliptic obferved by Eratofthenes to be 23° 51′ 20″.
224 The Coloffus at Rhodes overturned by an earthquake.
219 The art of furgery introduced at Rome.
218 Commencement of the fecond Punic war. Hannibal paffes the Alps and invades Italy.
216 The Romans defeated at Cannæ, May 21ft.
214 Syracufe befieged by Marcellus.
209 A cenfus at Rome: the number of citizens 227,107.
208 Afdrubal invades Italy; but is defeated and killed.
206 Gold firft coined at Rome.
202 Hannibal defeated by Scipio at Zama.
201 Conclufion of the fecond Punic war.
194 Sparta and Hither-Spain fubdued by the Romans.
192 A cenfus at Rome: the number of citizens 243,704.
191 Antiochus defeated by the Romans at Thermopylæ.
190 The firft Roman army enters Afia, and from the fpoils

EVENTS.

spoils of Antiochus brings the Afiatic luxury firſt to Rome.
188 The Spartans obliged to renounce the inſtitutions of Lycurgus.
179 A cenſus at Rome: the number of citizens 273,244.
173 The Jewiſh high-prieſthood ſold by Antiochus Epiphanes.
170 Paper invented in China.
   The temple of Jeruſalem plundered by Antiochus.
169 A cenſus at Rome: the number of citizens 212,805.
168 Macedon reduced to the form of a Roman province.
   The firſt library erected at Rome.
165 The temple of Jeruſalem purified by Judas Maccabeus.
164 A cenſus at Rome: the number of citizens 327,032.
162 Hipparchus began his aſtronomical obſervations at Rhodes.
161 Philoſophers and Rhetoricians baniſhed from Rome.
150 The third Punic war commenced.
146 Corinth deſtroyed.
   Carthage, the rival to Rome, is raſed to the ground by the Romans.
   A remarkable comet appeared in Greece.
143 Hipparchus began his new cycle of the moon, conſiſting of 111,035 days.
141 The Numantine war commenced.
135 The hiſtory of the Apocrypha ends.
133 Numantia deſtroyed by Scipio.
124 A cenſus at Rome: the number of citizens 390,736.
105 The Cimbri and Teutones defeated the Romans.
102 The Teutones and Ambrones defeated by Marius.
88 Rome beſieged by the chiefs of the Marian faction.
82 Sylla created perpetual dictator, at Rome.
69 A cenſus at Rome: the number of citizens 450,000.
66 Catiline's

66 Catiline's confpiracy.
55 Julius Cæfar makes his firft expedition into Britain. Craffus defeated and killed by the Parthians.
51 Gaul reduced to a Roman province.
50 A cenfus at Rome: the number of citizens 320,000.
48 The battle of Pharfalia between Cæfar and Pompey, in which the latter is defeated.
The Alexandrian library, confifting of 400,000 valuable books, burnt by accident.
45 The war of Africa, in which Cato kills himfelf.
The folar year introduced by Cæfar.
44 Cæfar, the greateft of the Roman conquerors, after having fought fifty pitched battles, and flain 1,192,000 men, is killed in the fenate-houfe by confp'rators.
42 The republicans defeated at Philippi.
31 The battle of Actium fought, in which Mark Anthony and Cleopatra are totally defeated by Octavius, nephew to Julius Cæfar.
30 Alexandria, in Egypt, is taken by Octavius, upon which Anthony and Cleopatra put themfelves to death, and Egypt is reduced to a Roman province.
29 A cenfus at Rome: the number of citizens 4,101,017.
27 Octavius, by a decree of the fenate, obtains the title of Auguftus Cæfar, and an abfolute exemption from the laws, and is properly the firft Roman emperor.
The pantheon at Rome built.
19 Rome at the height of its glory.
The temple of Jerufalem rebuilt by Herod.
Agrippa conftructed the magnificent aqueducts at Rome.
8 A cenfus at Rome: the number of citizens 4,233,000
5 The temple of Janus is fhut by Auguftus, as an emblem of univerfal peace, and
JESUS CHRIST is born on Monday, December 25.

AFTER

AFTER CHRIST.

1 THE Vulgar Christian era commenced from January 1; the Saviour of the world being then five years of age.
8 Jesus Christ disputes with the doctors in the temple.
14 A census at Rome, 4,037,000 citizens.
16 Mathematicians and magicians expelled from Rome.
17 Twelve cities in Asia destroyed by an earthquake.
27 Pilate made governor of Judea.
29 Jesus baptized in Jordan by John.
33 He is crucified at Jerusalem.
35 St. Paul converted.
39 St. Matthew writes his Gospel.
    Pontius Pilate kills himself.
    A conjunction of Saturn, Jupiter, and Mars.
40 The name of Christians first given at Antioch to the followers of Christ.
43 Claudius Cæsar's expedition into Britain.
44 St. Mark writes his Gospel.
50 London is founded by the Romans: 368, surrounded by ditto with a wall, some parts of which are still observable.
51 Caractacus, the British king, is carried in chains to Rome.
52 The council of the Apostles at Jerusalem.
55 St. Luke writes his Gospel.
56 Rotterdam built.
59 The emperor Nero puts his mother and brothers to death.
——— Persecutes the Druids in Britain.
60 Christianity introduced into Britain.
61 Boadicia, the British queen, defeats the Romans, but is conquered soon after by Suetonius, governor of Britain.
62 St. Paul is sent in bonds to Rome—writes his epistles between 51 and 66.

63 The

63 The Acts of the Apostles written.
   A great earthquake in Asia.
64 Rome set on fire and burned for six days; upon which began (under Nero) the first persecution against the Christians.
65 Many prodigies seen about Jerusalem.
66 St. Peter and St. Paul put to death.
70 While the factious Jews are destroying one another, with mutual fury, Titus, the Roman general, takes Jerusalem, which is rased to the ground, and the plough made to pass over it.
73 The philosophers banished from Rome by Vespasion.
79 The cities of Pompeii and Herculaneum destroyed by an eruption of Vesuvius.
80 The Capitol and Pantheon at Rome destroyed by fire.
83 The philosophers expelled Rome by Domitian.
85 Julius Agricola, governor of South-Britain, to protect the civilized Britons from the incursions of the Caledonians, builds a line of forts between the rivers Forth and Clyde; defeats the Caledonians under Galgacus on the Grampian hills; and first sails round Britain, which he discovers to be an island.
86 The Capitoline games instituted by Domitian.
88 The secular games celebrated at Rome.
93 The empire of the Huns in Tartary destroyed by the Chinese.
   The Evangelist John banished to Patmos.
94 The second persecution of the Christians under Domitian.
96 St. John the Evangelist wrote his Revelation—his Gospel in 97.
103 Dacia reduced to a Roman province.
105 A great earthquake in Asia and Greece.
107 The third persecution of the Christians under Trajan.
114 Armeni reduced to a Roman province.
    A great earthquake in China.
115 Assyria subdued by Trajan.

An

A moſt terrible earthquake, attended with dreadful ſtorms of thunder and lightning, deſtroys the greateſt part of Antioch.

Chriſtians, 11,000, picked out of the army by order of Trajan the emperor, and baniſhed.

117 Trajan is ſucceeded by Adrian, who rebuilt the walls of Rome.

The learned men in Trajan's time, were Plutarch his maſter, Pliny the younger, Suetonius, Florus, Aulius Gellius, Lucius Epictetus, and Galen the phyſician, came to Rome, and Scribonius Largus the phyſician, lived, Cerinthus the noted heretic, Quintus Curtius the hiſtorian, and Tacitus Cornelius, the hiſtorian.

119 Plutarch, the author of the lives, was a native of Cheronea; he came to Rome in the time of Veſpaſian and Titus, and returned to his own country about the death of Trajan, where two years after, he dies in an advanced age, leaving his works to immortalize his memory to the longeſt time; he died aged 69.

An inſurrection of the Jews, who murder 200,000 Greeks and Romans.

A violent earthquake at Antioch.

120 Nicomedia and other cities ſwallowed up by an earthquake.

121 The Caledonians reconquer from the Romans all the ſouthern parts of Scotland; upon which the emperor Adrian builds a wall between Newcaſtle and Carliſle; but this alſo proving ineffectual, Pollius Urbicus, the Roman general, about the year 134, repairs Agricola's forts, which he joins by a wall four yards thick.

130 Jeruſalem rebuilt by Adrian.
132 The ſecond Jewiſh war commenced.
135 The ſecond Jewiſh war ends, when they were all baniſhed Judea.
139 Juſtin writes his firſt apology for the chriſtians.
140 Dublin built.
141 A number of hereſies appear about this time.

146 The worship of Serapis introduced at Rome.
152 The emperor Antonius Pius stops the persecutions against the christians.
   An inundation of the Tyber, and an earthquake at Rhodes.
163 The fourth persecution of the christians, under Marcus Aurelius Antonius.
166 The Romans send ambassadors to China.
168 A plague over the known world.
188 The Capitol at Rome destroyed by lightning.
191 A great part of Rome destroyed by fire.
203 The fifth persecution of the christians under Severus.
205 An earthquake in Wales.
209 Severus's wall in Britain built.
218 Two comets appeared at Rome: the course of the most remarkable from east to west.
222 About this time the Roman empire begins to decline: the Barbarians begin their irruptions, and the Goths have annual tribute not to molest the empire.
225 Mathematicians allowed to teach publicly at Rome.
236 The sixth persecution of the christians, under Maximin.
241 The Franks first mentioned in history.
250 The seventh persecution, under Decius.
252 A dreadful pestilence broke out in Ethiopia, and spread over the world.
   The eighth persecution, under Gallus.
253 Europe ravaged by the Scythians and Goths.
258 The ninth persecution, under Valerian.
260 Valerian is taken prisoner by Sapor, king of Persia, and flead alive.
   The Scythians ravaged the Roman empire.
   The temple of Diana at Ephesus, burnt.
261 A great plague throughout the Roman empire.
262 Earthquakes in Europe, Asia and Africa, and three days of darkness.
274 Silk first brought from India; the manufactory of it introduced into Europe by some monks, 551; first worn by the clergy in England, 1534.
276 Wines

EVENTS.

276 Wines first made in Britain.
277 The Franks settled in Gaul.
284 The Dioclesian era commenced August 29th, or September 17th.
287 Carausius proclaimed emperor of Britain.
289 A great comet visible in Mesopotamia for 29 days.
291 Two emperors and two Cæsars march to defend the four quarters of the empire.
297 Alexandria destroyed by Dioclesian.
303 The tenth persecution, under Dioclesian.
306 Constantine the Great begins his reign.
308 Cardinals first began.
312 Pestilence all over the east.
313 The tenth persecution ends by an edict of Constantine, who favours the christians, and gives full liberty to their religion.
314 Three bishops, or fathers, are sent from Britain to assist at the council of Arles.
315 Crucifixion abolished.
321 Observation of Sunday enjoined.
325 First general council at Nicee, where 318 fathers attended, against Arius the founder of Arianism, where was composed the famous Nicene Creed, which we attribute to them.
328 Constantine removes the seat of empire from Rome to Byzantium, which is thereafter called Constantinople.
330 A dreadful persecution of the christians in Persia, which lasts 40 years.
332 Constantine causes all the heathen temples to be destroyed.
334 300,000 Sarmatians revolted from their masters.
336 Arius, the founder of the Arian heresy, dieth. Drepana, first called Helenople.
337 Constantine dieth, and leaveth the empire among his three sons, viz. Constantine, Constans, and Constantius.
340 Constantine, falling out with Constans about the limits of his empire, is slain.

Hereby Conſtans remains the maſter of the weſt, and Conſtantius of the eaſt.
341 The goſpel propagated in Ethiopia by Foumentius. Gaul invaded by the Franks.
344 Neocæſarea ruined by an earthquake.
350 Conſtans is killed by the tyrant Magnentius, who takes poſſeſſion of the weſtern empire.
351 Heathens firſt called Pagans.
353 Magnentius having been defeated by Conſtantius, and driven out of Italy, kills himſelf, and Conſtantius remains maſter of the whole empire.
358 An hundred and fifty cities in Aſia and Greece turned by an earthquake.
Romachus, three years king of Scotland, had his head cut off, and put upon a pole.
360 Firſt monaſtery founded near Poiétiers in France, by Martin.
361 Conſtantius is ſucceeded by Julian the apoſtate, reigned two years, who reſtabliſhes the pagan worſhip.
363 The Roman emperor Julian, ſurnamed the apoſtate, endeavours in vain to rebuild the temple of Jeruſalem.
364 The Roman empire is divided into the eaſtern (Conſtantinople the capital) and weſtern (of which Rome continued to be the capital) each being now under the government of different emperors.
373 Bible tranſlated into the Gothic language.
390 A fiery column ſeen in the air for 30 days.
395 Theodoſius, called the Great, dies, and the empire is divided between his two ſons, Arcadius and Honorius, the former ruling in the eaſt, and the latter in the weſt.
398 The learned men of this century were, Jamblicus, Themiſteus, the philoſophers, Euſebius the church hiſtorian, Oribaſius the phyſician, Juvenus, Sedulius, prieſts and poets, Septinius Afer, Terentianus Maurus, Auſonius, Rufus and Fortunatus the poets, Macedonius, Photinus and Priſcilian, the heretics.
Dathy, or Dahi Mckfiechra, grandſon of Moighneodhin,

EVENTS.

odhin, king of Ireland, the 119th king of Ireland of the Milesian race; after having harrassed the Britons, invades Gaul.

400 Bells invented by Bishop Paulinus, of Campagnia.
401 Europe over-run by the Goths, under Alaric.
404 Another irruption of the Goths.
    The kingdom of Calidonia or Scotland, revives under Fergus.
406 Third irruption of the Goths.
    The Vandals, Alans, and Suevi, spread into France and Spain, by a concession of Honorius, emperor of the west.
408 Christian religion propagated in Persia.
409 Rome taken and plundered by the Goths, Aug. 24.
412 The Vandals begin their kingdom in Spain.
413 The kingdom of Burgundy begun in Alsace.
419 Many cities in Palestine destroyed by an earthquake.
420 The kingdom of France begins upon the Lower Rhine, under Pharamond.
421 The Salique law promulgated.
426 The Romans, reduced to extremities at home, withdraw their troops from Britain, and never return; advising the Britons to arm in their own defence, and trust to their own valour.
432 Gospel preached in Ireland by St. Patrick.
444 All Europe ravaged by the Huns.
446 The Britons now left to themselves, are greatly harassed by the Scots and Picts, upon which they once more make their complaint to the Romans, (which they entitle, *The groans of the Britons*) but receive no assistance from that quarter.
447 Attila (surnamed the Scourge of God) with his Huns, ravage the Roman empire.
449 Vortigern, king of the Britons, invites the Saxons into Britain, against the Scots and Picts.
452 The city of Venice founded.
455 The Saxons having repulsed the Scots and Picts, invite over more of their countrymen, and begin to establish themselves in Kent, under Hengist.
458 Leo fits out a great fleet, consisting of 1113 ships.

476 The

476 The western empire is finished, 523 years after the battle of Pharsalia; upon the ruins of which several new states arise in Italy, and other parts, consisting of Goths, Vandals, Huns, and other barbarians, under whom literature is extinguished, and the works of the learned are destroyed.
480 A great earthquake at Constantinople, which lasted 40 days.
493 St. Patrick died the 17th of March, in the abbey of Saul, built by himself, and was buried there, being about a quarter of a mile from Down, aged 120 years.

Italy reduced by Theodoric, king of the Goths.
496 Clovis, king of France, baptized; and christianity begins in that kingdom.
500 St. Bridget's Church at Kildare built.

The learned men of this century were, Nonnus and Avitus the poets, Sozomon the historian, and Socrates, the church historian.

The famous men the fifth century in Ireland were, St. Albe, Dubrach, Finch, Benigne, Selulius, Feredeline, St. Catald, Kienan, &c.
508 Prince Arthur begins his reign over the Britons.
510 Paris made the capital of the French dominions
515 Constantinople besieged by Vitalianus, whose fleet is burnt by a speculum of brass made by Proclus.
516 The computing of time by the christian era, is introduced by Dionysius the monk.
517 Five years drought and famine in Palestine.
519 A bearded comet appears.
534 Belisarius, one of Justinian's generals, takes Carthage, and destroys the kingdom of the Vandals in Africa.
536 The manufacture of silk introduced at Constantinople by two Indian monks.
540 Belisarius takes Rome, and brings Vitige king of Italy, prisoner to Constantinople.

Antioch destroyed by the Persians.
541 Basilius the last consul elected at Rome.
542 Antioch rebuilt.
543 An earthquake all over the world.

The

The kingdom of Poland founded.
553 The empire of the Goths in Italy deſtroyed by Narſes.
557 A terrible plague all over Europe, Aſia, and Africa, which continues near fifty years.
565 Beliſarius died.
568 The Lombards founded a kingdom in Italy.
569 The Tower of London built.
The Turks firſt mentioned in hiſtory.
575 The firſt monarchy founded in Bavaria.
580 Antioch deſtroyed by an earthquake.
581 Latin ceaſed to be ſpoken about this time in Italy.
584 The origin of fiefs in France.
588 The city of Paris deſtroyed by fire.
589 Rome overflowed by the Tyber.
593 The Gaſcons eſtabliſhed themſelves in the country called by their name.
596 John, of Conſtantinople, aſſumes the title of univerſal biſhop.
597 Auguſtine the monk, comes into England with forty monks.
600 Eminent perſons who flouriſhed in the ſixth century in Ireland, were St. Collum Cille, St. Finian, St. Tarlah, St. Brendan, St. Congal, St. Kenny, St. Colman, St. Bridget, St. Ita, with ſeveral others.
604 St. Paul's church in London founded.
605 The uſe of bells introduced into churches.
606 Here begins the power of the popes, by the conceſſions of Phocas, emperor of the Eaſt.
Ethelbert, king of Kent, being by Auguſtine converted to the chriſtian faith, was the inſtrument of converting Sebert, king of the Eaſt-Saxons, whom he aſſiſted in the building of St. Paul's church in London, where had ſtood the temple of Diana; as alſo the church of St. Peter's, at Weſtminſter, then called Thorney, where the temple of Apollo ſtood; and himſelf built the cathedral church at Rocheſter, dedicating it to St. Andrew.
622 Mahomet, the falſe prophet, flies from Mecca to Medina, in Arabia, in the 44th year of his age, and 10th of his miniſtry, when he laid the foundation
of

of the Saracen empire, and from whom the Mahometan princes to this day claim their defcent: his followers compute their time from this era, which in Arabic is called *hegira*, i. e. "the Flight."

628 An academy founded at Canterbury.
630 The cathedral of Cork founded by St. Finbarr.
637 Jerufalem is taken by the Saracens or followers of Mahomet.
639 The epifcopal church of Killaloe was founded about this time, by the contribution of different kings.
641 Alexandria in Egypt is taken by the Saracens, and the grand library there burnt by the order of Omar their caliph or prince.
643 The temple of Jerufalem converted into a Mahometan mofque.
653 The Saracens now extend their conquefts on every fide, and retaliate the barbarities of the Goths and Vandals, upon their pofterity.
They take Rhodes, and deftroy the famous Coloffus. England invaded by the Danes.
660 Organs firft ufed in churches.
663 Glafs invented by a bifhop, and brought into England by a Benedictine monk.
669 Sicily invaded, and Syracufe deftroyed by the Saracens.
685 The Britons, after a brave ftruggle of near 150 years, are totally expelled by the Saxons, and drove into Wales and Cornwall.
698 The Saracens take Carthage, and expel the Romans from Africa.
700 Cracow built, and the firft prince of Poland elected.
704 The firft province given to the Pope.
713 The Saracens conquer Spain.
714 France governed by Charles Martel.
718 The kingdom of the Afturias in Spain founded by Pelagio.
719 Chriftianity promulgated in Germany.
725 Charles Martel, natural fon of Pepin, king of France, defeats and routs 370,000 Saracens near Tours, the greateft part of their numerous army, together

EVENTS. 23

ther with their general Abderomus, being killed on the spot.

726 The controversy about images begins, and occasions many infurrections in the eastern empire.
727 Tax of Peter's pence begun by Ina, king of Wessex.
735 Institution of the office of pope's nuncio.
746 Three years pestilence in Europe and Asia.
748 Computing of years from the birth of Christ, began to be used in history.
749 The race of Abbas become caliphs of the Saracens, and encourage learning.
The empire of the Saracens divided into three.
752 The exarchate of Ravenna abolished by Astolphus, king of the Lombards.
755 Commencement of the pope's temporal dominion.
762 The city of Bagdad upon the Tigris, is made the capital for the caliphs of the house of Abbas.
Burials, which formerly used to be in the highways, permitted in towns.
792 An academy founded in Paris.
794 The Huns extirpated by Charlemagne.
797 Seventeen days of unusual darkness.
800 Charlemagne, king of France, begins the empire of Germany, afterwards called the Western empire; gives the present names to the winds and months; endeavours to restore learning in Europe, but mankind are not yet disposed for it, being solely engrossed in military enterprizes.
801 A great earthquake in France, Germany and Italy.
807 Jan. 31. Jupiter eclipsed by the moon. March 17. A large spot seen on the sun for eight days.
808 The first descent of the Normans on France.
820 St. Mary's Abbey at Trim built.
826 Harold, king of Denmark, dethroned by his subjects, for being a christian.
832 Painters banished out of the eastern empire.
836 The Flemings trade to Scotland for fish.
838 The Danes in 60 ships arrive and take Dublin.
840 The Scots and Picts have a decisive battle, in which the former prevail, and both kingdoms are united

by

by Kenneth, which begins the second period of the Scottish history.

841 The sons of Louis le Debonnaire, falling out about the partition of their father's dominions, a bloody battle is fought near Fontenay in Burgundy, wherein the loss on both sides amounted to 100,000 men.

842 Germany separated from the empire of the Franks.
852 Armagh destroyed by the Danes on Easter-day.
853 London burnt by the Danes.
856 An earthquake over the greatest part of the known world.
861 Ruric the first prince of Russia began to reign.
864 The Danes begin their ravages in England.
867 Christianity propagated in Bulgaria.
868 Egypt becomes independent on the caliphs of Bagdad.
872 Bells and clocks first used in Constantinople.

University college in Oxford, as some say, was founded by king Alfred, some say he restored it only. Lately Dr. Ratcliff gave 5000l. to build a new front 40,000l. to erect a library, and 950l. a year for public uses. It has a master, twelve fellows, ten scholars and two exhibitioners: the vice-chancellor and protectors, are the visitors.

873 France distressed by locusts and pestilence.
874 Iceland peopled by the Norwegians,
Scotland invaded by the Danes.
875 A bearded comet appears in France.
878 Alfred the Great, after subduing the Danish invaders (against whom he fought 56 battles by sea and land) composes his body of laws; divides England into counties, hundreds, tythings; in 890 erects county-courts, having founded the university of Oxford in 886.
882 Cormack M'Cullen, king of Munster, and Archbishop of Cashel.
888 A great battle between Maolseachluin I. king of Ireland, and the Danes.
891 The first land-tax in England.

905 A very

EVENTS.

895 The monastery of Cluny founded.
902 The Danes, with a vast fleet, were overthrown by the people of Dublin, with a great slaughter.
905 A very remarkable comet appeared in China.
   Rome taken by the Normans.
911 The obliquity of the ecliptic observed by Thebit to be $23^\circ\ 33'\ 30''$
912 The Normans establish themselves in Normandy.
913 The Danes become masters of England.
915 Cambridge university founded.
923 Fiefs established in France.
925 Sigefroi elected first marquis of Brandenburg.
928 Marquisate of Misnia established.
937 Saracen empire divided by usurpation into seven kingdoms.
941 Arithmetic brought into Egypt.
961 Candia recovered from the Saracens.
967 Antioch recovered from the Saracens.
969 The race of Abbas extinguished from Europe.
975 Pope Boniface VII. is deposed and banished for his crimes.
977 Greece, Macedon, and Thrace, ravaged by the Bulgarians for ten years.
   The Bohemians subdued by Otho.
979 Coronation oath first used in England.
   Juries first instituted in ditto.
985 The Danes under Sueno, invaded England and Scotland.
987 The Carlovingian race in France ended.
991 The figures in arithmetic are brought into Europe by the Saracens from Arabia; letters of the alphabet were hitherto used.
993 A great eruption of Mount Vesuvius.
995 England invaded by the Danes and Norwegians.
996 Otho III. makes the empire of Germany elective.
999 Boleslaus, the first king of Poland.
   The obliquity of the ecliptic observed by Aboul Wafi and Abu Hamed to be $23^\circ\ 35'$.
1000 Paper made of cotton rags was in use; that of li-

nen rags in 1170; the manufactory introduced into England at Deptford, 1588.

The famous men of Ireland who flourished in the 9th and 10th century, were Albin, Clement, Claude, Donough, Andrew, Patrick (inventor of St. Patrick's purgatory) Johannes Scotus, Suibny, Probus, Cele, &c.

1002 Henry the emperor, assumed the title of king of the Romans.

1005 All the old churches are rebuilt about this time in a new manner of architecture.

1006 A plague in Europe for three years.

1007 A great irruption of Vesuvius.

1014 Sueno the Dane becomes master of England.

Sept. 28. Almost all Flanders laid under water by a storm.

On Good-Friday, 23d April, the famous battle of Clontarf was fought, wherein the Danes were completely defeated, with the loss of 11,000 men, and driven out of Ireland; but the Irish king, Brian Boro, was killed, aged 88.

1015 Children forbidden by law to be sold by their parents in England.

1017 Rain of the colour of blood for three days in Aquitain.

1022 A new species of music invented by Aretin.

1023 Elgina, wife of Canute the Dane being barren, shamm'd a lying-in, and so palm'd Sweyn a shoemaker's son on her credulous husband; this sham was king of Norway. She also put another bite upon her tame husband, Harold the son of a priest, who became king of England.

1026 Maolseackluin II. king of Ireland, submits himself and kingdom with 12000 horse to Bryan Boiroimhe, king of Munster, who gives Maolseackluin another year.

1027 Bryen Boiroimhluin, son of Kennedy, of the line of Heber Fionn, 12 years elected king of Ireland. This great monarch repaired the monasteries and churches the Danes had destroyed; having settled religion

religion upon its ancient footing, he built public
schools and libraries, and erected new academies.
William the first born king of England.
Olaus, king of Norway, an easy good tempered
prince, attempting to recover his kingdom, which
Carnute the Dane wrested from him, was barbarously murdered by his own subjects.

1035 Togrul-Beg, or Tangrolipix, the Turkish sultan,
establishes himself in Korasan.

The kingdoms of Castile and Arragon began.

1038 Christ Church built by Sitricus son of Amlaerus,
king of the Danes, of the city of Dublin, for secular canons.

The revenues of Bryen Boiroimhe, monarch of Ireland, were as follow: Connaught paid 800 beeves,
800 fat hogs; Tyrconnel paid 500 of each; Tir-
owen paid 60 of each, and 90 tons of Iron;
Rathargians of Ulster paid 500 beeves; Leinster
paid 500 fat hogs; Orgiels paid 500 beeves; Leinster paid beside 300 beeves and 300 tons of Iron;
Dublin Danes 150 hogsheads of wine; Ossory 60
beeves, 60 fat hogs, 60 tons of iron; Limerick
Danes, one ton of Claret daily. That great and
valiant prince was basely murdered by some run-
away cowardly Danes, on Good-Friday.

Bryen Boiroimhe soon after died of his wounds.

In the battle of Clontarf fell his son Murchard, and
many of the nobility: the Danes lost 11,000 men.

After the battle, Sitricus with the reliques of the
Danes, retired to Dublin.

1039 Maolseachluin II. restored to the throne of Ireland.

Waterford plundered and burnt by Dermot, king of
Leinster.

1040 The Danes, after several engagements with various
success, are about this time driven out of Scotland,
and never again return in a hostile manner.

Smyrna destroyed by an earthquake.

1041 First sermon at a coronation.

The Saxon line restored under Edward the confessor.

1043 The Turks become formidable, and take poffeffion of Perfia.
The Ruffians come from Scythia, and land in Thrace.
1049 The cathedral of Kilkenny fuppofed to have been built about this time by St. Canice.
1050 Broad feal of England firft ufed.
1054 Leo IX. the firft pope that kept up an army.
1055 The Turks take Bagdad, and overturn the empire of the Saracens.
1057 Malcolm III. king of Scotland, kills the tyrant Macbeth at Dunfinnan, and marries the princefs Margaret, fifter to Edgar Atheling.
Coventry, Warwick, by Leofric earl of Chefter, and his lady Godiva, hence came peeping Tom.
1060 French language and cuftoms firft introduced into England.
1061 Surnames appointed to be taken in Scotland by a parliament held in Forfar.
1065 Jerufalem taken by the Turks from the Saracens.
1066 The conqueft of England by William (furnamed the baftard) duke of Normandy, in the battle of Haftings where Harold is flain.
Bows and arrows introduced into England.
1068 Curfew bell eftablifhed by William the Conqueror; abolifhed in 1100.
1070 Feudal law introduced into England.
1074 Beheading of noblemen firft introduced into England.
1075 Henry IV. emperor of Germany, and the pope, quarrel about the nomination of the German bifhops. Henry, in penance, walks barefooted to the pope towards the end of January.
176 Juftices of the peace firft appointed in England.
An earthquake in England.
Afia Minor, having been two years under the power of Sølyman, is from this time called Turkey.
1080 Doomfday-book began to be compiled by order of William, from a furvey of all the eftates in England, and finifhed in 1086.
Tower of London built by ditto, to curb his Englifh
fubjects;

EVENTS.

subjects; numbers of whom fly to Scotland, where they introduce the Saxon or English language, are protected by Malcolm, and have lands given them.

1084 Dublin, erected into a bishopric; whose first bishop was one Patrick, an Easterling, and chosen by the city, who sent him to England, to be consecrated by Lanfranc, arbishop of Canterbury; and in 1152 had the archiepiscopal dignity added to it, as well as to Armagh, Cashel and Tuam, by Pope Eugene the third.

1086 The order of Carthusians established by Bruno.

1089 An university at Armagh, of considerable splendor, erected by St. Patrick.

1090 Dynasty of Bathineens or Assassins, begins in Irak, and continues for 117 years.

1091 The Saracens in Spain, being hard pressed by the Spaniards, called to their assistance Joseph king of Morocco; by which the Moors get possession of all the Saracen dominions in Spain.

500 houses in London were blown down by a tempest.

1096 First crusade to the Holy Land is begun under several christian princes, to drive the infidels from Jerusalem.

Duelling, the first public one; with small swords, introduced in 1588.

The cathedral of Waterford built by the Ostmen, and Malchus its first bishop.

1098 Order of St. Benedict instituted.

1099 Jerusalem taken by the crusaders; Godfrey elected king of it; and the order of knights of St. John instituted.

Westminster Hall, built by William Rufus; that edifice, as it now stands, was timbered and roofed with Irish oak, given to the king of England by Turlough M'Feig, king of Leahmoa, and most part of Ireland.

1100 Coats of arms first introduced into England. Same year Henry I. granted the privilege of making wills.

1101 Venice

1101 Venice reduced to ashes.
1107 The first king's speech, delivered by Henry I.
1110 Edgar Atheling, the last of the Saxon princes, dies in England, where he had been permitted to reside as a subject.
  Learning revived at Cambridge.
  Writing on paper made of cotton, common about this time.
1117 St. Giles's, an hospital for 14 leprous persons, built by the wife of Henry I. in which was a chapel, that presented each dying criminal with a bowl of ale on his journey to Tyburn.
1118 Order of the Knights Templars instituted, to defend the Sepulchre at Jerusalem, and to protect christian strangers.
1119 Bohemia erected into a kingdom.
1130 St. Mary's church built on the island of Devenish, near Silverhill, in the county of Fermanagh.
  Navigable rivers, and canals to join rivers, first made in England by Henry I.
1132 The kingdom of Portugal began.
1137 The pandect of Justinian found in the ruins of Amalphi.
  The city of York, with its cathedral and thirty-nine churches, destroyed by fire the 3d. of June.
1140 Canon law first introduced into England.
1141 Factions of the Guelphs and Gibellines prevailed about this time.
1143 The Koran translated into Latin.
1144 Peripatetic philosophy introduced into Germany.
1151 Four archbishops constituted, viz. Armagh, Dublin, Cashel, and Tuam; and 23 other bishops.
  Canon law collected by Gratian, a monk of Bologna.
1154 Christianity introduced into Finland.
1156 The city of Moscow in Russia founded.
1160 Order of the Carmelites instituted.
1162 Waterford in Ireland built.
1163 London Bridge, consisting of 19 small arches, first built of stone.

1164 The

EVENTS. 51

1164 The cathedral of Derry was built by Flathbert O'Brolcan, its first bishop; in this he was affisted by Maurice M'Loghlan, king of Ireland.
Teutonic order of religious knights begins in Germany.

1170 The English first land in Ireland. In 1168 Roderic O'Connor, put Dermot, king of Leinster, to flight, for committing a rape on the wife of Teighernan O'Rourke, king of Breifne: Dermot expelled his kingdom, fled to England to folicit affistance from Henry II. who being engaged in a war with France, referred him to Strongbow, earl of Pembroke, then at Bristol, who, on a promise of the king's daughter, Eva, in marriage, raifed men, and came over with him, and foon recovered his territories; bringing Maurice and William Fitz-Gerald with him, as cotemporaries.
The city of Cork built.

1171 Henry II. grants to Strongbow the whole province of Leinster.
Dublin is befieged and taken by Raymond le Gros; Waterford alfo furrenders to him and William Fitz Gerald.
Dynafty of Fatemites ended in Egypt; the fovereigns of this country henceforth called Sultans.

1172 Henry II. lands in Ireland with 400 knights, and 5000 men at arms, on the 18th of October, at Waterford, and is crowned king of Ireland; the clergy alfo, confirmed the kingdom to him, and when he had settled his affairs in Ireland, he returned to his own dominions, leaving Hugh de Lacy with 20 knights, in Meath, and the foldiers in proper garrifons, for the defence of the country, and beftowed upon the faid Hugh, the county of Meath, and confirmed it by his royal grant to his pofterity. To Robert Fitz-Stephen, and Maurice Fitz-Gerald (younger brother to faid William Fitz-Gerald) he gave the command of the city of Dublin, allowing them 20 knights for guard; and to William Aldelmel, Philip de Haftings, and
Robert

Robert de Bruis, attended by 20 knights, he left the government of Wexford.—Thus ended the monarchy of the Milesians, or ancient Irish, which commenced about 2,500 years before, in the persons of Heber and Heremon, two of the sons of Milesius, king of Spain.—From this time, Ireland became subject to the English government.—This year, Hugh de Lacy, Robert Fitz-Stephen, Maurice Fitz-Gerald, and Robert de Bruis, were appointed the first governors of Ireland, which at this time was divided into counties, when the office of Sheriff was first appointed.

Henry II. built a pavilion of platted twigs, near St. Andrew's church, city of Dublin, where he entertained several Irish princes.

1173 He by a grant of divers privileges, encouraged a colony from Bristol to settle in Dublin.

The first charter granted to Dublin.

Hugh de Lacy, an English governor of Meath, was such an oppressor of the poor, that Stanhurst says, a young man slew him to rid his country of a monster.

A conspiracy in England formed against Henry, on account of fair Rosamond, a concubine of his.

1174 Richard earl Strongbow erected the order of knights templars, at Kilmainham, near Dublin.

Richard earl Strongbow died of a mortification in his foot, and was buried in Christ church, Dublin.

Henry II. creates his younger son John, 12 years old, king or lord of Ireland, who grants charters to Dublin and other towns.

1176 England is divided by Henry into six circuits, and justice is dispensed by itinerant judges.

1177 In England a fat ox sold for twelve-pence, sheep four-pence, provender for twenty horses four-pence, bread for a hundred men, twelve-pence.

Almerick de St. Laurence, and his son Nicholas, were wounded in an engagement with the Ulster Irish in the county of Down, under the command of John Courcy, when 15,000 were killed: he

was anceftor to the barons of Howth, and to him
King John, then earl of Moreton, granted the lands
of Howth.
1179 At Oxon-hall, near Darlington, the earth fuddenly
rofe to an eminence refembling a mountain; remained fo feveral hours; then funk in as fuddenly
with a horrible noife, leaving a deep chafm, which
continues to this day.
The univerfity of Padua founded.
1180 Glafs windows began to be ufed in private houfes
in England.
1181 The laws of England are digefted about this time
by Glanville.
1182 Pope Alexander III. compelled the kings of England and France to hold the ftirrups of his faddle
when he mounted his horfe.
1183 7000 Albigenfes maffacred by the inhabitants of
Berry.
1184 The office of juftices in eyre, inftituted by Henry II.
the laft inftance of their holding a court in any of
the forefts is believed to be in the reign of Charles
the fecond.
1185 John de Courcy, earl of Ulfter, lord lieutenant of
Ireland.
1186 Stephen Riddle, the firft lord chancellor appointed
in Dublin.
1187 Jerufalem taken by Saladin.
1189 Sheriffs firft appointed in London.
1190 Patrick's church built, and Chrift church;—Dublin
rebuilt.
1191 Pope Celeftine III. kicked the emperor Henry IV's.
crown off his head while kneeling, to fhew his
prerogative of making and unmaking kings.
1192 The battle of Afcalon, in Judea, in which Richard
king of England, defeats Saladin's army, confifting of 300,000 combatants.
1193 Richard I. king of England, taken prifoner in Germany, and ranfomed for 100,000 marks.
1194 Sword of ftate carried at an Englifh king's coronation by a king of Scotland.

Dieu

Dieu et mon Droit! first used as a motto by Richard, as a victory over the French.

1195 Denmark and Norway laid waste by a dreadful tempest.

1198 Institution of the order of the Holy Trinity.

This year dies Roderic O'Connor, sometime king of Ireland, and in whom ended the Irish monarchy, and settled in the person of Henry II. king of England.

1200 Chimnies were not known in England.

Surnames now began to be used; first among the nobility.

Univerfity of Salamanca in Spain, founded.

First difpenfations granted by the pope.

The abbey of St. Peter and Paul in the county of Clare, built.

King John fold for 4000 marks, to William de Braufa, all the lands of Philip de Worcefter, and all the lands of Theobald Walter in Ireland.

1202 Affize of bread first appointed.

1203 The privilege of the De Courcy's (earls of Ulfter) ftanding covered before the kings of England, granted this year by king John, in the fecond year of whofe reign John de Courcy, earl of Ulfter, was fupplanted, and loft the king's favour; Hugh de Lacy, the younger, earl of Meath, who was formerly joined with him in the government of Ireland, alledging he had fpoken feveral difrefpectful words, highly reflecting on the king about the murder of his nephew Arthur, duke of Britany, in France (whofe right to the crown was before that of king John) at which the king being forely difpleaf'd, ordered the faid Lacy, who was then governor of Ireland, to feize the earl of Ulfter, and fend him prifoner to England. Lacy, who was the earl's grand enemy, gladly obeyed the command, and feveral times attempted to take him by force, but finding that would not do, he at laft hired fome of the earl's own fervants to betray their mafter into his hands, which took effect

1203 effect on Good-Friday, 1203; for on that day, the earl (according to the devotion of the times) was walking unarmed and barefoot, round the church-yard of Downpatrick, for penance; Lacy and his party came upon him unawares, and he having nothing to defend himself but the pole of a wooden crofs which ftood in the church-yard, was overpowered and forced to yield, after he had killed thirteen of Lacy's men. This great earl, after being thus betrayed, was fent prifoner to London, and after he had been confined fome time in the tower, a difpute arofe between king John, of England, and Philip, Auguft king of France, about the title to the Dutchy of Normandy, which, to hinder the greater effufion of human blood, was referred to two champions to decide: the French champion was ready, but none of king John's fubjects would anfwer the challenge; upon which the king was informed, that John de Courcy late earl of Ulfter, who was then a prifoner in the tower of London, was the only man in his dominions who could do it, if he would undertake it; the king being thus informed, fent twice to the earl for that purpofe, but he refufed it each time, faying, *not for him, for I efteem him unworthy the adventure of my blood, by reafon of the ungrateful returns he made for my fervices and loyalty to the crown, in imprifoning me unheard, at the fuit of my rival and enemy, Hugh de Lacy*: but the king fending the third time, to know if he would fight for the honour of his country, he made this anfwer, *that for the crown and dignity of the realm, in which many an honeft man liveth, againft his will (meaning the king) I fhall be contented to hazard my life.* The day of combat being appointed (in Normandy) the earl's own fword was fent for out of Ireland; but when the day came, and every thing was ready for the fight, and the champions were entered the lifts, in the prefence of the kings of England, France, and Scotland; the French champion not

liking

1203 liking the strong proportion of the earl's body, nor the terrible weapon he bore in his hand, when the trumpets sounded the last charge, he set spurs to his horse, broke through the lists, and fled into Spain, from whence he never returned. The French champion thus taking his flight, the victory was adjudged to the earl of Ulster; but the kings hearing of his great strength, and being willing to see some trial of it, they ordered an helmet of excellent proof, full faced with mail, to be laid upon a block of wood, which the earl with one blow cut asunder, and struck his sword so deep into the wood, that none there present but himself could draw it out again; which sword, together with his armour, are to this day preserved in the tower of London. After this noble performance, the king restored him to his former titles and estate, which was valued at that time at 25000 marks sterling per annum, a vast income in those days; and likewise bade him ask for any thing else in his gift he had a mind to, and it should be granted; upon which the earl replied, he had titles and estate enough, but desired that he and his successors, the heirs male of his family (after him) might have the privilege, after their first obeisance, to be covered in the royal presence of him and his successors, kings of England, which the king granted, and the said privilege is preserved in the family to this day. The earl afterwards arriving in England, attempted fifteen several times to cross the seas from thence into Ireland, but was every time put back by contrary winds, whereupon he altered his course, and went into France, where he died in the year 1210, leaving issue by Africa his widow, daughter to Godfred, king of the Isle of Man, and of the western isles of Scotland, Myles his heir and successor. Myles, who succeeded, was one of the bail or sureties for his father's fidelity, on his being released out of the tower in order to fight the French champion, as appears in the records

1203 cords of the fourth year of the reign of king John, in the said tower. He was kept out of the earldom of Ulster, by Hugh de Lacy, who had a grant of it from king John on taking earl John, and sending him prisoner to London; for on Myles's claiming the earldom on his father's death, said Lacy replied that he would maintain king John's last grant of it to himself, since earl John never returned into Ireland to reverse his outlawry; and the said Lacy being a great favourite of the king's, and a very powerful man, Myles was forced to quit his pretensions, but was created baron of Kinsale, and died in the beginning of Henry III's. reign.

1204 Constantinople taken by the French and Venetians.
The inquisition established.
Empire of Trebizond established.
The first parliament in England.
Where Amsterdam now stands, there was only a small castle and village.

1205 Foundation of Dublin castle laid.
Barons first summoned to parliament.

1206 The practice of physic was confined to ecclesiastics, from this time till about the year 1500.

1208 London incorporated, and obtained its first charter for electing a lord mayor and other magistrates from king John.
Order of *Fratres Minores* established.
The pope excommunicated king John.

1209 First bull-beating at Stamford in Lincolnshire.
Black Monday, so called on account of the slaughter committed by the Irish on a great number of the Bristol people, who inhabited Dublin, and went out to divert themselves in Cullen's wood, on Easter-Monday, when the mountain enemies fell upon them and destroyed 500 men, besides women and children.
The works of Aristotle imported from Constantinople into Europe.
Silk manufacture imported from Greece into Venice.

1210 Works of Aristotle condemned to be burnt at Paris.

Emperor Otho excommunicated by the pope.
Violent perfecution of the Albigenfes.
King John met at Dublin upwards of 20 Irifh princes who fwore allegiance to him, and there caufed them to eftablifh the Englifh laws and cuftoms.
Court of juftice firft erected in Ireland.
Pence and farthings were coined in Ireland, by order of king John.
St. Catherine's church at Waterford, founded by Elias, fon of a Norman.

1211 St. John the Evangelift's church in Kilkenny built.
1213 The caftle of Dublin finifhed by bifhop Cummin.
1215 Magna Charta figned by king John and the barons of England.
Court of Common Pleas eftablifhed.
Orders of the Dominicans and Knights Hofpitallers founded.
The doctrine of tranfubftantiation introduced.
1216 King Alexander, and the whole kingdom of Scotland excommunicated by the pope's legate.
Lewis, Philip of France's fon, laid claim to the crown of England, and landed with an army on the ifle of Thanet.
1217 Henry III. granted the city of Dublin to the citizens, in fee-farm, at 200 marks per annum.
1220 Aftronomy and geography brought into Europe by the Moors.
1222 A great earthquake in Germany.
1223 A comet of extraordinary magnitude appeared in Denmark.
1224 The cuftom paid in the city of Dublin, were three-pence for every fack of wool, fix-pence for every laft of hide, and two-pence for every barrel of wine.
The cathedral of Drogheda built.
Caftle of Sligo built by Maurice Fitz-Gerald, lord juftice of Ireland.
1226 A league formed againft the Albigenfes by the French king and many prelates and lords.
Marriage firft celebrated in churches.

1227 The

EVENTS. 39

1227 The Tartars, under Gingis-Kan, emerge from the northren parts of Asia, over-run all the Saracen empire, and carry death and desolation wherever they march.
    The priory of St. Mary and St. Edward at Limerick, founded by Simon Minor, a citizen of Limerick, in the reign of king John.
    St. Mary's-Abbey priory at Mullingar, built.
1228 University at Tholouse founded.
    Yarmouth becomes considerable for its fishery.
1230 Kingdom of Denmark distressed by pestilence.
    Kingdoms of Leon and Castile united.
    Prussia subdued by the Teutonic knights.
    University of Naples founded.
1231 The Almagest of Ptolomy translated into latin.
1233 The Inquisition begun in 1204, is now trusted to the Dominicans.
    The houses of London, and other cities in England, France and Germany, still thatched with straw.
1234 Coals discovered at Newcastle.
    Cyder called wine, made in England.
1236 Antelamus made bishop of Armagh, and primate of all Ireland.
    Leaden pipes for conveying water, invented.
1237 Water first conveyed to London by leaden pipes; it took near 50 years to complete it; the whole being finished, and Cheapside conduit erected only in 1285.
1238 University of Vienna founded.
1239 A writing of this year's date on paper made of rags still extant.
1240 England, miserably drained of its money by the Popes, to the amount of 120,000l. per annum of our modern money, equal in point of expence of living to 720,000l. in our days.
1241 First punishment of being hanged, drawn and quartered.
    The Hanseatic league formed.
1245 A clear red star, like Mars, appears in Capricorn.

1247 A marvellous and strange earthquake over Ireland, England, and all the western world.
1250 Painting revived in Florence, by Cimabue.
1251 Wales subdued, and Magna Charta confirmed.
1252 Magnifying glasses invented by Roger Bacon.
1253 The famous astronomical tables composed by Alonso king of Castile.
   Linen first made in England.
1254 Auricular confessions first introduced.
1256 Order of the Augustines established.
1258 Stephen Longsword, lord justice of Ireland, gave battle to O'Neill and the rebels of Ulster at Down, and slew 352, with O'Neill.
   Counties first sent members to parliament.
   The Tartars take Bagdad, which finishes the empire of the Saracens.
1260 The sect of Flagellantes appeared in Italy.
   Seaman's compass invented 1229, a Dutchman first used one at Venice 1260; improved at Naples 1302; its variation observed 1538.
1262 The petty kings of Ireland own themselves vassals to the English crown.
1263 Acho, king of Norway, invades Scotland with 160 sail, and lands 20,000 men at the mouth of the Clyde; but they are cut to pieces by Alexander III. who recovers the western isles.
1264 Clement IV. (the successor of Urban) confirms Charles in the kingdom, and crowns him at Rome.
1266 Cities and Boroughs first represented in parliament.
1268 The Tartars invade China.
1269 Hamburgh company incorporated in England.
   The obliquity of the ecliptic observed by Cozah Nassirodni to be 23° 30'.
   Maurice Fitz-Gerald, earl of Desmond, drowned between England and Ireland.
   The castle of Roscommon, built by Robert Ufford, lord justice of Ireland.
1272 Academy of Florence founded.
1273 The empire of the present Austrian family begun in Germany.

EVENTS.

1274 The first commercial treaty betwixt England and Flanders.

1275 The knee ordered to be bent at the name of Jesus.
 The city of London lends the crown of England 16,000l.

1279 280 Jews hanged for coining and clipping.
 Edward I. commanded groats, pence, half-pence, and farthings to be coined, and to pass current in England and Ireland.

1280 The city of Waterford burnt.
 Coals first dug at Newcastle, by a charter granted the town by Henry III.

1282 Lewellyn, prince of Wales, defeated and killed by Edward I. who unites that principality to England.
 A great pestilence in Denmark.
 8000 French murdered at the Sicilian vespers.
 Academy de la Crusca founded.

1283 Alexander III. king of Scotland, killed by a fall from his horse near Kinghorn.

1284 Edward II. born, and stiled Prince of Wales.

1285 Kingdom of Scotland is disputed by twelve candidates, who submit their claims to the arbitration of Edward king of England; which lays the foundation of a long and desolating war between both nations.
 Fencing-schools in England prohibited as introductory to duels.

1288 In England a bushel of wheat was sold for 4d.

1290 Jews were banished England for usury.

1291 Barristers first appointed by Edward I.
 Ptolemais taken by the Turks. End of the crusades.

1293 A regular succession of English parliaments from this year, being the 22d. of Edward I.
 Baliol, king of Scotland, appeared to a summons, and pleaded his cause in Westminster-hall, Oct. 14.

1294 Parliaments established in Paris.

1296 Scotch regalia and crown jewels taken, and brought to England with their coronation chair, now in Westminster-abbey.

1297 Admiral, the first in England.

1298 The prefent Turkifh empire begins in Bithynia, under Ottoman.

Silver-hafted knives, fpoons, and cups, a great luxury.

Tallow-candles fo great a luxury, that fplinters of wood were generally ufed.

Wine fold by apothecaries as a cordial.

The Scots defeated by the Englifh at Falkirk.

1299 Wind-mills invented.

An earthquake in Germany.

Spectacles invented by a monk of Pifa.

The year of Jubilee inftituted by Boniface VIII.

1300 From this time to 1500, the merchandife of the Eaft-Indies was brought into Europe by way of the Red-Sea and the Nile, and fometimes up the Euphrates, and by caravans to Aleppo.

Standard fixed by law for gold and filver.

Looking-glaffes made only at Venice.

Woollen fhirts frequently worn at this time.

Let no one prefume (fays an edict of Charles VI.) to treat with more than a foup and two difhes.

1301 A great part of Dublin burnt, with St. Werburgh's church; buildings continued to be made with wattles and thatch.

1302 The mariner's compafs invented, by which a voyage could be performed in three months, which before took up three years.

Univerfity of Avignon founded.

1307 Bills of exchange firft in ufe.

1308 The popes remove to Avignon in France for 70 years.

The firft mayor and bailiffs in Dublin.

1309 Crockery-ware invented.

Lord Jeffrey Genvil became a friar at Trim.

1310 The bakers of Dublin drawn on hurdles through the ftreets, tied at horfes tails, for ufing falfe weights.

Lincoln's inn fociety eftablifhed.

The knights of St. John take poffeffion of the ifle of Rhodes.

1314 The

EVENTS.

1314 The battle of Bannockburn, between Edward II. and Robert Bruce, which eſtabliſhes the latter on the throne of Scotland.
- The cardinals ſet fire to the conclave and ſeparate. A vacancy in the papal chair for two years. Philip IV. king of France, died by a fall from his horſe in hunting.

1315 Germany afflicted with famine and peſtilence.

1318 Armagh battle fought againſt Edward Bruce, who was there taken and beheaded at Dundalk, and with him 6200 Scots loſt their lives.

1319 Univerſity of Dublin founded.

1320 Gold firſt coined in Chriſtendom.
An earthquake in England.
A company of linen-weavers from the Netherlands, eſtabliſhed in London.

1322 Edward II. ſurrenders the crown to his ſon.

1323 A great eruption of Mount-Ætna.
Ships from Genoa, Sicily and Venice, come to England; but no Engliſh ſhips as yet traded to the Mediterranean.

1325 The firſt treaty of commerce between England and Venice.

1327 The firſt broad-cloth made in England, by Jack of Newberry.

1330 Gunpowder invented by a Monk of Cologn; firſt made in England, 1418.
Great guns invented by Swartz, a Cologne monk; uſed at the battle of Creſſy in 1346, when Edward had four pieces of cannon, which gained him the battle; they were uſed at the ſiege of Calais in 1347; in Denmark 1354; at ſea, by Venice againſt Genoa, 1377; firſt uſed in Spain, 1406; firſt made in braſs, 1535; of iron, 1547; invented to ſhoot whales, 1731; firſt uſed in England at the ſiege of Berwick 1405; bombs and mortars invented 1634.

1331 Two Weavers from Brabant, ſettled at York; which ſays king Edward, may prove of great benefit to us and our ſubjects.
Flemiſh weavers, dyers, cloth-drapers, linen-makers,

ſilk-

silk-throwfters, &c. fettled at Canterbury, Norwich, Sandwich, Colchefter, Maidftone, Southampton, &c. on account of the duke of Alva's perfecution, 1567: they taught the Englifh the making of baize, ferges, Norwich crapes, &c. The baize-makers chiefly fettled at Colchefter.

The caftle of Arklow taken by the Irifh, and a great number of the Englifh flain: fame year, a great famine in Ireland.

1332 The pope accufed of herefy.

1333 Wheat fold in Dublin at 6*d*. per bufhel.

1337 The firft comet whofe courfe is defcribed with an aftronomical exactnefs.

Europe infefted by locufts.

Luxury reftricted by an Englifh law, wherein the prelates and nobility were confined to two courfes at every meal, and two kinds of food in every courfe, except on great feftivals: it was alfo prohibited all who did not enjoy a free eftate of 100l. per annum, from wearing furs, fkins, or filk; and the ufe of foreign cloth was confined to the royal family alone, to all others it was prohibited.

1340 Heralds college inftituted in England.

Copper-money firft ufed in Scotland.

Parliamentary grants to the king were in kind;—30,000 facks of wool being in the grant.

Blankets firft made in England.

1344 Gold firft coined in England.

Creation to titles by patents, firft ufed by Edward III.

1346 *Ich Dien*, the Bohemian motto, firft ufed by the Prince of Wales after the battle of Creffy.

1347 Durham battle, in which David, king of Scots, is taken prifoner.

1350 Order of the Garter inftituted in England by Edward III. altered in 1577, and confifts of twenty-fix knights.

Dauphine is annexed to the crown of France, on condition that the king's eldeft fon fhould always bear the title of Dauphin.

1350 The

EVENTS. 45

1350 The jubilee of a hundred years reduced to fifty, by Pope Clement VI.
- Dyers, Brewers, &c. in the reign of Edward I. began to use sea-coal for fire.
1352 Turks first enter Europe.
1353 Asia and Africa desolated by locusts.
1354 The money in Scotland till now the same as in England.
 First method of alaying bullion of gold and silver.
1355 Harlots, or common prostitutes, obliged to wear striped hoods of party colours, and their garments the wrong side outwards.
1356 Battle of Poictiers, in which king John of France and his son are taken prisoners by Edward the Black Prince.
1357 John, king of France, brought to England, and ransomed for 3,000,000 crowns, but being unable to pay it, he returned to England, and died in prison 1364.
 Coals first brought to London.
1358 Arms of England and France first quartered by Edward III.
 University of Cologne founded.
 Tamerlane began to reign in Persia.
1360 Leather-money coined in France.
1361 Lionel, earl of Ulster, third son of Edward III. lord lieutenant of Ireland.
 A great plague in England and Ireland.
1362 The law pleadings in England changed from French to English, as a favour from Edward III. to his people.
 St. Patrick's cathedral, Dublin, burnt.
 Military order of Janizaries established among the Turks.
1364 Four kings entertained by a lord mayor of London at one table.
 The statute of Kilkenny passed.
1365 University of Geneva founded.
1368 Three clock-makers from Delft, arrived in England.

1369 John

1369 John Wickliffe, an Englishman, began to call in question the doctrine of the church of Rome about this time, whose followers were called Lollards.
1370 The office of grand-vizir established.
 A great pestilence in Ireland: a frost from September to April.
1374 Bull-running at Titbury, Staffordshire, instituted.
1376 Woollen-cloth made in Ireland.
1377 Inundation of the sea in Flanders.
 Population of England in 1377 was 2,092,978 souls
                 in 1483 — 4,688,000
                 in 1688 — 6,500,000
                 in 1786 — 8,000,000
1378 Greenland discovered by a Venetian.
1380 John Philpot, alderman of London, fitted out a fleet at his own expence, and took many prizes.
 Wat Tyler, the rebel, killed by the lord mayor.
1382 The people had an extravagant way of adorning their feet; they wore the beaks or points of their shoes so long, that they encumbered themselves in their walking, and were forced to tie them up to their knees; the fine gentlemen tied theirs with chains of silver, or silver gilt, and others with laces. This ridiculous custom was in vogue from the year 1382, but was prohibited, on the forfeiture of 20s. and the pain of cursing by the clergy 1467.
1384 The first act of navigation in England; no goods to be exported or imported by Englishmen in foreign bottoms.
1386 The first impeachment of a Chancellor, and the first by the Commons.
 Windsor castle built by Edward III.
1388 Battle of Otterburn, between Hotspur and the earl of Douglas.
 Four lords justices of England were banished into Ireland by parliament; it was not lawful for them to make laws or give council upon pain of death.
1389 Saffron first brought to England by a pilgrim; cultivated in 1582.

                                                   Wines

Wines fold at 20s. the tun; and the fecond fort at 13s. 4d.
1391 Cards invented in France; firft ufed for Charles the Sixth's amufement.
1392 Charles VI. king of France, loft his fenfes and often fo outrageous that his attendants were obliged to bind him.
1393 Canary Ifles difcovered.
1394 King Richard II. lands at Waterford in Ireland, September 2d, attended with 30,000 foot, and 4000 horfe, who arriving in Dublin, granted the the city a tax of a penny to be paid annually by every houfe; he was crowned at Waterford.
1397 The gilling and pickling of herrings invented, which before were all falted and dried for redherrings.
1399 Richard II. depofed September 29th, for violating his obligation with his people (his coronation oath) and committed to the tower by Henry, duke of Lancaufter; murdered in prifon February 14th.
Weftminfter-abbey rebuilt and enlarged—Weftminfter-hall ditto.
Order of the Bath jnftituted at the coronation of Henry IV. revived in 1725; confifting of 38 knights.
1401 Wellhmen forbid purchafing lands in England.
1402 David, prince of Scotland, ftarved to death at Falkland.
Tamerlane defeats and takes prifoner Bajazet, the Turkifh fultan.
1404 The ftatutes of Kilkenny and Dublin were confirmed in a parliament held in Dublin, under the earl of Ormond.
Hats invented in Paris; firft made in London, 1510.
1405 The firft bifhop that fuffered death in England by fentence of the civil power.
Chaucer Geoffry, the old Englifh poet, died aged feventy-two years.
1407 A great plague in London.

The

The fashion of wearing collars of SS, in honour of St. Simplicius, commenced.
1409 Thomas Cusack appointed first mayor of Dublin.
Painting in oil colours, invented at Bruges, by John Van Eyck.
1410 Guild-hall, London, built.
1411 University of St. Andrew's, Scotland, founded.
1412 Algebra brought from Arabia into Europe.
Sir William Gascoigne, lord chief justice of the king's bench, committed Henry, prince of Wales into custody, for assaulting him on the bench.
1413 Knights and citizens obliged to reside at the places they represented.
Henry V. landed at Clontarf, near Dublin, Oct. 1.
1414 Muskets first used in France, at the siege of Arras.
1415 Battle of Agincourt, gained over the French, by Henry V. of England.
Sir John Falstaff, a brave officer at Agincourt.
1416 Parliament of Ireland removed to Trim.
Three popes at one time at Rome.
1417 Paper made of linen rags invented.
1420 Maderia discovered by the Portuguese; vines and sugar-canes planted there.
1421 Earl of Desmond overthrown by the Irish, May 27.
Revenue of England amounted to £.55,754.
1422 First commission of array to raise the militia.
King Henry of England, crowned at Paris. The latter end of August, died that glorious and renowned conqueror of France, Henry V.
1424 Free-masonry forbid in England.
Sheep prohibited to be exported from England.
1425 Pumps first invented:—the old bridge of Dublin built, 1428.
1428 The siege of Orleans; the first blow to the English power in France.
Parliament petitioned against hops, as a wicked weed.
1430 Church benefices forbid to be held by foreigners.
Foreigners indulged with one half foreigners in juries.

National

EVENTS.

1430 National debt first contracted in Henry VI's. reign; the present national debt commenced, and was 5,000,000l. in 1697; was 46,603,100l. in 1717; was 64,593,797l. 16s. 9d. h. in 1747; was 74,780,886l. 8s. 2d.h. in 1757; was 110,603,836l. 8s. 2d.h. in 1762; was 127,497,619l. whole interest amounted to 4,526,392l. per annum, 1772; and the debt was upwards of 200,000,000l. in 1780; and 274,000,000l. in 1784.

1431 A great earthquake at Lisbon.
  Joan of Arc, burnt for a witch.
1432 Great inundations in Germany.
1437 The obliquity of the ecliptic observed by Ulug Beg to be 23° 30' 17".
1440 Printing invented by L. Coster at Haerlam in Holland; brought into England by W. Caxton, a mercer of London, 1471.
1445 Skiddy's castle, built by John Skiddy, who was that year bailiff of the city, and afterwards mayor; his descendants live in France, where they have acquired a good estate. This castle was rented by the crown until 1785 (when the ammunition was removed to a magazine erected in the south liberties) and was shortly afterwards taken down.
1446 The Vatican library founded at Rome.
  The sea breaks in at Dort in Holland, and drowns 100,000 people.
1447 A great plague and famine in Ireland: same year it was enacted by the parliament held in Trim, that every man should shave his upper lip, or otherwise to be treated as an Irish enemy.
1450 Cormac Mac-Carthy Mac-Tiege, surnamed Laider, founded the abbey called Bally vacadane, within four miles of Cork, for austen nuns.
1453 Constantinople taken by the Turks, which ends the eastern empire, 1123 years from its dedication by Constantine the Great, and 2206 years from the foundation of Rome.
1454 University of Glasgow in Scotland founded.

E   Attornies

Attornies in Norwich, Norfolk and Suffolk reſtraind, and the number reduced from 80 to 14.

1457 Glaſs firſt manufactured in England.

1460 Engraving and etching on copper invented.

The obliquity of the ecliptic obſerved by Purbachius and Regiomontanus, to be 23° 29'.

The fourth abbey in Youghall, reformed to obſervant friars, being before that time conventuals of the franciſcan order. The occaſion of its eſtabliſhment is ſaid to be thus: Maurice Fitz-Gerald was building a caſtle in the town, and while they were at work about the foundation, the workmen, on the eve of ſome feſtival, came and begged a piece of money from him to drink his health: the earl ordered his eldeſt ſon to give it; but he, inſtead of obeying his father's direction, abuſed the workmen; which his father was ſo concerned at, that, inſtead of carrying on the caſtle, he erected a houſe of grey friars, took upon himſelf the habit, and died here in the 80th year of his age, ann. 1256. This houſe, according to Ware, was the firſt franciſcan friary in Ireland. Wadding ſays, that ſeveral religious men were interred here.

1461 Berwick taken by the Scots.

1462 Mints eſtabliſhed in Dublin for coining groats, twopenny pieces, pence, half-pence, and farthings.

There were eleven pariſh churches in and about Cork, as appears by a charter granted by Edward IV. viz. 1. St. Mary Shandon; 2. St. Catherine: 3. St. Brendan, all on the North of the river. 4. Chriſt Church; 5. St. Peter's; 6. St. John; 7. St. Nicholas; 8. St. Bridget; 9. St. Mary Nard; 10. St. Stephen's; theſe five laſt on the South ſide of the river; and 11. St. Laurence's Chapel, near ſouth-gate; beſides the above, St. Finbarr's, St. Ann's, and St. Paul's, have been ſince built.

1463 An act paſſed in Ireland for the ſecurity of privilege to members of parliament during their ſitting, and for forty days before and after it.

Youghal

Youghal incorporated by Edward IV. by the intereſt of Thomas, the great earl of Deſmond: and in a parliament held at Wexford, before Thomas, earl of Deſmond, an act paſſed to ratify and confirm all letters patent, grants, franchiſes and privileges, confirmations, &c. to the ſuffrain, bailiff, portrieve, and commons; or to the mayor, bailiff, portrieve, and commons of the town of Youghal, by the king that now is, or any of his progenitors.

1464 Youghal college founded by Thomas, earl of Deſmond; confirmed by his ſon James in 1472, and by Maurice his brother 1496; the community at firſt conſiſted of a warden, eight fellows, and eight ſinging men, who lived in a collegiate manner, having a common table, and all other neceſſaries allowed them, with yearly ſtipends, the whole donation at the time of the foundation, being worth 600l. a year. In 1464, king Edward IV. granted letters patent to Robert Miles and Philip Chriſtopher, chaplains in the college church of the B. V. Mary of Youghal, to purchaſe lands for the uſe of this church, to the value of 20 marks yearly, notwithſtanding the ſtatute of mortmain; and the ſame patent pardons them for what they had purchaſed before this licence.

The foundation charter, and the appropriation of the ſeveral tythes to this houſe, were confirmed by Jordan, biſhop of Cloyne, under his ſeal, and that of William Roche, archdeacon of Cloyne, who was then the biſhop's coadjutor. Pope Alexander, by a bull, dated in 1494, confirmed theſe grants, and gave the warden and fellows a licence to purchaſe others, and unite them to the college. In 1590 Pope Julius beſtowed the vicarage of Kilmacdonough to this houſe, and confirmed the bulls of his predeceſſors in its favour. In 1468, Pope Paul granted an indulgence to ſuch perſons as contributed towards re-edifying the church of Youghal. In the charter of foundation, the patron is is ſtiled earl of Deſmond, lord of Decies, lord of Imokilly, lord of the regalities and liberties of the county of Kerry, and patron of this foundation.

1466 Another plague viſits Dublin and Meath.

1467 By virtue of an act of parliament, the great earl of Deſmond was beheaded at Drogheda, 15th of February.

1470 The way firſt found out for taking likeneſſes in Plaſter of Paris, by And. Veroceti.

Poſt-offices firſt eſtabliſhed in Paris in England, 1642; regulated by parliament, and made general, 1657; and in Scotland, 1695. Increaſed as follows:

		£.	
1644	it yielded	3,000	per annum.
1654	———	10,000	
1664	———	21,000	
1674	———	43,000	
1685	———	65,000	
1688	———	76,318	
1697	———	90,505	
1710	———	111,461	
1715	———	145,227	groſs amount.
1744	———	235,492	
1764	———	432,084	
1788	———	400,000	clear amount.

The mail firſt conveyed by ſtage coaches, began Aug. 2, 1785; began to be conveyed to Waterford by Milford Haven, 1787. The encreaſe of the revenue by the mail coaches was above 30,000l in 1789.

1471 Margaret, queen to Henry VI. with her ſon, taken priſoner at the battle of Tewkeſbury, May 4th.

1473 Study of the Greek language introduced into France.

1477 Univerſity of Aberdeen in Scotland founded.

Watches invented at Nuremberg, in Germany; firſt uſed in aſtronomical obſervations 1500. The emperor Charles V. was the firſt who had any thing that might be called a watch, though ſome call it a ſmall table-clock, 1530. Watches firſt brought to

EVENTS.

to England from Germany 1597; spring pocket ones invented by Hooke 1658.

1479 Union of the kingdoms of Arragon and Castile.
1480 Swifs soldiers first taken in the pay of France.
1482 Coast of Guinea discovered by the Portuguese.

Edward IV. granted the charter of Kinsale, which was called in Irish, *Cean Taile*, i. e. the head of the sea; alluding to the promontory called the Old Head. The corporation forfeited their charter upon the Spaniards landing in this town, anno. 1600, together with all their privileges; for on the 14th of October 1601, the burgesses came to sir George Carew, and requested him to restore their charter, seal, mace, and royal standard, which, upon the arrival of the Spaniards, they had delivered him to keep; the president said he could not return them without directions from England, but promised to write to the queen in their favour, which he did, and soon after had an order to restore them, on condition that they should at their own charges repair their walls.

King Edward IV. died in the 42d. year of his age; he was one of the handsomest men in all Europe, Edward V. succeeded his father the 9th of April, but was never crowned; this unfortunate prince, was but twelve years of age when he began to reign, which lasted but two years and twelve days, himself and his brother the duke of York, being both murdered by the protector, Richard, duke of Gloucester, their uncle, who afterwards usurped the crown: they were lodged in the tower, where it was customary for the kings of England to reside before their coronation; and the protector, upon the refusal made by Sir Robert Brackenbury, lieutenant of the tower, to be an accomplice of so barbarous a scene of villainy, gave the government of it for one night only, to sir James Tyrrel, who had suborned one Myles Forest and John Dighton, who in the dead time of the night, entered the chamber where the two princes lay, and stifled them. The following order was sent to the lieutenant of the tower, as some authors say,

To strive to shed king Edward's blood,
Refuse to fear,—pray hold it good.

So that by placing a comma after the word *refuse*, signifies to spare his life; whereas if it had been placed after the word *fear*, it would import taking away his life; hence by the misplacing of a single comma, death ensued.

 Jane Shore obliged to do penance in St. Paul's; starved to death by Richard III.

1483 Richard III. king of England, and last of the Plantagenets, is defeated and killed at the battle of Bosworth, by Henry (Tudor) VII. which puts an end to the civil wars between the houses of York and Lancaster, after a contest of 30 years, and the loss of 100,000 men.

1486 Henry establishes fifty yoemen of the guards, the first standing army.

 Henry, earl of Richmond, known by the name of Perkin Warbeck, claimed the crown of England, and was crowned king in Christ church, Dublin; he was afterward degraded to the base office of serving in the king's kitchen.

1489 This year a great rarity was sent to the earl of Kildare, viz. six hand-guns, or muskets, out of Germany, which his guards, during the time that they stood centinels before his house in Thomas-Court, bore on their shoulders, the earl being at this time lord deputy of Ireland.

 Maps and sea charts first brought to England by Barth. Columbus.

1490 William Groceyn introduces the study of the Greek language into England.

 The Moors, hitherto a formidable enemy to the native Spaniards, are entirely subdued by Ferdinand, and become subjects to that prince on certain conditions, which are ill observed by the Spaniards, whose clergy use the Inquisition in all its tortures; and in 1609, near one million of the Moors are

driven

driven from Spain to the oppofite coaſt of Africa, from whence they originally came.

Lord Barry, of Barry's-Court, fummoned to parliament as Lord Baron Barry. The family have long enjoyed the title of vifcount Buttevant, and were created earls of Barrymore 1627.

1491 This year was called the difmal year, by reafon of the continual fall of rain all the fummer and autumn, which caufed great fcarcity of all forts of grain, throughout the kingdom of Ireland.

1492 America firſt difcovered by Columbus, a Genoefe, in the fervice of Spain.

The Moors expelled from Granada, which they had poffeffed upwards of 800 years.

Wormwood and other plants ufed for preferving malt liquors, before the ufe of hops.

1494 Sir Edward Poyning, one of the king's counfellors, arrives in Ireland, and is made lord deputy; he calls a parliament at Drogheda, where he procured (among many others) the two following bills, viz. That no parliament fhould be called in the kingdom without affigning a reafon; and a bill to be tranfmitted for calling the fame under the great feal of Ireland to the king and council, with an approbation of the faid act; together with his majeſty's leave under the great feal of England, to fummon a parliament. Alfo the memorable law, which to this day is called by his name, viz. That the public ſtatutes of England, then lately ordained, be received alfo in Ireland.

Algebra firſt known in Europe.

1495 The venereal difeafe introduced into Europe.

1496 The Jews and Moors banifhed out of Portugal.

Gerald Fitz-Gerald, earl of Kildare, was declared a traitor by fir Edward Poyning, who was then deputy of Ireland; he had the earl fent prifoner to England, where his enemies, finding that the king favoured him, concluded their laſt article with this fharp expreffion, *that all Ireland was not able to rule him*; whereupon the king replied, *then he he shall rule all Ireland*; and made him lord lieutenant thereof, in which station he continued five years; he was the seventh earl of Kildare.

1497 The Portuguese first sail to the East-Indies by the Cape of Good Hope.

South America discovered by Americus Vespusius, from which it has its name.

Corn was so scarce this year, that a peck of wheat in Meath, was sold at five lesser ounces of silver, a gallon of ale 6d. and a barrel of oats in Ulster, was worth a cow.

1499 North America discovered for Henry VII. by Cabot, a Venetian.

In November, Perkin Warbeck, and his friend John Walters, who was mayor and citizen of Cork, were tried at Westminster by a jury of twelve men, found guilty of high-treason, and hanged at Tyburn. Their heads were afterwards set up on London-bridge. Philip Walters, the son of John beforementioned, was afterwards pardoned by the king's clemency. But lord Bacon says, that both the mayor and his son were executed with Perkin.

1500 Maximilian divides the empire of Germany into six circles, and adds four more in 1512.

Brazil discovered by the Portuguese. Florida discovered by John Cabot, an Englishman.

Painting in *chiaro obscuro* discovered.

A great plague in England.

Jubilee year. Most part of the town of Galway burnt.

Virtues of Jesuits Bark discovered; first brought to Europe, 1650.

August 1st, the charter of Cork was restored, it being forfeited by the rebellion of the citizens; and a new one granted to the corporation, with an enlargement of their privileges: they were also received into the favour of king Henry.

1501 The fort of Sligo taken by Rory O'Connor.

1502 A murrain in Ireland, which destroyed a great part of the cattle in the kingdom.

1503 Sugar-

1503 Sugar-baking first found out by a Venetian.
1504 A battle fought near Galway, between the earl of Kildare and Ulick Bourk, wherein the earl got the day, and flew 2000 men.
A pestilence raged this year in this province; and the next season was followed by a great dearth, of which also great numbers perished.
1505 Shillings first coined in England.
1506 Town of Trim burnt by lightning.
1507 Island of Madagascar discovered by the Portuguese.
1508 America first had negro slaves carried to it.
1509 Gardening introduced into England from the Netherlands, from whence vegetables were imported hitherto.
Henry VII. died 22d. of April; his son Henry VIII. was crowned 24th of June following.
1510 The obliquity of the ecliptic observed by Wernenus to be 23° 28′ 30″.
1512 Castle of Belfast demolished by the earl of Kildare. Royal Navy of England, first so called.
1513 Maximilian the emperor, enlisted as a subject, and fought as a captain under Henry VIII. against France.
The battle of Flowden, in which James IV. king of Scotland is killed, with the flower of his nobility.
Benefit of the clergy taken from murderers.
1514 Cannon bullets of stone still in use.
1515 The first Polyglot Bible printed at Alcala.
The kingdom of Navarre annexed to that of Castile by Ferdinand.
1516 The kingdom of Algiers seized by Barbarossa.
1517 Martin Luther began the Reformation.
Egypt is conquered by the Turks.
The kingdom of the Mamalukes in Egypt, overthrown by the Turks.
Queens of England, France and Scotland, in England at one time.
China first visited by the Portuguese; conquered by the eastern Tartars 1636.
1518 Discovery of New Spain, and the Straits of Magellan.

1521 Henry VIII. for his writings in favour of popery, receives the title of *Defender of the Faith* from his Holiness.
Phillippine Isles discovered by the Spaniards.
Whale-bone found by the English ships at Cape-Breton.
Richard Gold brought the king's sword, and presented it to the mayor of Cork.

1522 Rhodes taken by the Turks.
The first voyage round the world performed by a ship of Magellan's squadron.
Sir Edward Poyning died. A plague in the city of Limerick.

1525 Hops first used in malt liquors in England.
1526 The Inquisition established in Portugal.
Lutheranism established in Germany.
1527 Rome taken and plundered by the imperial army.
1528 Popery abolished in Sweden.
A malignant disorder, called the sweating-sickness, in Cork.

1529 The name of Protestant takes its rise from the reformed protesting against the church of Rome, at the diet of Spires in Germany.

1530 Union of the Protestants at Smalcalde, Dec. 22d.
Secretary of State's office established in England.
The revenue of Ireland, by the lord treasurer's accounts in *omnibus exitibus & proficuis*, did not at this time, exceed 3040l. per annum.

1531 A great earthquake at Lisbon.
— O'Sullivan tells the following story with great ostentation:—that an English ship took a Spanish vessel that was fishing near the Durseys. Upon which his grand-father, Dermót O'Sullivan, prince of Bear and Bantry (as he calls him) having notice of it, manned out a small squadron of ships, and brought in both the Englishman and the Spanish vessel to Bearhaven. The English captain he hanged, and set the other at liberty.

1532 The Court of Session instituted in Scotland.
Three blazing stars appeared in two years space.

Poisoning

Poisoning made treason.
1533 Insurrection of the Anabaptists in Westphalia.
Hemp and flax first planted in England.
1534 The Reformation takes place in England, under Henry VIII.
⁕ Barbarossa seized on the kingdom of Tunis.
1535 The Reformation introduced into Ireland.
Ten thousand friars and nuns turned out of the monasteries in England.
. The society of Jesuits formed.
Etching in copper with aquafortis, invented.
A most violent plague raged in the city of Cork.
1536 Annuities or pensions, first granted 1512, when 3l. 6s. 8d. was given to a lady of the court for services done, and 6l. 13s. 4d. for the maintenance of a gentlewoman, 1536; and 13l. 6s. 8d. a competent sum to support a gentleman in the study of the law, 1554.
1539 The first English edition of the bible authorised; the present translation finished 1611.
About this time cannon began to be used in ships.
Six hundred and forty-five religious houses suppressed in England and Wales.
This summer was so dry in Ireland, that the Lee at Cork, was almost dried up, and several other rivers also, for want of rain.
1540 The variation of the compass discovered by Sebastian Cabot.
The obliquity of the ecliptic observed by Copernicus to be 23° 28' 8''.
The order of Jesuits founded by Ignatius Loyola.
Use of quicksilver discovered in refining silver ore.
Sir Anthony St. Leger, gentleman of the king's privy chamber, and knight of the garter, was sworn lord-deputy of Ireland, before whom a parliament was held at Dublin, June 13, 33 Henry the VIII. in which it was enacted, that the king and his successors should be kings of Ireland. To whom the Irish and degenerated English, made their several submissions by indenture.
1541 Ireland

1541 Henry VIII. was proclaimed king of Ireland (of which before he was only ſtiled lord, but with kingly power) in St. Patrick's, near Dublin; in London 23d. of January, and confirmed by Pope Paul in June 1555.

1543 Silk ſtockings firſt worn by the French king; firſt worn in England by queen Elizabeth, 1561; the ſteel frame for weaving invented by the Rev. Mr. Lee, of St. John's college, Cambridge, 1589.

Pins firſt uſed in England; before which time the ladies wore ſkewers.

Iron cannon and mortars made in England.

Bankrupts in England firſt regulated by law.

1544 Good lands let in England at one ſhilling per acre.

Piſtols firſt uſed by the horſe.

1545 The famous council of Trent begun, and continued eighteen years.

Alderman Read of London, ſent as a common ſoldier for refuſing Henry VIII. an arbitrary benevolence.

Needles were firſt made in England by a native of India; the art loſt at his death; recovered by Chriſtopher Greening 1560, who was ſettled with his three children, Elizabeth, John, and Thomas, by Mr. Damer, anceſtor of the preſent lord Milton, at Long Crendon, in Bucks, where the manufactory has been carried on from that time to this preſent day.

Port-holes in ſhips of war introduced.

1546 Henry VIII. died of a fever and an ulcerated leg at Weſtminſter, the 28th of January, having reigned 37 years, 9 months and 6 days; he was born 28th of June 1491; married Catherine, infanta of Spain, widow of his brother Arthur, the 3d. of June 1509, whom he devorced, and married Ann Bullen, May 23, 1533; he was excommunicated by Pope Paul, Auguſt 30th, 1535; he put Ann Bullen, his ſecond queen to death, and married Jane Seymour, May 20th, 1536, who died in child-bed, October 12th, 1537; he diſſolved the religious foundations

tions in England 1539; married Ann of Cleves, January 6th, 1540; married Catherine Howard, his fifth wife, the 8th of August following, and beheaded her on Tower-hill, with lady Rochford, February 12th, 1542; married Catherine Parr, his fixth wife July 12th, 1543, who furvived him.

Public Stews fuppreffed, which before were licenced.

1547 Firft fheriffs in the city of Dublin.

Firft law in England eftablifhing the intereft of money at 10 per cent.

Slave—a ftatute made, enacting, that a runagate fervant, or any who lives idly three days, be brought before two juftices of the peace, and marked V. with a hot iron on the breaft, and adjudged the flave of him who brought him, for two years; he was to take the faid flave, and give him bread, water, or fmall drink, and refufe-meat, and caufe him to work by beating, chaining, or otherwife; and if, within that fpace, he abfented himfelf 14 days, was to be marked on the forehead or cheek, by an hot iron with an S. and be his mafter's, flave for ever; fecond defertion felony; lawful to put a ring of iron round his neck, arm, or leg; a beggar's child might be put apprentice, and on running away, a flave to his mafter;—obtained their freedom by arrival in England, 1772; abolifhed in Polifh Auftria, June 26, 1782; debated on in parliament, 1789.

1548 The Reformation gained ground in Poland.

1549 Lord Lieutenants of counties inftituted in England. A congregation of Proteftant Spaniards in London. Dermot O'Sullivan, of Bear-haven, was this year blown up in his caftle with gun-powder, by accident; and his brother Amiavus, who fucceeded him, was killed foon after.

1550 Horfe guards inftituted in England.

The bank of Venice eftablifhed about this time.

Bullets of iron firft ufed in England.

Knitting ftockings invented in Spain.

1551 George Brown, some time archbishop of Dublin, was the first of the Roman clergy that adhered to the Reformation of the Protestant church of England.
1552 The Paris massacre of Protestants, August 24th.
No taverns but in cities and towns, and those limited to a certain number.
Books of geography and astronomy destroyed in England, as being infested with magic.
The book of Common Prayer established in England by act of parliament.
1553 King Edward VI. died the 6th of July. Mary crowned queen, October 1st.
Queen Mary restores the Popish bishops, and countenances the mass.
Circulation of blood through the lungs, first made public, by Michael Servetus, a French physician; Cisalpinus published an account of the general circulation, of which he had some confused ideas, and improved it afterwards by experiments 1569; but it was fully confirmed by Harvey, 1628.
1554 Queen Mary ordered mass to be celebrated in Dublin.
The Protestant bishop of Meath expelled.
John Rogers the first martyr, was burnt in London, and bishop Hooper at Gloucester; bishop Ridley and Latimer, suffered the same inhuman deaths.
The kingdom of Astracan conquered by the Russians.
1555 The Russian company established in England.
Coaches first used in England. Wheat sold there for 2l. 3s. the barrel.
1556 Archbishop Cranmer was burnt at Oxford, and succeeded by Cardinal Pole.
1558 Queen Elizabeth began her reign.
Calais, which had been in the hands of the English for near two hundred years, surrendered to France.
Queen Mary died the 17th of November, aged forty-three years.
A great storm of hail in Northamptonshire, the
stones

EVENTS.

stones of which measured fifteen inches in circumference, and destroyed two towns, July 4th.

1559 The memorable, or wonderful year; so called by reason of the death of the pope, emperor, and several other great princes.

Church Service first performed in English, May 8th.

Custom-house, London, first in England burnt down, and rebuilt, 1718.

Act of uniformity passed; took place, 1662.

1560 The Reformation in Scotland completed by John Knox.

Bull-fights in Spain, first used.

1561 Livonia ceded to Poland.

1562 On the 3d. of April, the roof and part of the body of Christ church fell, by which the ancient monument of Strongbow was broke.

Ireland reduced into Shires, though we call them counties.

1563 Knives first made in England, by Thos. Matthews, on Fleet-bridge, London.

The first slave trade on the coast of Guinea by the English, was opened by John Hawkins, assisted by a subscription of sundry English gentlemen; he sailed from England with three ships, purchased negroes, sold them at Hispaniola, and returned home richly laden with hides, sugar, and ginger. v. Elizabeth.

Before this year, all English iron-wire was made and drawn by main strength alone, in the forest of Dean, and elsewhere, until the Germans introduced the drawing of it by a mill. The greatest part of the iron-wire and ready made wool-cards, hitherto imported.

1564 The first coach made in England, for the earl of Rutland, by Walter Rippon.

1565 The fort and town of Derry in Ireland, burnt.

Revolt of the Low Countries.

Malta attacked by the Turks.

Potatoes first brought to Ireland from New Spain.

During

During the government of sir Henry Sidney, Mac-Carty More, was created earl of Clancare. He went over to England and made a surrender of his estate to queen Elizabeth, which she regranted to him by letters patent; and after he had sworn fealty, conferred on him the above title, and paid the charges of his journey. He was, at the same time, made lord baron of Valentia. O'Sullivan Bear also took out a patent for his estate, wherein was a proviso, that he should pay all such rents and services as were due to the said earl of Clancare.

1566 The 39 articles of the church of England established.

1567 The earls of Ormond and Desmond at open war in Ireland.

The rebellion of Shane O'Neill, when O'Neill was betrayed and slain: this rebellion cost England 237407l. 3s. 9d. over and above the cess on the country, with the loss of 3500 soldiers.

Sixty-six constables hanged for rebellion.

The old Royal Exchange in London built.

The first physic-garden cultivated in England, by John Gerrard, surgeon of London; that at Oxford, endowed by the earl of Danby, 1652; that at Cambridge began 1763. Physic garden, Chelsea, began 1732.

1568 Labour of husbandmen at different periods, from 1568, to the year 1788, in England.

1568	———	4d. per diem.
1620	———	4h.
1632	———	6
1647	———	10
1662	———	6
1688	———	8
1698	———	8
1716	———	9
1740	———	10
1760	———	1 0
1788	———	1 4

Tracton-Abbey,

Tracton-Abbey, granted by queen Elizabeth, to Henry Guilford, gent. and fir. James Craig, on their paying 7l. 15s.—it was founded anno. 1224, for ciftertian monks, by the Mac-Carty's. The abbots of it formerly fat in parliament. The monks pretended to have a piece of the crofs, which, they faid, Barry-Oge, at a great price, obtained and gave them; this was fo firmly believed, that on every holy Thurfday, vaft multitudes reforted to pay their devotions to this fuppofed relick. The monks came from Alba Lauda, in Wales; and this houfe was called De Alba Tractu.

1569 Italian method of book-keeping brought to England.
Bonner, bifhop of London, died in the marfhalfea, Sept. 5th.
Lotteries for repairing the fortifications on the coafts of England, drawn at the weft end of St. Paul's cathedral, for pieces of plate.
Perfian trade began; opened through Ruffia, 1741.

1570 Gauging invented.
The Dutch lay the foundation of their Commonwealth.
Duelling, in civil matters, forbidden in France.

1571 Felt hats made in England.
The firft printing in Irifh characters brought into Ireland by Nicholas Walfh, chancellor of St. Patrick's, Dublin.
Diffenters firft feparated from the church of England.
Ifland of Cyprus taken by the Turks.
They are defeated at Lepanto.
Marcley Hill, near Hereford, was moved from its fituation on Saturday evening, Feb. 17th; continued in motion till Monday following; carried along with it the trees, hedges, and cattle on its furface; overthrew a chapel in its way; formed a large hill 12 fathom high, where it fettled, and left a chafm 40 feet deep and 30 long, where it flood before.
A law, enacting that every perfon above feven years

of age, should wear on Sundays and holidays a cap of wool, knit made, thickened and dressed in England, by some of the trade of cappers, under the forfeiture of three farthings for every day's neglect; excepting maids, ladies, and gentlewomen, and every lord, knight, and gentleman, of twenty marks of land, and their heirs, and such as have borne office of worship in any city, town, or place, and the wardens of the London companies.

This year, queen Elizabeth gave a silver collar of S. S. to Maurice Roche, mayor of Cork, for his assistance against the rebels.

1572 A new star in Cassiopæia observed by Cornelius Gemma. It appeared in November, and disappeared in March.

— Fans, muffs, masks, and false hair, first devised by the harlots in Italy, and brought into England from France.

Presbyterian meeting-house, the first in England, at Wandsworth, in Surry, Nov. 20.

1575 A great plague broke out in Dublin, on the 7th of June, and continued till the 17th of October, which carried off three thousand persons.

The sheriffs of the city of Dublin, held their courts at Glasmanouge (now united to the city) in the time of the plague, as being remote more from it.

1576 The exercise of the Protestant religion authorised in France: this toleration followed by a civil war.

The earl of Clanrickard taken prisoner, and sent to the castle of Dublin.

Sir William Drury was appointed lord president of Munster; and two years after, was elected lord justice of Ireland.

1577 Three hundred people died at the assizes of Oxford, by the stench of the prisoners.

Sir Francis Drake began his voyage round the world, and returned in 1580.

Rory Oge O'Moore burnt Naas, Catherlough, Leighlin-

EVENTS.

Leighlin-bridge, Ballymore, Rathcool, and many other towns in Leinster.

1578 The first treaty of alliance betwixt England and the States General, January 7th.

1579 The Dutch shake off the Spanish yoke, and the Republic of Holland begins.
English East-India Company incorporated—established 1600.
English Turkey company incorporated.
The arch rebel, James Fitz-Maurice, lands in Kerry with Allen and Saunders.
The rebels defeated by the earl of Ormond.
Calendar first regulated by Pope Gregory.
Linen staining first known in England.
Youghal suffered much in the wars of the earl of Desmond; it was taken and sacked by him in this year; and being regained by captain White, it was again retaken by the seneschal of Imokilly. White, and most of his men being slain; by this means Youghal was left quite desolate, not a man staying in it, except one poor friar; but the old inhabitants were invited to return, a garrison of 300 men being left for their protection. The mayor, who had refused a garrison, and had perfidiously yielded the town to Desmond, was taken and hanged at his own door.

1580 James Usher, born in Dublin; afterwards Archbishop of Armagh.
Parochial register first appointed in England.
Kingdom of Portugal seized by Philip of Spain.
Customs of England amounted to but 14,000l. in this year; to 50,000l. in 1592; to 148,000l. in 1614; to 168,000l. in 1622; to 500,000l. in 1642; to 1,555,600l. in 1720; to 1,593,000l. in 1721; to 1,094,000l. in 1744; to 2,000,000l. in in 1748; its officers deprived of voting for members of parliament, 1782.

1581 Copper money first used in France.
Sedans first introduced in England.

Pope

1582 Pope Gregory introduced the New Stile in Italy; the 5th of October being counted 15th.

Doctor Saunders the pope's nuncio, died of a famine and the bloody flux in a wood, where his carcass was partly devoured by wolves.

Tide ebbed and flowed three times in one hour, at Lyme, in Dorsetshire.

1583 Tobacco first brought from Virginia into England.

The first proposal of settling a colony in America.

A remarkable circumstance happened in Dorsetshire; a field of three acres, with the trees and fences, at Black-moor, moved from thence, passed over another field, and settled in the highway at Hearn.

1584 By an inquisition taken at Cork, Nov. 4, Ballynamony was found to be an ancient corporation.

Stephen Skiddy, alias Scudamore, by his will, bearing date the 28th of May, and the 27th of queen Elizabeth, bequeathed, among other legacies, that the master, wardens and commonality of vintners of the city of London, and their successors, should, out of certain rents mentioned in his will, pay yearly the sum of 24 l. sterl. at the common hall of the said vintners for the time being, to the mayor of Cork, in Ireland, or his deputy, on the 25th of March and 29th of September for ever; to be by him distributed among ten of the honest poor of the said city, of the age of 40 years at the least. The mayor of the staple is governor of the said hospital and his successors. Every alderman nominates a person to the said hospital in turn, as is done in St. Stephen's hospital.

The Irish from their peculiar customs, their appearance and dress, were in regard to the English, a foreign, we might almost say, a remote nation. When the chieftain O'Neal, went upon his visit and interview with queen Elizabeth, he was accompanied, and continued to be attended in England by a guard of Gallowglasses, armed with the battle-axe, after the manner of their country, their heads bare, their hair flowing on their shoulders,

ders, and their linen vests with large sleeves, dyed with saffron. He was received and treated as an independent chief.

1585 Algerine pirates first put to sea.
Fishery of Newfoundland claimed by the English.

1587 Mary queen of Scots, is beheaded by order of queen Elizabeth, after eighteen years imprisonment.
Copperas first made in England, by Cornelius de Vos, a merchant.

1588 This being the remarkable year of the defeat of the Spanish armada, by Drake and other English admirals, and their being afterwards' dispersed by storms and tempests, several of their great ships perished on the Irish coast. On Septem. 10th, the vice-president of Munster had advice, that two great ships were lost upon the coast of Connaught, in which 700 persons were drowned, and 150 taken prisoners: there were also lost, in the same province, three great ships in Sligo haven, in which were 1500 men; in Tyrawly, one ship and 400 men; in Clare-island, one ship and 300 men; in Dunglass, one ship and 400 men; in O'Flaharty's country, one ship and 200 men; in Irrise, two vessels, the men of which were saved by other vessels; in Munster, there were two ships and 600 men lost in the river Shannon; besides one ship burnt, the men of which escaped in another ship; in Tralee, one ship and 24 men; in Dingle, one ship and 500 men; in Desmond, one ship and 300 men; with another lost in Loughfoile in Ulster, which had in her 1100 men; the whole of their loss on the coast of Ireland, was 17 ships and 5394 men.
Henry IV. passes the edict of Nantes, tolerating the Protestants.
Duelling with small swords introduced into England.
Fire-ships first invented.

1589 Sir Francis Drake, with five ships of the line, chased into Cross-haven by the Spaniards in a much larger fleet, and moored his ships under shelter of

Corribiny-hill; the Spaniards sailed up the harbour of Cork, and were surprised at not seeing the ships they had been in chase of; thus having missed their prey, they sailed out again.

Coaches first introduced into England; hackney act 1693; increased to 1000 in 1770.

This year saffron was first brought to England by a pilgrim.

Tyrone enters into a conspiracy with the Spaniards.

1590 The city of Dublin granted the priory of All-Saints for the foundation of an university.

Sail-cloth first made in England.

Telescopes invented at Middleburg, in Zealand, by the children of one Jansen, a spectacle-maker, who in play, set some glasses at a distance from each other in their fingers, which they held up against a steeple, on which they observed the weather-cock to appear much larger, and to come very near them; of this they acquainted their father, who soon improved the hint, and made it public.

Band of pensioners instituted in England.

Tea and Porcelain of China first mentioned.

Chest at Chatham enforced by law.

Criminals were ordered transportation instead of execution. Henry VIII. executed 72000.

Iron mills for flitting iron, the first in England, was set up at Dartford.

Jupiter's satellites discovered by Jansen.

1591 The East-India company began. The English make their first voyage to India.

Queen Elizabeth erected an university in Dublin, dedicated to the blessed Trinity, on the foundation of an old monastery called All-Saints; the first stone was laid by Thomas Smith, Esq; mayor of the city, attended with the regalia, March 13th. Adam Loftus, archbishop of Dublin, was the first provost; Lucas Challoner, William Daniel, James Fullerton, and James Hamilton, were the first fellows; Abel Welsh, James Usher, and James Lee, the first scholars.

The

EVENTS. 71

The firſt patent for Printing.
1593 Above 18,000 people died of the plague in London.
Cadiz in Spain, taken by the English, under the earl of Eſſex.
1594 The Jeſuits expelled from France.
The obliquity of the ecliptic obſerved by Byrgius to be $23° \ 30''$
Cork-ſtreet, in the town of Kinſale, was this year burnt to the ground.
1595 Tyrone rebells, and takes the fort at Black-Water, in Ireland.
Sir John Hawkins's expedition againſt Spaniſh America.
The obliquity of the ecliptic obſerved by Tycho-Brache to be $23° \ 29' \ 25''$.
1596 A great earthquake at Japan.
Another in Kent, where the hills became vallies full of water.
1597 The firſt act for the relief of the poor.
1598 Tyrone defeats the Engliſh forces under Sir Henry Bagnell, who is killed.
1599 The earl of Eſſex, lord lieutenant of Ireland, lands at Dublin the 15th of April: he makes a bad truce with Tyrone, and returns to England, for which he was impriſoned by the queen.
1600 The earl of Ormond made priſoner by the rebels.
St. Helena firſt poſſeſſed by the Engliſh; ſettled 1651.
Ballincolly, a large caſtle, was an ancient ſeat of the Barrets; this caſtle was garriſoned by Cromwell, and, in the late wars for king James; William Barret was created a baronet, June 4, 1665, the title now extinct.
1601 The earl of Eſſex beheaded February 25th.
The Spaniards landed at Kinſale with 4000 men, and were beat out the 25th of October.
An act paſſed to prevent men riding in coaches, as effeminate.
Inſurance of ſhipping began in England.
Lord deputy Mountjoy built the fort on Hawlbowlin.
1602 The largeſt ſhip in the royal navy of England, at the

the death of queen Elizabeth, was 1000 tons, 340 mariners, and 40 cannon.

Decimal arithmetic invented by Simon Stephen, of Bruges.

Kinalmeaky (formerly part of Carbery) forfeited by O'Mahony in the earl of Defmond's rebellion; was by queen Elizabeth granted to Grenville and Beecher, English undertakers, by whom it was first planted and got the name of a barony. It afterwards gave title to the noble Lewis Boyle, lord viscount Kinalmeaky, and baron of Bandon-bridge, who was unfortunately slain at the fight of Liscarrol. It was formerly a mere fastness, being all wood and bog, so that the army could not pass it, being obliged to go round by Kinsale, in their march from Cork to the siege of Dunboy, in Bearhaven; but it is now as well improved as any part of the country.

1603 Queen Elizabeth (the last of the Tudors) dies, and nominates James VI. of Scotland as her successor.

Sir Walter Raleigh condemned November 17.

A law enacted, that no victualler should sell less than one full quart of the best beer for 1d. and two quarts of the smaller sort for 1d.

Sir James Fullerton, also obtained a patent from king James I. for several concealed church lands; by virtue of which patent he laid claim to the college of Youghal; but sir Richard Boyle gave him a sum of money for his title.

1604 A proclamation against tobacco (used formerly for physic) and a tax laid on it, without the consent of parliament, of 6s. 8d. per pound, besides 2d. formerly. It came from the Spanish West-Indies; prohibited to be planted here, 1624; subjected to excise laws, 1789.

Sir Richard Boyle, in consideration of 1000l. paid to the king, obtained a patent for all Sir Walter Raleigh's lands in Ireland, in which the college of Youghall is particularly mentioned.

The

The following remarkable incident, happened at the siege of Bommel. Two brothers, who had never seen, but had often been in quest of one another, met here by accident. The eldest, who was called Hernando Diaz, having heard the other addressed by the name of Encisso, the surname of their mother which he had taken, a custom usual in Spain, interrogated him concerning several domestic affairs, which produced a discovery. As they were tenderly embracing each other, a cannon ball carried off both their heads, without separating the bodies, which fell down together to the ground.

1605 Gunpowder-plot discovered at Westminster; being a project to blow up the king and both houses of parliament.

A proclamation published in Ireland, commanding the popish clergy to depart the kingdom.

The city of Cork and its liberties, were separated from the county of Cork, and made a distinct county. The same year, the corporations of Bandon, Cloghnakilty, &c. began to settle their future form of government.

The first idea of attraction, taken up by Keplar.

1606 Oaths of allegiance first administered in England.

Henry Garnet, the jesuit, on a confession of being concerned in the gunpowder-plot, was executed near St. Paul's, March 28th.

Christianus, king of Denmark, came into England.

The lord Kinsale obtained letters of leave and recommendation to the king, from the lords justices and council; among other particulars, they inform his majesty, that he had given good testamony of his loyalty to the crown, in the service at Kinsale, beside several other acts of fidelity and forwardness at other times, both in civil and martial affairs; upon which, he obtained an annual pension of 133l. 6s. 8d. from king James I.

The first ambassador sent to Turkey from England.

1607 The bible translated as it now stands, by order of king James I.

Towards the end of this year, and beginning of the next, there was a most dreadful pestilence in the city of Cork, which by degrees, ceased of itself.

A conspiracy of the Irish in Ulster, to surprise the castle of Dublin.

1608 Allum first made in England.

Colonies sent from England to Virginia.

Saturn's satellites first discovered.

King James, by his charter, dated at Westminster, Jan. 20, an. reign 6, 1608, confirms all the privileges, subsidy and poundage excepted; and incorporates them by the name of the mayor, bailiffs, and commonality of Youghal. Grants to the mayor the office of admiral, and its perquisites, from Ardmore-head, and Cable-island, up to Tooreen; as also the custom of murage, cranage, keyage, and anchorage of all goods imported and exported. The mayor, bailiffs, &c. to be exempted from all juries held out of the town, except the suit concerns the king. All causes to be tried by the townsmen. All lands, &c. anciently belonging to the corporation confirmed. Two weekly markets viz. on Wednesday and Saturday, with two annual fairs on St. Luke and Ascension-day, granted to the corporation, with courts of pye-powder, &c. Power to have a staple and a mayor, and constables of the same, as the city of Dublin has. The mayor may appoint an alderman for his deputy. All waifs, strays, goods of felons, &c, granted to the corporation. The mayor, recorder, and bailiffs, to be justices of the peace, and to hold sessions of gaol delivery, &c. for the town. No freeman to be impleaded out of the town. The mayor to be coroner, say-master, and feodary. All perquisites arising therefrom to be for the use of the corporation. The mayor and recorder to be justices of the peace, in the county of Cork; and the mayor to be of the quorum. The mayor may appoint

clerk

clerks of the market, a clerk of assize, and a clerk of the assay, and no other person to intermeddle. He can appoint a sword-bearer, and may have a sword carried before him. All ships to load and unload at the key, and no where else, unless by the mayor's licence. A court of record to be held every Friday, by the mayor, recorder and bailiffs, or the deputy; as also every Tuesday, to take cognizance of all actions, real and personal. The corporation has power to distinguish themselves into several guilds and fraternities (of which there are several in this town.) The late king James also incorporated this place, by a new charter, April 18, 1688, which appoints Thomas Ronayne, esq; mayor; William Fitz-Gerald and Thos. Vaughan, jun. bailiffs, with 19 aldermen, 24 burgesses, a recorder, and town-clerk. But this charter is of no force.

1609 The independency of the United States acknowledged by Spain.

The mulberry-tree first planted in England.

New river cut, finished in three years time; the manager, Mr. Hugh Middleton, knighted by king James; runs 50 miles, and has about 200 bridges over it; brought to London, 1614.

The cities of Dublin, Waterford, Cork, Limerick, Tredagh, Galway, Ross, Wexford, Youghal, Kinsale, and Knockfergus, had their charters renewed by the lord-deputy.

1610 Galileo, of Florence, first discovers the satellites about the planet Jupiter, by the telescope, lately invented in Germany.

Henry IV. is murdered at Paris, by Ravaillac, a priest.

Thermometers invented by Diebel, a Dutchman.

1611 Baronets first created in England by James I.

An earthquake at Constantinople; 200,000 persons died there of the plague.

Bartholomew Legat, a bishop, burnt for an Arian heretic in London.

First

First voyage of the English on the whale fishery.
The tranquility of Ireland was so well established, that king James reduced the army to 176 horse, and 1450 foot; additional judges were appointed, circuits established throughout the kingdom, and sir John Davies observes, *that no nation under the sun loves equal and indifferent justice better than the Irish.*

1612 The north-west passage to China attempted in vain by the English.

A considerable part of the city of Cork was burnt down by an accidental fire.

Prince Henry died November 6th.

King James I. on the 13th of April, 1612, directed a letter to sir Arthur Chichester, lord-deputy of Ireland, in behalf of Owen Mac-Swiney, alias Owen Hogy, of Mashanaglass, to accept the surrender of his lands, and to grant a patent to restore them to him. This Owen was particularly recommended to that prince, by the lord Danvers, president of Munster, and sir Richard Morrison, vice-president, for having performed many faithful services in that king's reign, and in queen Elizabeth's. He had also testimonials from sir C. Cornwallis, who was ambassador in Spain, of his loyal and dutiful behaviour, and how much he suffered for it in his fortune and reputation during his abode there, by the malignity of his countrymen. Owen Mac-Swiney, son to the above Owen, was attainted, anno 1642, for being concerned in the Irish rebellion, and forfeited his estate.—Mashanaglass signifies a strong hold or fortress.

The castle of Dundaneere, built by Barry-Oge, stands near the confluence of the Brinny and Bandon rivers. The East-India company of England had a settlement here for carrying on iron-works, and building large ships; for which uses they purchased the woods and lands for 7000l. The following year two ships of 500 tons were

launched,

launched, and a dock was erected for building more; they kept a garrison in the castle.

1613 King James I. in a letter to sir Arthur Chichester, proposes that Cork should be divided into two counties; but the project was for that time opposed by the first earl of Cork.

A parliament called, which had not been for twenty years before.

1614 Napier of Marcheston, in Scotland, invents the logarithms.

Powdering the hair first introduced.

The lord of Kerry and lord of Clare, dispute precedency, which was adjudged to the former.

A convocation held in Dublin, which established the articles of religion.

Dying cloth in the wool first invented.

1615 The Irish parliament dissolved.

Sir Thomas Overbury poisoned in the tower.

Bands for lawyers first used by judge Finch; for clergymen in about 1652.

Sir Oliver Lambert was sent to the island of Ila, to reduce some seditious Scots.

1616 The first permanent settlement in Virginia.

Shakespear died, aged 53, at Stratford upon Avon.

Sir Richard Boyle, first earl of Cork, created baron Boyle of Youghal; it was in this town that the first potatoes were landed in Ireland, by sir Walter Raleigh. The person who planted them, imagining that the apple which grows on the stalk, was the part to be used, gathered them; but not liking their taste, neglected the roots, till the ground being dug afterwards to sow some other grain, the potatoes were discovered therein; and, to the great surprise of the planter, vastly increased; from those few, this country was furnished with seed. It is said sir Walter brought them, together with tobacco, into Ireland, from Virginia. He also brought the celebrated Affane cherry, at the same time, from the Canary islands.

1617 Coining with a die first invented.

The city of Waterford's liberties, revenues, and ensigns of authority, seized by order, under the great seal, for several crimes.

August 9th, sir Walter Raleigh, sailed from the harbour of Cork, on his last unfortunate expedition to the West-Indies.

1618 On the 7th of November, Mr. William Gold, who was the foregoing year mayor of Cork, delivered up in open court, to his successor, four charters, viz. those of Edward IV. Henry VIII. queen Elizabeth, and the charter of king James I. as also one quietus of the exchequer, for the fee-farm rent of the city.

The town of Pleurs in Italy, was buried by a slice of the Alps falling, and all the inhabitants, near 2,200, perished; a town in the same neighbourhood was buried in the same manner in the 13th. century.

Sir Walter Raleigh beheaded October 29th.

A great comet seen in England.

1619 The order of baronets first instituted in Ireland, September 30th, by James I.

A rebellion in Bohemia, Austria, and Hungary.

Proclamation, directing houses to be built with brick walls.

W. Harvey, an Englishman, confirms the doctrine of the circulation of the blood, which had been first broached by Servetus, a French physician, in 1553.

1620 The broad silk manufacture from raw silk, introduced into England.

Barbadoes discovered by sir William Courteen.

Navarre united to France.

Copper-money first introduced in England.

The famous doctor Usher made bishop of Meath.

The first peruke worn in France; introduced into England, 1660.

Gaming-houses licenced in London.

1621 New England planted by the Puritans.

The two parties of Whigs and Tories, formed in England.

Sir Fitz-Gerald Aylmer, of Donedea, in the county of Kildare, was the firſt baronet in Ireland; he was created the 25th of January, by letters patent of James I.

Thomas viſcount Thurles, father to the firſt duke of Ormond, drowned.

1622 A dreadful fire happened in Cork, which conſumed the greateſt part of the city; and the ſhoe-makers received a new charter from king James I.

The Palatinate reduced by the Imperialiſts.

Licences firſt granted for public houſes.

Maſſacre of the Engliſh by the Dutch at Amboyna.

1623 The knights of Nova Scotia inſtituted.

The Auguſt aſſizes for the county at large, were held at Bandon, by the intereſt of the earl of Cork.

1624 Doctor Uſher made archbiſhop of Armagh.

Concealing the death of baſtard children, deemed murder.

The Thames made navigable to Oxford, by act of parliament.

1625 King James dies, and is ſucceeded by his ſon, Charles I.

The iſland of Barbadoes, the firſt Engliſh ſettlement in the Weſt-Indies, is planted.

A great plague in London, of which 35,417 perſons died.

The crown of England pawned with the Dutch for 300,000l.

Hackney-coaches began in London, and were only 25 in number.

Chriſt church in Bandon built; the oldeſt grave ſtone in this church is dated 1629, over one Mr. Crofts, one of the firſt burgeſſes of this corporation.

The forts of Cork and Waterford having been quite neglected: the earl of Cork lent 500l. to the lord preſident Villers, with which theſe forts were made defenſible. When lord Wimbleton arrived

rived at Kinsale, with the king's forces, lord Cork took ten companies of foot, many of them being weak and wounded, and lodged and dieted them near three months, upon his tenants; he supplied the general with 500l. and entertained him and all his officers nobly, at Lismore.

1626 Charles I. crowned, February 2d.

The inhabitants of London and Westminster, &c. commanded by proclamation to keep all their urine throughout the year, for making salt-petre.

The king ordered the lord-deputy to make a lord high-steward, &c. for the trial of the lord Dunboyn by his peers, for killing a man in the county of Tipperary.

1627 Sir Dominick Sarsfield was created lord viscount Kinsale, to the great prejudice of this ancient and noble family, and set up his arms in the town; but upon a fair hearing before the earl Marshall, of England, he was obliged to renounce the title of Kinsale, and take that of Kilmallock.

The king ordered that Nathaniel Catlin, his second serjeant at law, should have precedency of the attorney-general and solicitor-general.

England declared war against France.

1628 The building of Boston in New-England.

1629 The crown of England redeemed from the Dutch by iron ordnance.

A great eruption of Vesuvius.

Board wages first commenced with the king's servants.

This year, an unusual appearance happened at Cork; for notwithstanding the sun shone out very bright, the sky was darkened, all of a sudden by an infinite multitude of stairs, which seemed, like a black dense cloud, to hang over the city. When they had passed the town, they were observed by the citizens, to fight furiously for several hours, with a great noise, picking and wounding each other with their bills, whereby great numbers of them fell down to the earth, and were slain; many

1629 of which, with the wounded, were taken up by the citizens and country people.

The author (Thomas Carve) says, that the like is related by Leonelavius in Pand, to have happened anno 1587, in the month of December, on the confines of Croatia, near Wihitzium, in Hungary, where flocks of wild geese were seen to fight with each other; and this happened before the invasion of the Turks.

In the year 1756, the like happened in North-America, and was related in the public papers of a battle seen at New York, between a great flock of eagles and hawks.

The earl of Cork says, that during the time of his being in the government of Ireland, which was four years, having but 100l. a month allowed him; he spent, besides his allowance, above 6000l. in maintaining hospitality and the dignity of the state; nor, during that time, was there the least complaint made of him to his majesty, or to the lords of the council of England. Adding, which government I ruled with an upright heart, and clean hands. He payed off all persons, both in the civil and military list, without having the least assistance of treasure from England, and without leaving the king a penny in debt; and whereas he found an empty treasury, he left 7000l. in it (after paying every man) in the hands of the lord Mount-Norris. He says, that during the government of the lord Falkland, the king's great north tower, in the castle of Dublin, fell down; but he had it re-edified with battlements, and platformed it with lead, and six-inch plank upon the lead, so as cannon was mounted thereon; for which he paid out of his purse 1200l. which, says he, if it had been done at the king's charge, 2000l. would not effect it.

1630 King Charles II. born the 29th of May.

Callico first imported by the East India company.

The

1631 The transit of Mercury over the sun's disk, first observed by Gassendi.

The earl of Castlehaven condemned and beheaded in England for beastly crimes.

The western coasts of this county were infested by a dangerous pirate, Nut, who not only robbed on the seas, but also made several descents on the coast. In a letter from the lord president St. Leger, to the government, he informs them, that Nut had three ships under his command, his own being a twenty gun ship, of 300 tons burden; a ship which he took belonging to St. Maloes, of 160 tons, was his vice-admiral; and the third, which he had taken, belonging to Dieppe, also mounted fifteen guns. At the time this letter was wrote, viz. in May, Nut lay with his fleet at Crookhaven, where he victualled, watered, and took his wife on board. Soon after, the government sent him a pardon, which he at first, refused; but in a little time, he accepted it.

June 30th, two Algerine rovers landed their men in the dead of the night at Baltimore, and having plundered the place, they made a great number of the inhabitants prisoners, with 100 of the English, and carried them all to Algiers. The earl of Strafford, in his letters, mentions the insolency of those rovers, who again infested the coast in 1636, being assisted by the French, whom he calls most christian Turks; for they frequently landed their captives in France, and drove them in chains to Marseilles, whence they shipped them to Algiers. The earl proposed to lay out 40,000l. of the country's money, in order to attack them, even to their own ports. In a letter of his to Mr. secretary Cook, 15th of September, 1636, he tells him,—the Turks still annoy this coast; they came of late into Cork harbour, took a boat which had eight fishermen in her, and gave chace to two more who saved themselves among the rocks, the townsmen looking on, at the same time, without means or power to assist them. The

EVENTS.

1632 The battle of Lutzen, in which Guftavus Adolphus, king of Sweden, and head of the proteftants in Germany, is killed.

June 3d. the lord-deputy Wentworth fent an ingot of filver, of 300 ounces, to the king, being the firft fruits of his majefty's mines in Munfter.

1633 Galileo condemned by the Inquifition at Rome.

Loufiana difcovered by the French.

William Prynne, tried by the ftar-chamber, ftood in the pillory 1634, again in 1637, and took his feat in the long parliament, November 28th, 1640.

Lacquer varnifh, firft ufed in the ftead of gilding.

Saw-mills firft erected near London.

There was this winter, a prodigious flood in the river Lee; which, among other damages done to the city of Cork, carried away both the north and fouth bridges, and the caftles erected thereon.

The firft exportation of corn and butter was to Spain, as appears by lord Strafford's letters, which met with very great fuccefs, the merchants making large returns in fpecie. About the fame time they began to barrel up their beef and butter, with hoops bound about with twigs after the Englifh manner, and fet two letters, B. C. the mark of Briftol, on their barrels.

1634 This year, fir Roger Coppinger, mayor of Cork, carried away the city charter, and alfo the fword and mace.

Sedan-chairs firft in ufe.

Grandier burnt in France, for witchcraft.

By an order of council, Auguft 15th, the mayor elect was either to give up the butt of fack, as formerly given him by the corporation for his entertainment in lieu of 20 nobles, or pay the chamberlain 20l. at his election.

1635 Province of Maryland planted by lord Baltimore.

Regular pofts eftablifhed from London to Scotland, Ireland, &c.

Thomas Parr, died November 15th; he lived in the
reign

reigns of nine kings and queens of England, and was 152 years old.

Parliament of Ireland diffolved.

King Charles wrote to the government of Ireland, to iffue out a proclamation to preferve the ayries of hawks in this kingdom.

1636 The fhip Royal Sovereign, built; then the largeft in the world.

Patent for copper and brafs coin in England.

A tranfit of Mercury over the fun's difk, obferved by Caffine.

1637 Stamp-office for cards and dice erected.

1638 A fea-fight between the Spaniards and Dutch.

William Chappel was confecrated lord bifhop of Cork, &c. he had been a moft fubtle difputant, of which Dr. Borlace tells the following ftory: *That at a commencement at Cambridge, in the prefence of James I. he fo warmly oppofed the refpondent Dr. Roberts, that unable to folve his arguments, he fell into a fwoon in the pulpit; whereupon the king undertook to maintain the thefis, againft whom Mr. Chappel fo well profecuted his argument, that his majefty openly gave God thanks,* that the opponent was his fubject, and not the fubject of any other prince: *and alluding to this paffage, the titular dean of Cork, long afterwards, refufed to enter into a difpute with him, although he was preffed to it by the lord prefident St. Leger; alledging, that it had been a cuftom with him to kill his refpondent.*

Monks-town is the neareft parifh, in Kerrycurihy, to Cork: the caftle was built by the family of Archdeacon: it is large and in ruins, and is flanked by four fquare turrets.

1639 A furveyor of wreftling, within three miles of London, appointed; in fuch efteem was that exercife.

A tranfit of Venus over the fun's difk, firft obferved by Mr. Horrox, Nov. 24th, O. S. 3 h. 15 P. M.

An order of council was paffed for making a new
wooden

wooden bridge at the north end of the city of Cork.

The king being resolved to go in person to York, to suppress or pacify the Scots, the lord Dungarvan, eldest son to the earl of Cork, attended his majesty, and raised 100 men at his own charge. At the same time, the earl says, *I sent two more of my sons, each with* 100 *horse, to attend the king, the raising and accoutring of which troops, cost* 5000*l.* And when the king marched into the north with his army, the earl being then seventy-four years of age, and not able personally to attend him, sent his son the lord Broghill to his majesty, to present him with 1000 broad pieces of gold. Also, when the new Irish army was to be disbanded, the earl of Cork entered into bonds of 8000l. upon which the treasurer of Ireland was furnished with money, viz. 4000l. in London, and the remainder he ordered the receiver of his rents to pay into the treasury here.

1640 King Charles disobliges his Scottish subjects; on which their army, under general Lesley, enters England, and takes Newcastle, being encouraged by the malecontents in England.

The massacre in Ireland, when 40,000 English protestants were killed.

The independency of Portugal recovered by John duke of Braganza.

The first anabaptist meeting house established in England.

Judge Berkely arrested on his seat in the court of king's-bench, and sent to prison, for giving his opinion in favour of ship-money.

Castle-Magner, the seat of Richard Magner, agent for the Irish inhabitants of Orrery and Kilmore. When Cromwell was at Clonmell, he went to pay his court to him; but being represented as a very troublesome person, and one who had been very active in the rebellion, Cromwell sent him with a letter to colonel Phaire, then governor of Cork, in which was an order to execute the bearer. Magner, who suspected foul play, had scarce left Clonmell, when he opened the letter, read the contents, and sealed it up, instead of proceeding towards Cork, turned off to Mallow, and delivered it to the officer who commanded there, telling him, Cromwell had ordered him to carry it to colonel Phaire. This officer had often preyed upon Magner's lands, for which he was resolved to be revenged. The officer, suspecting no deceit, went with the letter, which greatly surprised the governor of Cork, who knew him to be an honest man, and immediately sent an express to Cromwell for further directions. Cromwell being extremely chagrined to be so served, sent orders to let the officer have his liberty, and to apprehend Magner, who took care to get out of his reach. This castle and lands were granted to the family of Bertridge for 49 arrears; it is now the estate of sir Standish Hartstonge.

A committee from the house of commons, went to England to impeach the earl of Stafford, who was afterwards beheaded.

1641 The castle of Dundareck (which signifies Mount-Prospect) forfeited by Dermot Mac-Carthy, in the rebellion.

Coffee first brought to England by Mr. Nathaniel Conopius, a Cretan, who made it his common beverage, at Baliol college, Oxford.

On Saturday, the 23d. of October (a day dedicated to St. Ignatius) broke out the dreadful rebellion, and general defection of the Irish.

Sir Phelim O'Neal, having taken Dundalk, marched with 4000 men to Liffengarvy.

Drogheda besieged by 14,000 rebels.

The forfeited estates in Ireland sold, amounting to two millions and an half of acres.

In the rebellion of 1641, the earl of Cork shut himself up in the town of Youghal, in which he suffered

fered very great hardships, and died in it during
those troubles.
The castle of Macromp, altered into a more modern
structure by earl Clancarty. It was built in king
John's time, soon after the conquest by the Ca-
rews (according to sir Richard Cox) but others
attribute it to the Daltons; it was repaired and
beautified by Tiege Mac-Carty, who died in it
1565, who was father to the celebrated Cormac
Mac-Tiege. It is at present inhabited by Robert
Hedges, esq; who keeps it in good order. Sir
William Penn, the famous admiral was born in it.

1642 News-papers first published in England, Aug. 22d.
their annual produce to government in 1788, was
129,000l. their number printed 15,564,203.
The castle of Poulne-long, i. e. Ship-pool, built by
the Roaches (as appears from their arms over the
chimney-piece) was taken by the Bandonians,
whereby they gained a correspondence to and
from Kinsale. It is now in the possession of Thos.
Herrick, esq;
King Charles impeached the refractory members,
which began the civil war in England.
Sir Isaac Newton born on Sunday 25th December.
The castle of Limerick surrendered to the Irish.
The battles of Kilrush, Tymachoo, Raconnel, Rofs,
and Ballintober.

1643 Galway surrendered to the Irish, August 6th.
King Charles demanded a cessation of arms with the
Irish, September 7th.
Excise on beer, ale, &c. first imposed by parliament.
Barometers invented by Torricelli.
Charter and other records of Cloughnakilty, saved by
Mr. Walter Bird, who at the hazard of his life es-
caped with them to Bandon, in the Irish rebellion.
Two full companies of lord Forbes's regiment were
slain in the town, 1642; the third company be-
ing Bandonians, made good their retreat a full
mile, to an old fort on the highway to Rofs,

which they maintained till the reft of the regiment came to their relief.

Ballincarrigg caftle built by Randel-Oge Hurley, or, as fome fay, by his wife.

At Anna ftood a ftrong caftle, that in the wars of 1641 ftood a fiege of 4 years; being in the midft of a bog, was deemed impregnable; but was taken by treachery in 1745, and the whole garrifon put to the fword in cold blood.

1644 The people of Dublin numbered 2565 men, and 2986 women, proteftants; 1202 men, and 1406 women, Roman catholics.

1645 Archbifhop Laud, beheaded January 10th.

1646 Peace concluded with the Irifh catholics.

Blarney caftle, taken by Roger earl of Orrery (then lord Broghill.) It was the feat of the earls of Clancarty, and ftrongly fortified. The city of Cork was greatly annoyed by it in 1641; in queen Elizabeth's time, it was reckoned one of the ftrongeft fortreffes in Munfter; the walls are 18 feet thick, and it was likewife flanked with baftions.

1647 The famous battle of Knocknicofs, on the 13th of November, between the half-ftarved Englifh, under the lord Inchiquin, and a numerous army of the Irifh, under the lord Tauf, whereon depended the fate of this province, and where the Englifh obtained a complete victory.

The common prayer prohibited by proclamation, June 20th.

The Scots deliver up king Charles I. to the parliament, for 400,000l.

Owen Rowe burns the country about Dublin, fo that 200 fires were feen from a fteeple there.

1648 A vote paffed, that writs fhould no longer run in the king's name.

Supreme authority voted to be in the houfe of commons.

A new ftar obferved in the tail of the Whale, by Fabricius.

Wind-guns invented.

Charles

Charles II. proclaimed king, by the lord lieutenant at Youghal.

Prince Rupert arrived at Kinsale with 16 frigates, and raises some forces for Scilly, but was blocked up all the summer by the parliament's navy.

1649 King Charles I. brought before the pretended high-court of justice, the 20th of January, sentenced to death by Bradshaw, the 27th, and beheaded at Whitehall the 30th, aged 48 years; he was buried in St. George's chapel, Windsor.

Kingly government abolished by parliament.

Oliver Cromwell voted general of all the parliament forces in Ireland. The British army, under the lord of Ardes, joined the king's party, and soon after besieged Londonderry.

The king's army, under Ormond, encamped at Finglass, near Dublin.

Tredagh surrendered to the lord Inchiquin; who having soon after taken Dundalk and other garrisons, returned to the camp at Finglass.

Colonel Jones sallying out of the city, totally routed the king's forces at Rathmines, killing 4000, and taking prisoners, 2517, with all the artillery and baggage.

Oliver Cromwell landed at Dublin, with 9000 foot, and 4000 horse; began his battery next day, and took Drogheda by storm, after being twice repulsed. Dundalk immediately submitted.

Cromwell came before Wexford, and summoned the town, which he took in three days by storm, putting 2000 to the sword.

Owen Rowe and Ormond, came to an agreement.

After the taking of Ross, Cromwell besieged Waterford, but drew off again.

The garrisons in the county of Cork revolt to him. —He marched out of winter quarters, and took many small places in Munster.

Sixty houses blown up, including a tavern full of company, opposite Barkin-church, Tower-street, by the accidental blowing up of some barrels of gunpowder at a ship-chandler's, Jan. 4; a child in a cradle was found unhurt on the leads of the church.

The lady of lord Roche defended the castle of Castle-Town Roche, in a most gallant manner for several days, against the parliament forces, who besieged the castle with a battery erected for the purpose.

When Cromwell was preparing to invest Kinsale, the mayor of the town delivered up the keys to him; which instead of returning (as customary) to the magistrate, he handed them to colonel Stubber, the governor; it was whispered to Cromwell, that Stubber was not over strict in any religion; may be not, replied Cromwell, but as he is a soldier he has honour, and therefore we will let his religion alone at this time.

William III. born, November 4th.

Pendulums first applied to clocks by Huygens.

1650 Fornication made capital for the second offence.

Incest and adultery, capital for the first offence.

Bread first made with yeast by the English.

The first coffee-house in England was kept by Jacob, a Jew, at the sign of the angel, in Oxford; Mr. Edwards, an English Turkey merchant, brought home with him a Greek servant, who kept the first house for making and selling coffee in London, 1652. The rainbow coffee-house, near Temple-bar, was in 1657, presented as a nuisance to the neighbourhood.

Kilkenny surrendered to Cromwell.

Clonmell besieged and surrendered after a vigorous defence, which cost Cromwell 2000 men.

The battle of Macromp fought, where the Irish were routed.

Ormond sent to treat with Cromwell about the terms, on which the protestants of his party might be relieved.

Cromwell embarked for England at Youghal, and left the command to Ireton, his son-in-law.

The

The battle of Skirfolas fought, and the Irish routed by sir Charles Coote.
Waterford surrendered.

1651 The sect called Quakers, appeared in England.
Donough, lord Muskerry, with 4000 Irish, marching to the siege of Limerick, defeated on Knockinchally-hill, by 1000 English, commanded by lord Broghill.
King Charles II. crowned in Scotland, January 1st, entered England with the Scots army, Aug. 6th; lay concealed in the royal oak, September 4th, and escaped to France a second time, Oct. 15th.
Limerick surrendered to Ireton, who died there.
The last battle fought in Ireland, was at Knocknaclathy, where the Irish were utterly overthrown by the parliament forces, October 29th.

1652 Rofs, in the county of Kerry (a castle in an island) yielded up to Ludlow, after he had caused a small ship to be carried over the mountains, and set afloat in the lough, which terrified the enemy.
The lord of Mayo was condemned in Connaught, and shot to death.
The Dutch colony at the Cape of Good Hope, established.
Galway surrendered; which was the last town of importance, May 12th.
Admiral van Trump beat the English fleet, and sailed through their channel with a broom at his maintop, November 29th.
At Kilkenny was held the first high court of justice, for trial of such as were accused of barbarous murders in the rebellion,
Another was held in Dublin, where sir Phelim O'Neal was condemned and executed.

1653 A sea-fight between the English and Dutch on the coast of Holland, when the Dutch lost 30 men of war, and their admiral Van Trump was killed, July 29th.
Rump parliament turned out by the army, April 20.
It was declared that the rebellion was ended.

Cromwell

1654 Cromwell assumes the Protectorship.
  The air-pump invented by Otto Guericke, of Magdeburg.
  Gravelins had 3000 people killed by an explosion from a magazine.
  Peace made between the two Republics, at the supplication of Holland, who, in the two years war, lost 700 merchant ships, besides many of the navy. Respect to the English flag, stipulated by an article in the treaty.
  The fine broad-cloth of England sent to Holland to be dyed.
1655 Archbishop Usher died the 31st of March.
  The Jews admitted into England, after an expulsion of 365 years.
  The English, under admiral Penn, took Jamaica from the Spaniards.
  One of Saturn's satellites observed by Huygens.
  Tripoli reduced by Admiral Blake.
  In this year the city and county of Londonderry was restored to the society, who had been deprived of it by a decree in the star-chamber, 1636.
1656 The river Thames ebbed and flowed twice in three hours, October 3d.
  The first manufacture of wove stockings in France.
1657 Mugletonians began.
1658 Cromwell died, and was succeeded in the Protectorship by his son Richard.
  The earl of Clancarty was first summoned to parliament as baron of Blarney, by queen Elizabeth, and created viscount of Muskerry, and earl of Clancarty, in 1658, the 10th of Charles II.
1659 The officers to the army in favour of the king's restoration, surprized the castle of Dublin and Jones in it, and declared for a free parliament.
  Bradshaw, the Regicide, died October 31st.
1660 They accepted his majesty's declaration from Breda, and concurred to his restoration.
  Franking letters first claimed.
  King Charles II. proclaimed at Cork, on the 29th

of May; fame day colonel Phaire was fent prifoner to Dublin.
King Charles II. was reftored by Monk, commander of the army, after an exile of twelve years in France and Holland.
Charles II. gave a collar of SS to the mayors of Dublin.
The people of Denmark being oppreffed by the nobles, furrendered their privileges to Frederic III. who became abfolute.
Baize manufacture firft introduced into England, at Colchefter.
King George I. born 28th of May.
King Charles II. made his entry through London to Whitehall, being the day of his reftoration, and his birth-day, May 29th.
Lewis XIV. married to the infanta of Spain; June the 19th.
Poft-offices firft eftablifhed in England.
Tea, coffee, and chocolate, firft mentioned in the ftatute books.
January 30th, the carcaffes of Oliver Cromwell, Henry Ireton, and John Bradfhaw, were hanged at Tyburn, and buried under the gallows.
Afparagus, artichokes, cauliflowers, lemons and oranges, firft brought to England.
King James II. married to the lady Ann Hyde, September the 3d.

1661 The duke of Ormond appointed lord lieutenant of Ireland, October the 4th.
Logwood allowed by law to be ufed for dying.
Queen of Bohemia vifited England, May the 17th, and died there.
The obliquity of the ecliptic obferved by Helvetius to be $23° 29' 7''$.

1662 Mary, king William's queen, born April 30th.
The court of claims fat at the king's inns, Dublin, February the 15th.
. The Royal Society eftablifhed at London, by Charles II.

The

The Lacteals discovered by chance, in opening a dog, by Ascellius, July 23; in birds, fish, &c. by Mr. Hewson, surgeon of London, 1770.

1663 The plot of Jephson, Thompson, Blood, &c. to seize the castle of Dublin, discovered June 1st.

Turnpike gates erected.

Carolina planted: 1728, divided into two separate governments.

Prussia declared independent of Poland.

Castlemartyr, formerly Ballymartyr; it was incorporated by the interest of the earl of Orrery, who erected it into a borough, with the nomination of the chief magistrate, recorder, town-clerk, clerk of the market, and other proper officers, to the earl and his heirs for ever, and with a privilege of sending two members to parliament.

1664 War proclaimed by England against the Dutch.

Sir William Penn, with part of his majesty's fleet, sailed from Dover, November 23d.

A blazing star seen in England, December 24th.

A protestant militia raised in Ireland, Sept. 16th.

The New Netherlands in North America conquered from the Swedes and Dutch, by the English.

Cattle were prohibited to be imported into England, from Ireland and Scotland.

Exportation of corn from England, permitted by law; bounty granted, 1689.

1665 This year, the magistracy of Dublin was honoured with the title of lord mayor; Sir Daniel Bellingham being the first that bore that title; 500l. per annum being allowed by the crown to support that honour.

Signals at sea, first devised by James II.

The plague raged in London, and carried off 68,000 persons.

The magic lantern invented by Kircher.

The first London Gazettee, published Feb. 15th.

A great plague at Lyons in France, when 60,000 persons died.

A glorious

A glorious victory obtained by his majesty's fleet, under prince Rupert, over the Dutch, wherein 18 capital ships were taken, and 14 destroyed, June the 3d.

1666 War with France, January 26th; with Denmark, the 19th of October following.

September 2d. about one o'clock in the morning, a dreadful fire broke out in London, which consumed 113,000 houses; the city gates, guildhall, 86 churches, among which was St. Paul's cathedral, and 400 streets; the ruins of the city were 436 acres, extending from the tower to the temple-church, and from the north-east gate to Holborn-bridge and Fleet-ditch. It broke out near the monument, and burnt four days and nights without intermission.

The duke of Ormond, lord lieutenant, made a progress through this county, and was escorted by the horse militia of each barony, who made a fine appearance, the earl of Orrery, and chief gentry of the county, being their officers, most of whom served in the civil wars.

The lord lieutenant and council, considered about sending 105,000 bullocks, for the relief of London lately burnt.

Tea first used in England.

Insurance-offices first set up in London.

Dying and dressing of woollen-cloth, perfected in England by one Brewer, from the Netherlands.

The militia arrayed; those of Leinster encamped on the curragh of Kildare; those of Dublin in the city; being on account of an expected invasion from France.

Captain O'Brien (son to the earl of Inchiquin) in the Advice man of war, brought in three Dutch prizes which he had taken; one of them was an Indiaman of 800 tuns burthen, with a very rich cargo, besides thirteen chests of silver, each containing 1800l.

The

The LIST for CIVIL AFFAIRS.

Containing the several entertainments, by the year, of all officers and others, serving in our courts of justice, in the several provinces of Ireland: officers belonging to the state; officers of our customs; officers of the excise; creation-money; with other perpetuities and particular payments for our service; which we require henceforth to be duly paid out of our revenues there, by the hands of our vice-treasurer, or receiver-general for the time being, according to the cautions here mentioned; the same to begin for, and from the first day of April, 1666.

☞ *These following payments are the constant fees to be continued to the several officers, without change from time to time.*

	l.	s.	d.
The right honourable Arthur, earl of Anglesey, vice-treasurer, and general-receiver.	50	0	0
Sir Robert Meredith, knt. chancellor of the exchequer.	100	0	0
John Bysse, esq; lord chief baron of the exchequer.	600	0	0
Sir Richard Kennedy, kt. second baron of the exchequer.	300	0	0
John Povey, esq; third baron of the exchequer.	220	0	0
Sir Audly Mervin, knt. his majesty's prime serjeant at law.	20	10	0
Sir William Domvile, kt. his majesty's attorney-general.	75	6	0
Sir John Temple, knt. his majesty's solicitor-general.	75	0	0
Philip Fernely, esq; his majesty's chief remembrancer.	30	0	0

EVENTS.

	l.	*s.*	*d.*
Sir James Ware, knt. his majesty's auditor general, for his ancient fee per annum 184l. 6s. 3d. and for an augmentation thereof, allowed by the former establishment 50l. in all.	234	6	3

The Court of Exchequer.

Sir Allen Brodrick, knt. his majesty's surveyor-general.	60	0	0
Francis Lee, escheator of the province of Leinster.	6	13	4
Escheator of the province of Ulster.	20	5	0
Escheator of the province of Munster.	20	5	0
Escheator of the province of Connaught.	20	5	0
Henry Warren, esq; second remembrancer.	7	17	6
Nicholas Loftus, esq; cleark of the pipe.	15	0	0
Roger Moore, esq; chief chamberlain.	10	0	0
Sir Robert Kennedy, bart. second chamberlain.	5	0	0
Maurice Keating, comptroller of the pipe.	7	0	0
John Longfield, usher of the exchequer, for his fee per annum, 2l. 10s. and for his allowance for ink for the exchequer, 10l. per annum; in all per annum	12	10	0
Thomas Lee, transcriptor and foregin opposer.	15	0	0
Edward Ludlow, summonitor of the exchequer.	7	5	0
John Burniston, marshal of the four-courts.	4	0	0
Sir Theophilus Jones, knt. clerk of the pells.	30	0	0
John Exham, clerk of the first fruits, and twentieth parts.	27	10	0
Thomas Gibson, crier of the court of exchequer.	1	14	4

The Court of King's-Bench.

	l.	*s.*	*d.*
The right honourable James, baron of Santry, lord chief justice of his majesty's bench.	800	0	0
Sir William Aston, knt. second justice of the said court.	300	0	0
Thomas Stockton, esq; third justice of the said court.	300	0	0
Sir William Usher, knt. clerk of the crown, of the said court.	7	10	0

The Court of Chancery.

The most reverend father in God, Michael, lord archbishop of Dublin, lord chancellor of Ireland.	1000	0	0
Sir John Temple, sen. knt. master of the rolls.	144	3	4
Dr. Dudley Loftus, one of the masters of the chancery.	20	0	0
Robert Mollom, esq; another master of the chancery.	20	0	0
George Carleton, clerk of the crown in chancery.	25	0	0
The said George Carleton, clerk of the hanaper, for his fee per annum 10l. 10s. and for an allowance of paper and parchment for the chancery, per annum 25l. In all per annum	35	10	0
	1244	13	4

The Court of Common-Pleas.

Sir Edward Smith, knt. lord chief justice of the common-pleas.	600	0	0
Sir Jerome Alexander, knt. second justice of the said court.	300	0	0
Robert Booth, esq; third justice of the said court.	300	0	0

EVENTS.

	l.	s.	d.
Sir Walter Plunkett, knt. prothonotary of the said court.	7	10	0
	1207	10	0

Star-Chamber.

	l.	s.	d.
Sir George Lane, knt. clerk of the star-chamber.	10	0	0
George Rutlidge, marshal of the star-chamber.	10	0	0
	20	0	0

Officers attending the State.

	l.	s.	d.
Sir Paul Davis, knt. secretary of state, for his fee	200	0	0
The said sir Paul Davis, for intelligences	100	0	0
The said sir Paul, clerk of the council, for his ancient fee, per ann. 7l. 10s. and for an allowance for paper and parchment 40l. In all	47	10	0
Richard St. George, esq; Ulster king at arms	26	13	4
Richard Carvy Athlong, pursivant	10	0	0
Phillp Carpenter, esq; chief serjeant at arms, at 5s. 6d. per diem.	100	7	6
George Pigott, second serjeant at arms, for like allowance,	100	7	6
George Wakefield, pursivant,	20	0	0
William Rowe, pursivant,	20	0	0
Arthur Padmor, pursivant,	20	0	0
Thomas Lee, keeper of the council-chamber.	18	5	0
Six trumpeters and a kettle-drum, at 60l. each per ann. 420l. for their fee, and 6l. per ann. each board-wages 42l. In all	462	0	0
	1125	3	4
	Charge		

REMARKABLE

Charge of Circuits.

	l.	s.	d.
The chief and other justices of assizes in every the five circuits twice a year, per annum.	1000	0	0
Robes for the judges, viz three in exchequer, three in the king's-bench, three in the common-pleas, master of the rolls, and three of the king's council, at 13l. 6s. 8d. a piece per ann. making in all	173	6	8

Incidents.

Liberates under the seal of the exchequer yearly, viz. the chancellor of exchequer, 13l. 6s. 8d. the chief remembrancer, 6l. 13s. 4d. clerk of the pipe, 6l. 13s. 4d. the usher, 10l. the second remembrancer, 5l. the chief chamberlain, 5l. the second chamberlain, 5l. clerk of the common-pleas of the exchequer, 5l. summoniter and comptroller of the pipe, 5l. the customer at Dublin for wax, paper, parchment and ink, 3l. 15s. In all per ann.	82	10	8
Rent of a house for the receipts	25	0	0
Keeper of the house for the receipts	5	0	0
Singers of Christ church in Dublin, for singing in the exchequer, and praying for his majesty, at 10s. for every term per annum.	2	0	0
Pursuivants of the exchequer for carrying writs.	71	5	0
Paper and parchments to the courts	150	0	0
The nobility, bishops, and counsellors, which shall reside and keep house in Ireland for impost of wines, according to his majesty's special grace.			

	508	13	4

Besides impost of wines.

EVENTS.

Provincial Officers.

	l.	s.	d.
William Halfy, efq; chief juftice of the province of Munfter.	100	0	4
John Nayler, fecond juftice of Munfter	66	13	0
Henry Batthurft, attorney of the province of Munfter.	13	6	4
William Carr, efq; clerk of the council of the faid province.	7	10	0
Walter Cooper, ferjeant at arms there	20	0	0
Oliver Jones, chief juftice in the province of Connaught.	100	0	0
Adam Cufack, efq; fecond juftice of that province.	66	13	4
John Shadwell, efq; attorney for the faid province.	20	0	0
Sir James Kuff, knt. clerk of the council there.	7	10	0
Thomas Elliot, ferjeant at arms there	20	0	0

Officers of the Cuftoms.

Dublin.

Thomas Worfop, cuftomer of the port of Dublin.	7	10	0
William Maul, efq; comptroller,	7	10	0
William Scott, efq; fearcher,	5	0	0
	20	0	0

Wexford.

George Wakefield, cuftomer,	10	0	0
Hugh Polder, comptroller,	5	0	0
	15	0	0

Waterford and Rofs.

Sir John Stephens, cuftomer,	15	0	0
Frederick Chriftian, comptroller,	15	0	3
Thomas Tint, fearcher,	6	13	4
	36	13	4

	l.	*s.*	*d.*
Cork.			
Richard Scudamore, customer,	6	13	4
Robert Williams, searcher,	5	0	0
	11	13	4
Kinsale.			
Robert Southwell, customer,	13	6	8
John Brown, searcher,	6	13	4
	20	0	0
Dingle-Icoush.			
John Selby, customer,	5	0	0
Limerick.			
The customer,	13	6	8
Montford Westrop, comptroller,	13	6	8
John Lynch, searcher,	5	0	0
	31	13	4
Galway.			
John Morgan, customer,	13	6	8
The searcher,	5	0	0
	18	6	8
Drogheda, Dundalk, and Carlingford.			
Thomas Willis, customer,	7	10	0
John Bulteele, comptroller,	7	10	0
Hugh Montgomery, searcher,	5	0	0
	20	0	0
Carrickfergus.			
Roger Lindon, customer,	7	10	0
Samuel Wilby, searcher,	6	13	4
	14	3	4
Strangford.			
Nicholas Ward, customer,	7	10	0

Newcastle,

EVENTS.

Newcastle, Dundrum, &c.

	l.	*s.*	*d.*
Robert Hard, searcher at Newcastle, Dundrum, Killaleagh, Bangor, Holywood, Belfast, Olderfleet, St. David, Whitehead, Ardglasse, Strangford, Ballintogher, and Donaghadee,	6	13	4

Creation-Money.

The duke of Ormond	40	0	0
The marquis of Antrim	40	0	0
The earl of Castlehaven	20	0	0
The earl of Desmond	15	0	0
The earl of Westmeath	15	0	0
The earl of Arglasse	15	0	0
The earl of Carbury	15	0	0
The earl of Cavan	15	0	0
The earl of Donegal	15	0	0
The earl of Clanbrazil	20	0	0
The earl of Inchiquin	20	0	0
The earl of Orrery	20	0	0
The earl of Montrath	20	0	0
The earl of Tyrconnel	20	0	0
The earl of Clancarty	20	0	0
The earl of Mount-Alexander	20	0	0
The earl of Carlingford	20	0	0
The lord viscount Grandison	10	0	0
The lord viscount Willmot	10	0	0
The lord viscount Valentia	10	0	0
The lord viscount Dillon	10	0	0
The lord viscount Nettervil	10	0	0
The lord viscount Killulla	10	0	0
The lord viscount Magennis	10	0	0
The lord viscount Sarsfield and Kilmallake	10	0	0
The lord viscount Renelaugh	10	0	0
The lord viscount Wenman and Tuam	10	0	0
The lord viscount Shannon	13	6	8

The lord vifcount Clare   10 0 0
The lord baron of Cahir   11 5 0
                                         484 11 8

Where creation-money is granted to one and the fame perfon for two honours, that fum which is granted with the higheft title, is only to be paid.

1667 Dr. Jonathan Swift, dean of St. Patrick's, Dublin, born Nov. 30th.

The peace of Breda, which confirms to the Englifh the New Netherlands, now known by the names of Pennfylvania, New-York, and New-Jerfey.

The Englifh fleet deftroyed at Chatham by the Dutch.

Sheernefs blown up by the Dutch fleet.

The militia of the city of Cork confifted of 600 foot and 60 horfe, all ready for duty.

A general peace proclaimed in Cork between England, France, Denmark, and Holland.

1668 The peace of Aix la Chapelle.

St. James's Park planted, and made a thoroughfare for public ufe by Charles II.

Bridge-town in Barbadoes burnt, April 18th.

Earl of Orrery impeached, but acquitted with honour, on which his majefty prefented him with 7000l. he died 1679, aged 59.

The high fpire of St. Audoen's fteeple in Dublin, blown down.

1669 War with the Algerines, September 6th.

The ifland of Candia taken by the Turks.

1670 The Englifh Hudfon's-Bay company incorporated.

The obliquity of the ecliptic obferved by Mengoli to be $23° 28' 24''$.

Blood feized the duke of Ormond with an intent to hang him at Tyburn, but prevented Dec. 6th.

Blue-coat hofpital in Dublin, built by the contribution of the citizens.

A fignal victory obtained by captain Beech, and
                                                   fome

some more of his majesty's ships, over the Algerines.

The wooden-bridge over the Liffey, commonly called the Bloody Bridge, built.

Henry Jenkins of Yorkshire, died aged 169.

Maiming and wounding, made capital.

Cabinet council first instituted.

Muslins from India, first worn in England.

Salt-mines in Staffordshire, discovered.

Charles-Fort at Kinsale, began and received that name by the duke of Ormond, who came to review it; it cost 73000l. on the works to the sea, 100 pieces of brass cannon were mounted, carrying from 24 to 42 lb. ball.

The channel to the south of the King's-marsh, now called Dunscombe's-marsh, was cut, and the quay on the same began to be filled up.

By a bye-law of the corporation, made November the 8th, the sons of a freeman, at the age of 21 years are admitted to be free, without paying any fine except officers fees.

1671 Blood attempted to steal the crown out of the tower, May the 9th.

The play-house in Smock-Alley fell, and killed several, besides divers bruised and hurt, Dec. 26th.

The apprentices in Dublin assembled with an intent to break down the wooden-bridge, twenty of whom were seized and committed to the castle, but afterwards as they were carrying to bridewell, under a guard of soldiers, they were rescued, and four of them killed in the fray; hence it was called Bloody Bridge. The occasion of this riot was on account of a ferry belonging to the city, which the building of this bridge effected.

This year a proclamation was issued for all the corporations to renew their charters; the city of Cork appointed Henry Bathurst, esq; to be their agent for the renewing of theirs.

1672 Admiral earl of Sandwich, blown up in an engagement with the French, May 28.

Shoulder-

Shoulder-knots first used.

Louis XIV. over-runs great part of Holland, when the Dutch opened their sluices, being determined to drown their country, and retire to their settlements in the East-Indies.

African company established.

The obliquity of the ecliptic observed by Richer to be 23° 28' 54".

Farthings first coined by Government, August 16th.

The Dutch fleet defeated at Southwold-Bay, by the duke of York, May the 28th.

Tobago, in the West-Indies, taken from the Dutch, December 20th.

According to sir William Petty, there were no more than 1,000,000 people in Ireland.

1673 The prince of Orange made Stadtholder.

Prince Rupert defeats the French fleet, Aug. 11th.

An alphabetical list of the noblemen and gentlemen in the commission of the peace for this county, in the year 1773, exclusive of the mayors of Cork and Youghal, the Sovereign of Kinsale, and the provost of Bandon, all for the time being.—Note, Thus marked *, or thus †, were appointed since the year 1750.

Adderly, Thomas, esq;
Aldworth, Boyle, esq;
Aldworth, Richard, esq;
*Aldworth, St. Leger, esq;
*Anderson, William, esq;
*Ashe, Richard, esq;
*Atkin, Walter, esq;
*Austen, William, esq;
*Ball, Robert, esq;
*Beecher, Edward, esq;
Bernard, Arthur, esq;
*Bernard, Francis, sen. esq;
Bernard, Francis, jun. esq;
*Bernard, James, esq;
*Bernard, John, esq;

*Bernard, Roger, esq;
Berkeley, rev. Robert,
*Bligh, rev. Robert,
*Bousfield, Benjamin, esq;
*Bowerman, Henry, esq;
*Bowles, George, esq;
*Brereton, George, esq;
*Brown, rev. Edward,
*Brown, Richard, esq;
*Brown, rev. St. John,
*Bullen, John, esq;
*Bullen, Robert, esq;
*Butler, Thomas, esq;
Callaghan, Robert, esq;
*Capell, Joseph, esq,

Carey

EVENTS.

*Carey, Peter, esq;
*Carey, William, esq;
*Chester, Richard, esq;
*Chinnery, Broderick, esq;
*Chinnery, rev. George,
Chinnery, Nicholas, esq;
*Colthurst, sir John, bart.
*Colthurst, John, esq;
*Connor, Roger, esq;
Conron, Christopher, esq;
*Coote, Chidley, esq;
*Coppinger, Maurice, esq;
Corker, Thomas, esq;
*Cotter, sir Js. Lawr. bart.
*Cowley, William, esq;
*Creagh, Michael, esq;
Creed, John, esq;
*Crofts, Wills, esq;
*Croker, Taylor, esq;
*Crofs, Philip, esq;
Dalacourt, Robert, esq;
*Davies, Henry, esq;
Davies, Rowland, esq;
Davies, rev. Michael,
*Deane, Jocelyn, esq;
*Deane, sir Rob. Tilson, bart.
*Devonshire, Abraham, esq;
*Donoghue, John, esq;
*Drew, Francis, esq;
*Durdin, Alexander, esq;
*Earberry, Matthias, esq;
*Elphin, right rev. Jemmett, lord bishop of
*Evans, Eyre, esq;
*Evans, Nicholas Green, esq;
*Evans, rev. Thos. Waller,
*Eyre, Richard, esq;
*Falkiner, Riggs, esq;
*Fitz-gerald, Richard, esq; of Mitchelstown,

*Fitz-gerald, Robert, esq;
Fitzgerald, Robert Uniacke esq;
Fitzmaurice, hon. John,
*Fitzsimons, Walter, esq;
*Freeman, Joseph, esq;
*Freeman, Matthew, esq;
Freke, sir John, bart.
French, Savage, esq;
*Fuller, William, esq;
Gibbons, Thomas, esq;
Gifford, Arthur, esq;
*Godsell, James, esq;
*Gould, Michael, esq;
*Gorden, Robert, esq;
Grady, Standish, esq;
*Gray, Francis, esq;
*Gray, Richard, esq;
Gumbleton, Richard, esq;
*Hendley, Matthias, esq;
*Herrick, Falkiner, esq;
*Hewitt, rev. Henry,
*Hewitt, Isaac, esq;
*Hingston, rev. James,
Hoare, Edward, esq;
Hoare, Samuel, esq;
*Hednett, rev. William,
*Honner, Robert, esq;
*Hull, William, esq; of Cahermul,
*Hull, William Richard esq;
*Hungerford, Thos. esq;
*Hutchinson, Massey, esq;
*Jackson, Rowland, esq;
*Jeffries. Js. St. John, esq;
*Jephson, Denham, esq;
Jervais, Samuel, esq;
*Jones, Edward, esq;
*Kearney, James, esq;
†Kenny, rev. John.

Knight,

†Knight, Christopher, esq;
†Lawton, Hugh, esq;
†Leader, William, esq;
†Lisle, right hon. John, lord baron of
†Lloyd, Edward, esq;
Longfield, John, esq;
†Longfield, Richard, esq;
†Lumley, William, esq;
Lysaght, John, esq;
†Lysaght, Nicholas, esq;
†Lysaght, William, esq;
†M'Carthy, Ruby, esq;
†Mannix, Henry, esq;
†Marshall, John, esq;
†Massey, Hugh, esq;
†Meade, David, esq;
†Mellefont, Richard, esq;
†Mockler, rev. James,
Moore, Emanuel, esq;
†Morris, Abraham, esq;
†Morris, Jonas, esq;
†Mount-Cashel, right hon. Stephen, lord viscount,
†Newenham, sir Edw. knt.
†Newenham, Robert, esq;
– Newman, Adam, esq;
Newman, Richard, esq;
†O'Callaghan, Daniel, esq;
†O'Leary, Denis, esq;
Parker, John, esq;
†Parker, Matthew, esq;
Parker, Robert, esq;
†Parsons, Thomas, esq;
†Peard, Christopher, esq;
†Pearde, Henry, esq;
†Philpott, Usher, esq;
†Purcell, James, esq;
†Purcell, rev. Richard.
†Purdon, Bartholomew, esq;
†Purdon, George, esq;
†Puxley, Henry, esq;
Roberts, Randal, esq;
†Roberts, William, esq;
†Roche, Edmond, esq;
Rogerson, John, esq;
†Rye, John, esq;
†St. Leger, Warham, esq;
†Sealy, George, esq;
†Shannon, right hon. Richard, earl of, *custos rot.*
†Snow, William, esq;
†Spaight, Thomas, esq;
†Spread, William, esq;
†Stawell, George, esq:
†Stawell, Samson, esq;
†Stawell, William, esq;
†Steele, Robert, esq;
†Strangford, right hon. and rev. Philip, lord viscount.
†Sullivan, rev. John,
†Supple, Edmond, esq;
†Supple, James, esq;
Supple, William, esq;
†Swayne, Benjamin, esq;
†Tanner, Jonathan, esq;
†Thornhill, Edw. Badham, esq;
†Tisdall, rev. Michael,
Tonson, Richard, esq;
†Tottenham, Cliffe, esq;
†Townsend, Edward Mansell, esq;
†Townsend, Richard, esq;
†Townsend, rev. Richard,
Townsend, rev. Horatio,
†Townsend, John, esq; of Mardyke
Travers, Boyle, esq;
Travers, Robert, esq;

Travers,

†Trave fe, Walter, esq;
†Underwood, Richard, esq;
†Unacke, John, esq;
†Wallis, Henry, esq;
†Warren, Robert, esq;
†Watkins, Westrop, esq;
White, Richard, esq;
†White, Simon, esq;
†Widenham, rev. Thomas,
†Witheral, Joseph, esq;
Wrixon, Henry, esq;

☞ *The reader will please to note, that the above list should be placed among the articles of* 1773.

1674 The Dutch agree to honour the English flag.

A witch tree, in sir Walter Baggot's park, in the county of Stafford, which took two men five days in felling it; it lay 40 yards in length, the stool 5 yards and 2 feet diameter, 14 loads of wood broke in the fall, and 48 loads in the top; there were 8,660 feet of board and plank; it cost 10l. 17s. sawing; the whole substance was computed to be 97 tons.

October 7, ann. 1674, there was an order of council, that a grant should pass under the seal of the city of Cork, of the place of prior of the hospital of St. Stephen, to William Worth, esq; to hold the same as Richard Ward, esq; enjoyed it, which grant the said William Worth, esq; is to deposit into the hands of the mayor, together with the resignation of the said Mr. Ward; and also, all deeds and leases relating to the lands of the said hospital, in the north liberties of the city, until a proper instrument be perfected by the said William Worth, relinquishing all other titles to the same employ, but what he shall receive from the corporation; which deed being perfected, the said grant is to be delivered to the said William Worth, esq;   Signed John Bayly, mayor.

1675 Coffee-houses suppressed on account of the liberty taken with the politics of the times.

Callicoe printing, and the Dutch-loom engine, first used in England.

Peter Fox and five more, pretending to be passengers in a rich ship in Holland, bound for France, murdered the master and some of the crew, and brought her to Ireland; they were all executed at St. Stephen's-Green.

Phosphorus, artificial fire, discovered.

1676 Essex-bridge in Dublin, built by sir Humphry Jarvis.

The following subsidies were, this year, raised in this county. The earl of Cork, 110l. He paid more than any nobleman in Ireland; for I find the duke of Ormond then paid but 100l.—the earl of Barrymore, 30l.—earl of Carbery, 15l.—earl of Clancarty, 40l.—earl of Orrery, 20l.—Lord Courcy, 2l.—Lady Clancarty, 15l.—the bishopricks of Cork and Ross, 32l. 16s.—the bishoprick of Cloyne, 4l. 4s.—the county of Cork and city of Cork, 1364l. 18s.

The south bridge of the city of Cork, built by the corporation.

1677 Lady Mary of England, daughter to James duke of York, married to William, prince of Orange.

Violins invented.

The micrometer invented by Kircher.

1678 The peace of Nimeguen.

The habeas corpus act passed.

A strange darkness at noon-day, Jan. 12.

The wife of William Peters, at the bunch of keys in High-street, Dublin, was delivered of four sons, who all lived to be baptized, September 14th.

Several rich French prizes brought into Kinsale, by the prince William, a Dutch man of war; as were some Dutch prizes, by the Invincible, a French ship of war.

Draw-bridges made on the north and south bridges of the city of Cork, by order of lord Shannon, the governor.

Burying in woollen, first began.

June 10th, The corporation of the city of Cork, by a bye-law, changed the mode of chosing a mayor

and

and sheriffs which was. The mayor and two
sheriffs made choice each man of three persons out
of the council, being nine in all; who, with the
present mayor and sheriffs, made twelve. These
twelve went into the castle, and there continued
till they made choice of three other persons out
of the common council, to be offered to the freemen as candidates for the mayoralty, one of whom
they elected by votes; in case of disagreement of
the twelve men until 12 o'clock at night, the
mayor and sheriffs made choice next day of three
more, and proceeded as before upon a choice of
three persons to be candidates to the freemen for
the place of mayor. The mode adopted was,
that the mayor and sheriffs, as formerly, should
chose three persons, who were to retire, as before,
to the castle; and if they disagreed until twelve
at night, the mayor was next day, at 11 o'clock,
to call a council, the majority of which were to
agree on three persons to be on the election for
mayor.

1680 A great comet appeared, and from its nearness to
our earth, alarmed the inhabitants. It continued
visible from Nov. 3, to March 9.

William Penn, a Quaker, receives a charter for plant-
ing Pennsylvania.

1681 The votes of the house of commons began to be
printed.

Dr. Oliver Plunket, titular primate of Ireland, was
executed at Tyburn for high-treason, July 1st.

Bomb-ketches invented by the French.

1683 Earl of Essex cut his throat in the tower, July 13th.
Siege of Vienna raised by 100,000 Turks, Sep. 10th.
King George II. born October 30th.
A severe frost that lasted thirteen weeks.
India stock sold from 360 to 500 per cent.
City Tholsel, Dublin, built.
Kilmainham hospital built at the charge of the army,
by the duke of Ormond.

Penny-poſt ſet up in London and ſuburbs, by one Murray, an upholſterer, who afterwards aſſigned the ſame to one Dockwra; afterwards claimed by the government, who allowed the latter a penſion of 200l. a year, in 1711. Firſt ſet up in Dublin, 1774.

Ann, queen of England, married to prince George, of Denmark.

1684 A great part of the caſtle of Dublin was conſumed by a fire that began about two in the morning; his excellency the earl of Arran, narrowly eſcaping. The great magazine of powder, as alſo the tower in which the ancient records of the kingdom were kept, was happily preſerved; which elſe had laid the city in ruins.

1685 Charles II. died, aged 55, and was ſucceeded by his brother, James II.

The duke of Monmouth, natural ſon to Charles II. raiſed a rebellion, but was defeated at the battle of Sedgmore, and beheaded.

The edict of Nantz was revoked by Louis XIV. and the Proteſtants were greatly diſtreſſed.

James II. and his queen, crowned April 23d.

Titus Oates, D. D. whipt, May 20th.

Alderman Cornish hanged, and Mrs. Grant burnt, October 23d.

1686 The earl of Tyrconnel, ſworn lord lieutenant of Ireland, who, not being able to prevail on the magiſtracy of the city of Dublin to admit Roman catholics to their freedom, had a *quo warranto* brought againſt the city charter, and appointed popiſh judges in every court.

The Newtonian philoſophy publiſhed.

1687 There were exported from Ireland this year, 11360 pieces of new draperies, and 1,129,716 yards of frizes.

An inundation in Dublin, and Eſſex bridge broken down, at which time a carriage paſſing over, fell into the river, the coachman and one horſe periſhed.

White

EVENTS.

White paper firſt made in England.
The Proteſtant diſſenters, to avoid perſecution, go in great numbers to America.
The palace of Verſailles, near Paris, finiſhed by Louis XIV.

1688 The Revolution in Great Britain begins Nov. 5.
King James abdicates, and retires to France, Dec. 3.
King William and queen Mary, daughter and ſon-in-law to James, are proclaimed February 16.
Viſcount Dundee ſtands out for James in Scotland, but was killed by general Mackay at the battle of Killycrankie; upon which the Highlanders, wearied with repeated misfortunes, diſperſed.
Smyrna deſtroyed by an earthquake.
The nation, repreſented by its parliament, now fixed the ſo long-conteſted bounds between the prerogative of the crown, and the rights of the people.
They preſcribed the terms of reigning to the prince of Orange, and choſe him for their ſovereign, in conjunction with his conſort, Mary.
February 25th, the people of Bandon diſarmed the garriſon, but ſoon ſurrendered, and purchaſed their pardon for one thouſand pounds.
James, duke of Ormond died, July 21ſt.
The art of ſoftening bones, firſt found out.
Charity ſchools firſt began in England.
King James heard maſs in a chapel belonging to a monaſtery, on the north ſide of the city of Cork; he was ſupported through the ſtreets of the city by two franciſcan friars, and attended by many others of the ſame order in their habits. The poſſeſſions of this houſe were originally granted to Andrew Skiddy, by queen Elizabeth, who aſſigned them to the earl of Cork, and by him given to his ſon, the lord Broghill, afterwards earl of Orrery. This houſe is now entirely demoliſhed.

1689 The prince of Orange landed at Torbay November 4th, 1688; proclaimed king, Feb. 13th, 1689.
King James's abdication voted by the houſe of commons, January 28th.

1689 March 12th, 37 French men of war arrived in Kinfale, and on the 14th, 5000 French landed.

King James's parliament sat till the 20th of July, and passed an act of repeal of the act of settlement; and by an act of attainder, attainted near 3000 Protestants.

King James issued a proclamation for making brass money current in Ireland, June 18th.

William and Mary crowned April 11th.

Lord chief justice Jeffereys died in the tower, April 18th, to which place he had been committed Dec. 12th, 1688, by the lord mayor of London.

The college of Dublin turned into a barrack for popish soldiers, when the provost and fellows were dispossessed. Dr. Moore, a popish priest, nominated provost, who, contrary to expectation, conducted himself with prudence, and paid great attention to the preservation of the books and manuscripts.

The church tythes appointed by act of parliament to be paid to the Roman clergy.

The Protestants of Ireland disarmed by order of Tyrconnel.

Duke Scomberg landed at Bangor with 10,000 men, August 13th. Killed at the battle of the Boyne.

One thousand Enniskilliners, under colonel Lloyd, routed 5000 Irish going to Sligo, and killed 700 of them, September 7th.

The brass coin raised by calling in the half-crowns, and stamping them anew for crowns, at Dublin, December 3d.

On the failure of brass, king James had his image impressed on pewter, which was also to have been made current, had it not been for king William's victory at the Boyne.

The land-tax passed in England.

The toleration-act passed in ditto.

Several bishops were deprived for not taking the oaths to William.

William Fuller, who pretended to prove the prince

of Wales fpurious, was voted by the commons to be a notorious cheat, impoftor, and falſe accuſer.

Epiſcopacy aboliſhed in Scotland.

1690 The battle of the Boyne, gained by William againſt James in Ireland.

Limerick was beſieged. Sarsfield ſurprized and deſtroyed the great guns, with tin boats, ammunition and proviſions, at Ballynedy, within ſeven miles of the beſieger's camp, to which they were coming.

The town attacked, but not carried.

The ſiege is raiſed.

King William returns to England.

Judges were appointed for the circuits of Munſter, Leinſter and Ulſter.

Londonderry beſieged April 20th; raiſed July 31ſt, after which the Dartmouth frigate forced her way up to the town.

James II. ſailed from Breſt with 17 ſhips of war, and landed at Kinſale.

Admiral Herbert attacked the French fleet in Bantry Bay.

Mr. Richard Maunſell of Cork, narrowly eſcaped being hanged for refuſing to take the braſs money.

The day before the ſiege of Derry, 2000 Enniſkilliners met major-general M'Carthy with 6000 men, whom they took priſoners, routed his army, and deſtroyed near 2000 men, with the loſs of about 20 men on their ſide.

The city of Cork made a reſiſtance for five days againſt a regular army, under the command of the earl of Marlborough; the garriſon, conſiſting of 4500 men, ſurrendered on Michaelmas-day, and were made priſoners of war. Mac-Elligot, the governor, took 500l. from the inhabitants to ſave it from fire, and the next day ſet fire to it at both ends.

The magiſtrates of Cork, reaſſuming their places, proclaimed king William and queen Mary, and put the city into ſome order.

October 3d, Earl Marlborough ſtormed Charles-fort,

fort, when it furrendered; it confifted of 1200 men, who had provifions for 12 months.

Sir Coudefley Shovel took a frigate out of the harbour of Dublin, in fight of the Irifh.

June 14th, King William landed at Carrickfergus.

June 18th, Colonel Lutterell, governor of Dublin, iffued an order, forbidding more than five Proteftants to meet together on pain of death.

June 30th, King William in viewing the Irifh army by the Boyne, narrowly efcaped being killed by a cannon ball which grazed his right fhoulder.

July 2d, King James fled to Waterford, from thence to France.

Sept. 22d, The duke of Grafton was mortally wounded by a mufket ball : a black fmith, who ftood at the back of the old poft-office, oppofite Sullivan's quay, taking aim at the duke when he was giving the word of command, fhot him through the heart, of which he died in a few hours. He was killed on a piece of ground adjoining the fouth-mall, which to this day is called Grafton's Alley.

October 15th, Kinfale furrendered.

Excife on beer and ale, firft impofed by act of parliament, November 25th.

1691 When fir Richard Cox was fent to govern this county and city, and the militia thereof, notwithftanding many Proteftants were difperfed and loft to their country, he raifed in three weeks eight complete regiments of dragoons, and three of foot, which eleven regiments contained 6000 men.

Bottle-hill, midway between Cork and Mallow, is remarkable for a ftout ftirmifh, fought there between the Englifh and king James's forces, on the 29th of April, wherein the former got the victory.

On the 12th of October, the Breda frigate, lying at anchor in Cork harbour, with a number of Irifh on board, took fire and blew up.

Mark Baggot, taken in Dublin as a fpy in woman's cloaths, was condemned and hanged.

The

1691 The lord Tyrconnel died at Limerick a day before the army approached it.

Part of the English army paſſed over the Shannon, where the Iriſh army was encamped, who preſently retreated.

Sligo ſurrendered to lord Grenard.

Athlone attacked, and the Engliſh-town taken.

This year an act paſſed for the raiſing 2500l. for the relief of the inhabitants of Bandon, to be levied in the counties of Cork, Limerick, Clare, Kerry, Tipperary and Waterford, in the following manner:—

On the county of Cork, and in the city of Cork	889	7	0
County of Limerick — — —	282	5	6
The city and county of the city of ditto	55	18	6
The county of Clare — — —	363	0	0
Kerry — — —	153	15	0
Tipperary, including Holy-Croſs	615	0	0
Waterford — — —	184	15	6
The city and county of the city of ditto	55	18	6

The ſaid money to be put into the hands of the right honourable the lord viſcount Dungarvan, lord high treaſurer of Ireland, Francis Bernard and Edward Riggs, eſqrs. or any two of them, which they are to diſpoſe of as they ſhould ſee fit, for the relief of the ſaid inhabitants of Bandon.

The Engliſh and Dutch Smyrna fleets anchored in the port of Kinſale, and the grand fleets of both nations at the mouth of the harbour, extending from the Old-head to Youghal. Thus, the importance of Kinſale was again known to England, when upon a falſe alarm, that the French fleet was approaching, the men of war could draw into a line of battle, without any trouble or concern for the merchantſhips, which were ſecured in the harbour; nor was this the only benefit England received from Kinſale this ſummer; for the Virginia and Barbadoes fleets likewiſe took ſanctuary there, till an opportunity preſented to convoy them ſafe to their reſpective ports

Count

Count Schomberg (second son to the late duke) created duke of Leinster.

Monsieur St. Ruth sent from France, to command the Irish army.

General Ginckle goes to the camp at Mullingar.

Sunday July 12th, was fought the decisive battle of Aughrim, when, after many severe conflicts and doubtful states, victory was declared in favour of king William. The Irish loss amounted to 7000 men, with their general St. Ruth, who fell by a cannon shot as he came down the hill of Kilcomaden. The loss of the English did not amount to more than 600 killed, and 960 wounded.

July 26th, Galway surrendered upon articles.

October 5d, Civil and military articles were agreed on for Limerick, and all the other forts then in possession of the Irish.

October 18th, The French fleet, consisting of 18 men of war, 4 fire-ships, and 20 ships of burden, arrived in the Shannon, with ammunition and provisions for the relief of Limerick; in two days after the articles were signed, there was news of their being come to Dingle-Bay.

November 1st, The last of the Irish march out of the English-town, many of whom were shipped off for France; 120 of whom were cast away on a rock in the Shannon. Their horse were shipped off at Cork afterwards.

March 23d, A proclamation was published, declaring the war of Ireland to be at an end.

Dec. 6th, The transport ships return from France, and bring an account of the mean reception of the Irish who went there, which made several regiments desert, who were not shipped off.

Dec. 23d, Lord Lucan, and the rest of the Irish officers, went off at Cork.

1692 The English and Dutch fleets, commanded by admiral Russel, defeat the French fleet off La Hogue.

The massacre of Glencoe in Scotland, Jan. 31, O. S.

Earthquakes

EVENTS.

Earthquakes in England and Jamaica, Sept. 8.
Hanover made an electorate of the empire.
Royal College of physicians incorporated. 15th Dec.
Jan. 19th, A great frost in Ireland, which held till the middle of February.
July 18th, Four French men of war, that were disabled by admiral Ruffel in the battle of La Hogue, were brought into Kinsale by the king's ships; and on the 1st of August, sir George Rook, with the squadron under his command, and 40 English and Dutch merchantships, arrived in the same harbour.

1693 Two French privateers entered Kenmaire river, and cut out a rich vessel of 300 tons, which was soon retaken by the Monck man of war.
The flesh-shambles of Cork erected by the corporation in the center of the city, at the expence of 481l. 5s.
About one hundred men were killed at Dublin, by the blowing up of a magazine, containing a quantity of gunpowder.
Bayonets at the end of loaded muskets, first used by the French against the confederates, in the battle of Turin.
Bank of England established by king William.
The first public lottery was drawn this year.
Commissioners appointed to enquire into the forfeited lands and goods in Ireland.
The battle of Landen in Flanders, where Luxemburg beat the English, July 29th.

1694 The tower of Limerick fell suddenly; it contained 218 barrels of powder, which by the striking of the stones, took fire, and blew up; it greatly shattered the town, killing about 100 persons, and wounded many others.
Hackney coaches and chairs established by act of parliament.
Queen Mary died at the age of 33, and William reigned alone.
Stamp duties instituted in England.

A ship-

A ftipftaff was fent by the houfe of commons againft James French and Simon Dring, fheriffs of the city of Cork, for quartering foldiers on private houfe-keepers.

1695 Batchelors taxed ;—again in 1785.

Greenwich hofpital began to receive 6d. per month from every feaman.

Marriages taxed ;—again in 1784.

Kilmainham hofpital founded.

The Devonfhire man of war, had her deck blown up by accident, in Kinfale harbour, and thirty men wounded.

In the winter of this year, and a good part of the following fpring, there fell in feveral places of this province, a kind of thick dew, which the country people called butter, from its colour and confiftence, being foft, clammy, and of a dark yellow, as doctor St. George Afhe, then lord bifhop of Cloyne, has recorded in the philofophical tranfactions; it fell always in the night, and chiefly in marfhy low grounds, on the top of the grafs, and on the thatch of cabins, feldom twice in the fame place; it commonly lay a fortnight without changing colour, but then dried, and turned black; cattle fed as well where it lay, as in other fields; it often fell in lumps, as big as the end of one's finger, thin and fcatteringly; it had a ftrong ill fcent, fomewhat like that of church-yards and graves; and there were moft of that feafon very ftinking fogs, fome fediment of which the bifhop thought might poffibly have occafioned this ftinking dew; it was not kept long, nor did it breed worms or other infects; yet the country people, who had fcald or fore heads, rubbed them with this fubftance, and faid it healed them.

October 2d, This day was kept as a day of thankfgiving in Dublin, for the prefervation of his majefty's perfon, and the taking of Namur in the fight of the French army, though 100,000 ftrong.

Captain

Captain Walſh, a ſubject of England, but commanding a French privateer on theſe coaſts, was taken and hanged, April 15th.

The parliament of Ireland met, and voted a ſupply of 163,325l. Auguſt 27th.

The rolls, records, and papers, relative to the acts of attainder, and other acts of king James's parliament, were cancelled and publickly burnt, October 2d.

1696 The peace of Ryſwick.

Elections made void by bribery.

The town of Youghal having manned out a boat, with about 40 ſeamen and ſoldiers, took a French privateer that lay at anchor under Cable-iſland. The privateer had ſeized on ſome boats belonging to the town, and ſent in one of them for proviſions, keeping the reſt as hoſtages. The French loſt five men in the engagement, and Patrick Comerford their captain, with the lieutenant and ſixteen more, were wounded.

Lords commiſſioners of trade, firſt appointed.

French Proteſtants ſettled in Ireland, and improved the linen manufacture.

1697 The magazine at Athlone blown up by lightning.

The chamberlain was ordered to pay ſeven guineas to Mr. Walker, on his producing the great charter of king Charles I. which was loſt and miſſing ſeveral years.

About this time, ſeveral members in Dublin, and other corporation towns, aſſociated for promoting reformation of manners, by bringing ſwearers and lewd perſons to public puniſhment.

The old pariſh of St. Michan's, Dublin, including all that part on the north ſide of the river, was by act of parliament divided into three pariſhes, viz. the new St. Michan's, St. Paul's, and St. Mary's.

Upon the Commons addreſs, king William gave 300ol. to Trinity College.

This year, B. Van Homrigh, eſq; one of the commiſſioners of the revenue, was lord mayor of the city of Dublin; and being a person very serviceable to the crown and city, he obtained a collar of SS *a royal donation*, for the chief magistrate of that city, to the value of near 1000l. The former collar having been lost in king James's time.

The English parliament passed a vote for reducing the army to 7000 men, and these to be native subjects; the king, to his great mortification, was obliged to dismiss even his Dutch guards.

1698 Whitehall palace burnt, January 4th.
- William Molyneux, author of Ireland's Case, died in Dublin, October 13th.

The old barrack of Cork built.

Trading people have ever aimed at exclusive privileges; of this there are two extraordinary instances: two petitions were this year presented from Folkstone and Aldborough, stating a singular grievance that they suffered from Ireland, by the Irish catching herrings at Waterford and Wexford, and sending them to the Streights, and thereby forestalling and ruining petitioners markets.

In this year, according to captain South's account, in the Phil. Transact. No. 261, p. 591, there were in the city of Cork 58 seamen, 34 fisherman, 91 boatmen, in all 183; whereof 111 were papists; but the number is at present so great, they are not easily to be reckoned.

The lords and commons of England addressed king William to employ his influence in Ireland, to suppress the woollen manufacture therein; to which he answered the lords, that his majesty will take care to do what their lordships required; and to the commons he answered, I shall do all that in me lies to discourage the woollen trade in Ireland.

1699 The Scots settled a colony at the isthmus of Darien in America, and called it Caledonia.

The treaty of Carlowitz, between the emperor and the Turks.

The parliament of England vested the forfeited estates

tates of Ireland in thirteen truftees, to be fold
for the public ufe, notwithftanding feveral grants
already made.
Tuckey's-bridge built, from Tuckey's-quay to the
eaft-marfh, by captain Dunfcombe.
An Englifh law paffed this year to prevent the Irifh
exporting woollen goods, of which the following
is the preamble: " For as much as wool and woollen manufactures of cloth, ferge, baize, kerfies,
and other fluffs, made or mixed with wool, are
the greateft and moft profitable commodities of
this kingdom, on which the value of lands, and
the trade of the nation do chiefly depend; and
whereas quantities of like the manufactures have
of late been made, and are daily encreafing in the
kingdom of Ireland, and in the Englifh plantations in America, and are exported from thence to
foreign markets, heretofore fupplied from England, which will inevitably fink the value of lands,
and tend to the ruin of the trade and woollen manufactures of this realm; for the prevention thereof, and for the encouragement of the woollen manufactures of this kingdom, &c."
Peter the Great quitted his dominions, animated by
the noble ambition of acquiring inftruction, and
of carrying back to his people the improvement
of other nations.

1700 Charles XII. of Sweden, began his reign.
King James II. died at St. Germains, in the 68th
year of his age.
India filks prohibited to be worn in England.
Died at Windfor, the duke of Gloucefter, in the
12th year of his age; a prince of early hopes, and
the only remaining bloffom of the prefent royal
family.
About this time the firft auction was in Britain, by
Elifha Yale, a governor of Fort-George in the
Eaft-Indies, of the goods he brought home with
him.

1700 Exports from G. Britain in 1700, were 7,302,716l. 8s. 7d. imports were 5,970,175l. 1s. 10d. In 1788 exports were 18,296,166l. 12s. 11d. the imports were 17,804,024l. 16s. 1d.

The lands by which the blue-coat hospital is supported, were set so low that there were but eight boys kept; but they are since considerably increased in value, and at present there are 40 children provided for, with sufficient food, raiment and schooling; and when of a competent age, are bound out apprentice to trades and the sea service. This building owes its foundation to Dr. Edward Worth, formerly bishop of Killaloe, and dean of Cork, sometime before the restoration of Charles II.

The exports of linen from this kingdom amounted to but 14,112l. but in 1709, an act having passed in Ireland, enabling the lord lieutenant to appoint trustees for the disposal of the revenue granted for the encouragement of the linen manufacture; his grace the duke of Ormond, accordingly appointed trustees from each province, and assembled them on the 10th of October, 1711, when the deed of their appointment was read, and they proceeded to the execution of their trust. From this board, called the trustees of the linen and hempen manufactures of Ireland, has the important object of their appointment, received the most zealous and unremitting attention.

Charles XII. then only 18 years of age, made a descent on Copenhagen, and impatient to reach the shore, leaped into the sea sword in hand, when the water rose above his middle; his example was followed by his army, who put to flight the Danish troops that attempted to oppose their landing. Charles, who had never in his life before heard a general discharge of muskets loaded with ball, asked major Stuart, who stood near him, what the whistling which he heard meant; it is the noise of the bullets, replied the major, which they fire against your majesty: very well, said the king, this shall henceforth be my music.

1701 Society for the propagation of the gospel in foreign parts, established.

The Hanoverian succession to the crown of England signed by king William, the 12th day of June.

Charles XII. no sooner raised the siege of Copenhagen, in consequence of his treaty with the king of Denmark, than he turned his arms against the Russians, who had undertaken the siege of Narva, in Ingria, with 80,000 men. Charles, with only 8000 men, advanced to the relief of the place, and having carried without difficulty, all the out-posts, he resolved to attack the Russian camp. As soon as the artillery had made a breach in the entrenchments, he ordered an assault to be made with screwed bayonets, under favour of a storm of snow, which the wind drove full in the face of the enemy. The Russians for a time, stood the shock with firmness; but after an engagement of three hours, their entrenchments were forced on all sides with great slaughter, and Charles entered Narva in triumph. About 8000 of the enemy were killed in the action, many were drowned in the Narve, by the breaking down of a bridge under the fugitives, near 30,000 were made prisoners, and all their magazines, artillery, and baggage, fell into the hands of the Swedes. Charles dismissed all his prisoners, except the officers, whom he treated with generosity. When the Czar was informed of the disaster, he was chagrined, but not discouraged. " I knew that the Swedes would beat us, said he, but in time they will teach us to beat them."

On the death of Charles II. of Spain, the duke of Anjou, second son of the dauphin of France, was crowned at Madrid, by the name of Philip V.

The emperor dignified the elector of Brandenburgh with the title of King of Prussia.

Grand alliance formed between the Emperor, the king of England, and the States-General.

Lewis XIV. in violation of the treaty of Ryfwick, acknowledged the Pretender king of Great Britain, and Ireland, under the title of James III.

1702 King William died, aged 50, and was fucceeded by queen Anne, daughter to James II.

The French fend colonies to the Miffifippi.

War declared againft France on the fame day, at London, the Hague, and Vienna.

Voltaire fays, after the taking of Baden, by the marquis de Villars, a voice called out *we are undone;* on hearing this all his troops fled. He ran after them, crying "Come back, my friends, the victory is ours, *long live the king!*" The trembling foldiers repeated, long live the king, but continued to fly, and the marquis found the utmoft difficulty in rallying the conquerors.

The confederate fleets failed for Vigo, where the Spanifh galleons, under efcort of 23 fhips of war were arrived. As the wealth on board thefe galleons was confidered as the chief refource of the monarchy, and even of the whole houfe of Bourbon, Lewis XIV. expecting to fhare in it, the utmoft precaution had been taken to preferve them. They were carried up into a bafon, through a narrow entrance, one fide of which was defended by a fort, the other with platforms mounted with cannon; a boom was thrown acrofs the mouth of the bafon, and within the boom the French fquadron was drawn up; but all thefe obftacles was not fufficient to difcourage the confederates, when animated by the hopes of fo rich a prize. The French admiral fet fire to his fhips, and the galleons followed his example. The Britifh tars foon extinguifhed it, and fix fhips of war were taken, feven funk, and nine burnt; of thirteen galleons, nine fell into the hands of the conquerers, and four were deftroyed; the booty was immenfe, and the confternation of the houfe of Bourbon inexpreffible.

Borge,

EVENTS.

Borge, a feat near Frederickftadt in Norway, funk into an abyfs one hundred fathoms deep, which inftantly became a lake, and drowned fourteen perfons, with 240 head of cattle.
Apothecaries exempted from civil offices.
Semper Eadem, firft ufed for the motto of the arms of England.

1703 The obliquity of the ecliptic obferved by Bianchini to be $23° 28' 25''$.
Kidder, bifhop of Bath, and his lady, killed by the fall of a ftack of chimnies.
The commons of Ireland expelled Mr. Afgill the houfe, for his book, afferting the poffibility of tranflation to the other world without death.
Captains Kerby and Wade, fhot at fea for cowardice April 4th.
The Grand Seignior depofed, and his throne ufurped by his brother, Sept. 29th.
The duke of Ormond, lord lieutenant of Ireland.

1704 Gibraltar taken from the Spaniards by admiral Rooke.
The battle of Blenheim won by the duke of Marlborough and allies againft the French.
The court of exchequer inftituted in England.
Foundations of the barracks at Dublin laid.
Pruffian Blue firft difcovered at Berlin.
Mr. Rochford, attorney-general, ftabbed with a knife in St. Andrew's church, Dublin, by Mr. Chefwick.
Battle of Hochftet, where the duke of Marlborough defeated the confederate forces of French and Bavarians, under the command of monfieur Tallard who was killed in the engagement; 13000 were taken prifoners, and the remainder moftly flain or fcattered, Auguft 13th.
The number of Popifh clergy in each county in the kingdom of Ireland, returned to the clerk of the council, purfuant to an act of parliament for regiftering the Popifh clergy; 1080 in the whole kingdom, of which number 4 were in the city, and 58 in the county of Cork.

The

1705 The particulars of the siege of Barcelona, as related by Voltaire, are too much to the honour of this country to be omitted. The earl of Peterborough, says he, a man in every respect resembling those imaginary heroes that the Spaniards have represented in their romances, proposed to the prince of Hesse Darmstadt to force, sword in hand, the entrenchments which covered fort Montjoui and the town. The enterprize was accordingly executed with success; but with the loss of the brave prince of Hesse, who was killed in the attack. The garrison, however, still held out; when a bomb, directed at Montjoui, happened to enter the magazine of powder, it blew up with a terrible explosion, and the fort instantly surrendered. The town soon after offered to capitulate; and the duke of Popoli, the governor, came to the gate, in order to adjust the articles with Peterborough: but before they were signed, tumultuous shouts being heard, " You betray us!" exclaimed Popoli. " Whilst we, with honour and
" sincerity, are here treating with you, your troops
" have entered the town by the ramparts, and
" are murdering, plundering, and committing
" every species of violence."—" You are mistaken," replied Peterborough: " these must be
" the troops of the prince of Darmstadt. There
" is only one expedient left to save your town:
" allow me freely to enter it with my Englishmen.
" I will soon make all quiet, and return to the
" gate to finish the capitulation." These words he uttered with an air of dignity and truth, which, joined to a sense of present danger, induced the governor to comply. Attended by some of his officers, he hastened into the streets, where the licentious soldiery, but more especially the Germans and Catalans, were pillaging the houses of the principal inhabitants. He drove them from their prey; he obliged them to quit even the booty they had seized; and he happily rescued from

their

their hands the duchefs of Popoli, when on the point of being dishonoured, and restored her to her husband. In a word, after having quelled every appearance of diforder in the town, he returned to the gate, and finished the capitulation with the governor;—to the no small astonishment of the Spaniards, in general, at finding fo much honour and generofity in a people, whom they had hitherto been accustomed to confider only as mercilefs heretics.

1706 The treaty of union betwixt England and Scotland, signed July 22d.
The battle of Ramillies, won by Marlborough and the allies.
Great eclipfe of the fun, May 1st.
The act of bankruptcy commenced in England.
A great part of the walls of the city of Cork being in a ruinous condition, there was an order of council to have feveral of the breaches stopped, and all the stairs leading thereto taken down; and the fame year, a great part of the city wall facing the east-marsh, was taken down accordingly.
Auguftus, king of Poland, depofed, and Staniflaus elected.

1707 The first British parliament.
The allies defeated at Almanza.
The custom-houfe of Dublin began to be built.
Sir Cloudefley Shovel was caft away on the rocks of Scilly, where his body was thrown afhore, October 22d.
Fires occafioned by fervants, punifhable.
Modena and Milan furrendered to the allied armies.
The Pretender (Chevalier de St. George) failed from Dunkirk with a French fleet, 6000 land forces, and 10,000 arms, with an intention to enter the Firth of Forth, but fir George Byng, with a fuperior force, obliged him to go back to Dunkirk, with the lofs of one ship.

1708 Minorca taken from the Spaniards by General Stanhope.

The

The battle of Oudenarde won by Marlborough and the allies.

A Ruffian ambaffador arrefted by a lace-merchant, which occafioned a law for their protection.

Prince George of Denmark, hufband to queen Anne, died October 28th, aged 56 years.

The foundation of the exchange in Cork laid.

An epidemic fever vifited Cork, from the month of Auguft until January following, and again in 1718,—1719,—1720, and 1721, as taken from doctor Rogers's effay on the endemical difeafes thereof.

Lille furrendered to the combined army.

The Czar propofed a peace to Charles, who made the following anfwer: "I will treat at Mufcow." When Peter heard this haughty anfwer, he replied, "My brother Charles always affects to play "the Alexander; but he will not, I hope, find "in me a Darius."

1709 A general naturalization of foreign Proteftants enacted in England.

Mr. Euftace murdered his wife in Smithfield, Dublin, and made his efcape, but being purfued by a conftable, they fired a piftol at each other, and both died on the fpot.

The ftatute in favour of literary property, paffed.

Lewis XIV. offered the following terms of peace:— to yield the whole Spanifh monarchy to the Houfe of Auftria, without any equivalent; to cede to the Emperor, his conquefts on the Upper Rhine; to give Furnes, Ypres, Menin, Tournay, Lille, Conde, and Mabenge, as a barrier to Holland; to acknowledge the Elector of Brandenburgh as king of Pruffia; the duke of Hanover as ninth elector of the empire: to own the right of queen Anne to the Britifh throne; to remove the Pretender from the dominions of France; to acknowledge the fucceffion to the crown of Great Britain in the Proteftant line; to reftore every thing required by the duke of Savoy; and to agree to the cef-

fion

fions made by the king of Portugal, by his treaty with the confederates. All which were rejected.

The famous battle of Malplaquet: few battles in any age, have been fo fierce and bloody; and none perhaps fo long contefted, fince the improvement of the art of war, in confequence of the invention of gunpowder; 120,000 men were engaged on each fide, and the confederate army gained nothing but the field, with the lofs of 20,000 men, the enemy but half the number.

Tournay, one of the ftrongeft and moft ancient cities in Flanders, taken by the confederate army.

Poltowa, well ftored with every neceffary wanted by Charles's army, befieged by him, which brought on a general engagement in which he loft 9,000 flain, and 6000 with the king's military cheft taken; 12,000 fled, but were obliged to furrender, for want of boats to take them over the Borifthenes; Charles, accompanied with 300 guards, with difficulty efcaped to Bender.

1710 Queen Anne changed the Whig miniftry for others more favourable to the intereft of her brother, the late Pretender.

The cathedral church of St. Paul, London, rebuilt by fir Chriftopher Wren in 37 years, at the expence of one million fterling, by a duty on coals.

The Englifh fouth-fea company began.

Lewis XV. of France, born February 4th.

The new law paffed for adjufting the affize of bread.

Indian kings had audience of queen Anne, April 19.

This year the laft prefentment for killing wolves, was made in the county of Cork.

Doway, St. Venant, Bethune, and Aire, taken by the confederate army.

The battle of Elfinbury, where the Danes were beat by the Swedes.

1711 Robert Harley, efq; (afterwards earl of Oxford) was ftabbed by Anthony Guifcard, who was then under examination before a committee of the privy council, March 8th, fince which time, it is

made

made felony of death without benefit of clergy, to affault, ftrike, or wound any privy counfellor in the execution of his office. Stat. 9, Anne. c. 16.

Great plague began at Copenhagen, May 22d.

James, duke of Ormond, fworn lord lieutenant of Ireland, July 3d.

An engagement between the Turks and Ruffians; the latter were beat and obliged to offer terms, which were agreed upon.

1712 The Sultan ordered Charles XII. to quit his territories, who replied he could not go without 1000 purfes; the Sultan ordered him 1200; he then demanded 1000 more, which were refufed, and the bafhaw of Bender was defired to bid him depart, which he likewife refufed, and with his retinue, confifting of about 300, threw up entrenchments on which they were attacked by 20,000 Turks, who took them prifoners before they had time to draw their fwords. Charles, who was on horfe-back between the camp and his houfe, took refuge in the latter, attended by a few general officers and domeftics; with thefe he fired from the windows upon the Turks, killed 200, and bravely maintained his poft, till the houfe was all in flames, and one half of the roof fell in. In this extremity a centinel, named Rofen, had the prefence of mind to obferve, that the chancery houfe, which was only about fifty yards diftance, had a ftone roof, and was proof againft fire; that they ought to fally forth, take poffeffion of that houfe, and defend themfelves to the laft extremity. There is a true Swede, cried Charles, rufhing out like a madman, at the head of a few defperadoes, but was foon made prifoner with his companions.

A furious battle took place between general Steenbock with 12000 men, and double that number of Danes and Saxons; and though the latter had every advantage of pofition, they were entirely routed,

routed, and driven out of the field with great
slaughter.

The expedition against Quebec (from Old and New-
England) failed partly from the lateness of the
season, and partly from an ignorance in the navigation of the river St. Lawrence; ten transports
and 2000 men were lost.

The duke of Marlborough dismissed by Q. Anne.

The wooden bridge at the north end of the city of
Cork was taken down, and a fair bridge erected in
its place; the piers, arches, and butments being
faced with hewn stone.

The queen agreed to a suspension of arms; the immediate delivery of Dunkirk was the condition
of that indulgence, which was delivered up to
brigadier-general Hill, and its fortifications demolished.

General Albemarle defeated by Marshall Villars,
and lost 10,000 men.

Duke of Hamilton and Lord Mohun killed in a duel
in Hyde-park.

Robert Walpole, esq; sent to the tower, January 17th.

Wednesday, May 7th, Mary Easberry was burnt at
gallows-green, for poisoning her husband Daniel
Easberry, tallow-chandler, who lived in Paul-street.

1713 The peace of Utrecht, whereby Newfoundland,
Nova Scotia, New Britain, and Hudson's Bay,
in North America, were yielded to Great Britain;
Gibraltar and Minorca, in Europe, were also confirmed to the said crown by this treaty.

The wooden bridge at the south end of the city of
Cork was taken down, and a handsome stone
bridge erected at the corporation charge.

1714 Queen Anne died at the age of 50, and was succeeded by George I.

Interest reduced to *five per cent*.

A parliamentary reward offered for discovering the
longitude.

The Protestant doors in the city of Dublin marked
with chalk, June 16th.

The Czar made himself master of Abo, Borgo, defeated the Swedes at Tavestius, penetrated as far as Vaza, gained a complete victory over them at sea, and took the isle of Oeland,

Charles XII. had now kept his bed for ten months with an affected sickness, at Demetica, when he received a letter from his sister, to inform him that his ministers wanted to make peace with Russia and Denmark, which effectually roused him; on which he wrote to the senate, that if they pretended to assume the reigns of government, he would send them one of his boots, from which they should receive their orders, and set out on his return immediately. On his arrival he gave his only surviving sister in marriage to Frederic, prince of Hesse-Cassel.

Ormond dismissed, and Marlborough restored.

1715 Lewis XIV. died, and was succeeded by his great-grand-son Lewis XV. the late king of France.

The rebellion in Scotland began in September, under the earl of Mar, in favour of the Pretender. The action of Sheriffmuir, and several others.

The obliquity of the ecliptic observed by Louville to be 23° 28' 34".

The greatest eclipse of the sun that had been for 500 years.

A great snow fell, which continued two months.

North-Gaol built by a tax on the inhabitants, and the Green coat hospital began to be erected the same year.

Iron first discovered at Virginia in America,

Castle-Bernard, formerly Castle-Mahon (once the residence of O'Mahony) rebuilt by Judge Bernard.

Lord Bolingbroke, the earl of Oxford, and the duke of Ormond, impeached; Ormond and Bolingbroke escaped to the Continent; but Oxford, after an imprisonment of two years, was brought to his trial, and dismissed for want of accusers.

The duke of Berwick gives the following character

of

1715 of Lewis the XIV.—"No prince was ever so little
"known as this monarch; the Protestants have
"represented him as a man not only cruel and
"false, but difficult of access. I have frequently
"had the honour of audiences from him, and
"have been very familiarly admitted to his pre-
"sence: and I can affirm, that his pride was only
"in his appearance. He was born with an air of
"majesty, which struck every one so much, that
"no body could approach him without being
"seized with awe and respect; but as soon as you
"spoke to him, he softened his countenance, and
"put you quite at ease. He was the most polite
"man in this kingdom; and his answers were ac-
"companied with so many obliging expressions,
"that, if he granted your request the obligation
"was doubled, by the manner of conferring it;
"and if he refused, you could not complain."

M'Intosh and Forster lead the Scotch rebels to Pres-
ton, where they were attacked, and surrendered to
general Carpenter. Several reduced officers were
immediately shot as deserters; the noblemen and
gentlemen were sent prisoners to the tower, and
the common men were confined in the castle of
Chester and other secure places.

The duke of Argyle, with only 3,300 men, attacked
and defeated the earl of Mar at the head of 9000
men at Drumblaine.

Dec. 22d, The Pretender landed at Peterhead in
Scotland, where he was joined by the earl of Mar,
and conducted to Perth, where a regular council
was formed, and a day fixed for his coronation at
Scoon; but the arrival of the duke of Argyle
obliged them to retire to Montrose, where seeing
no hope of retrieving their affairs, they embarked
for France, accompanied by several other persons
of distinction.

At the siege of Stralsund, the bombs fell as thick as
hail upon the houses, and half the town was reduced to ashes. One day, as Charles was dictating

some letters, a bomb bursting in the neighbourhood of his appartment, his secretary dropt his pen. "What is the matter?" said the king, with a degree of chagrin, as if ashamed that any one belonging to him should be capable of fear,— "The bomb!" sighed the intimidated scribe, unable to write another word. "Write on," cried Charles, with an air of indifference, "What relation has the bomb to the letter I am dictating?"

1716 The Pretender married the princess Sobieska, grand-daughter of John Sobieska, late king of Poland.

An act passed for septennial parliaments.

The Emperor's army, commanded by prince Eugene, defeated the grand vizer at Peterwaradin.

The famous quadruple alliance, formed between France, England, Holland, and the Emperor, against the violent ambition of Spain. By this treaty the duke of Savoy was dignified with the title of King of Sardinia.

Christ church in the city of Cork, being in a ruinous condition, was taken down and rebuilt in 1720; the first sermon being preached therein on Sunday the 27th of November that year, by the reverend Philip Townsend. The corporation gave 200l. towards this building.

Earl of Derwentwater and viscount Kenmure, beheaded in London February 24th.

Justice Hall and parson Paul, hanged July 13th, for being concerned in the rebellion.

River Thames dry both above and below the bridge, whereby foot passengers went across with great ease, September 14th.

The battle of Glanmire fought on Saturday the 16th of June, occasioned by the regiment who lay in the old barrack, having turned out for their arrears and pay, which being detained from them some time past, they marched out of the barrack, and went up to lower Glasheen, with drums beating

ing and colours flying, croffed the lee, went to
the foot of Dublin hill, and encamped themfelves
in a field belonging to Peter Healy, where they
halted a few days, and then marched to Glanmire;
at this time they were purfued by a regiment of
foldiers (who landed that morning at the Cove
of Cork) with two brafs field pieces, upon which
the mutineers made a ftand at the further fide of
the bridge, headed in particular by one of themfelves, a Dutchman, named John Chriftopher
Gurvy, and fome others of their own regiment,
who made a refolute defence; their ammunition
having failed, they made ufe of their buttons as a
fubftitute for bullets, when at laft they gave way,
and retreated in diforder: the Dutchman, together with Coffy and Holland, two of the ring-
leaders, were taken, tried by a court-martial,
and fhot at gallows-green; many others were fe-
verely whipt.

1717 The Turks befiege Belgrade, but were repulfed by
an inferior army under prince Eugene, on which
the Turks ceded Belgrade to the emperor.
Guineas reduced by parliament from twenty-two to
twenty-one fhillings.
Britifh linen exported duty free.

1718 A proclamation publifhed by the lords juftices of
Ireland, offering 10,000l. reward for the appre-
hending the late duke of Ormond, January 9th.
England offered 5000l. for apprehending him.
Colonel Henry Luttrell fhot in a hackney-chair, as
he was returning home from Lucas's coffee houfe,
Dublin.
The marquis de Palcotti, brother to the dutchefs of
Shrewfbury, killed one of his fervants in London;
he was tried for it, found guilty, and executed.
The famous Quaker, Sir William Penn, died.
War with Spain in the month of December.
Betridge's alms-houfe in Cork, began to be built.
War was declared in Cork againft Spain.
Alexis, the only fon of Peter of Ruffia, by his firft
wife

wife, having led an abandoned life, he made him sign a solemn renunciation of his right to the crown, and least that deed should not prove sufficient to exclude the Czarowitz from the succession, he was condemned to suffer death, which event took place and suddenly. This was supposed to be in consequence of Peter having a son, (Peter) by his beloved Catherine, who soon after died.

Sir George Byng engaged the Spanish fleet near the coast of Sicily, and took or destroyed 21 ships out of 27; 14 were of the line.

The king of Sweden sat down (a second time) before Frederickshall, in the month of December, when the ground was as hard as iron, and the cold so intense, that the soldiers frequently dropped down dead. In order to animate them, he exposed himself to all the severities of the climate, as well as to the dangers of the siege, sleeping even in the open air, covered only with a cloak. One night as he was viewing them carrying on their approaches by star-light, he was killed by a half-pound ball, from a cannon loaded with grape shot. Though he expired without a groan, the moment he received the blow, he instinctively grasped the hilt of his sword, and was found with his hand in that position, so truly characteristic of his mind.

Baron de Goertz, impeached for slanderously misrepresenting the nation to Charles, and beheaded.

1719 The Mississippi scheme at its height in France.

Lombe's silk-throwing machine, containing 26,586 wheels, erected at Derby; takes up one-eight of a mile; one water-wheel moves the rest; and in 24 hours it works 318,504,960 yards of organzine silk thread.

Great thunder and lightning in Dublin, which continued from two o'clock in the afternoon, till five the next morning.

The new barrack in Cork built.

EVENTS.

1719 In this year the charitable infirmary was begun to be erected in the old church-yard of Saint Mary Shandon; the work was supported by the voluntary subscriptions of several worthy persons, and the shell of the house was finished in 1721. The building is, in length, 70 feet, and 24 broad, and is capable of receiving 24 sick persons, on three floors, four chambers on a floor, and two persons in each chamber. In every chamber there are fire places, and all other conveniencies for the sick, and a fair gallery on each floor for them to walk in. Here are also a kitchen and store-room, a chamber for medicines, with a convenient room adjoining for the surgeon, and other offices; under ground, for the nurse-tenders, &c.

On the 15th of October, 1719, the corporation granted to captain Thomas Deane, a piece of ground adjacent to St. Peter's church, to erect a school and alms-house thereon. And the house was built accordingly for the education of forty poor children, twenty of each sex, who are clothed and taught gratis to read, write, &c. by a master and mistress, who are lodged and accommodated in the same building, and have 14l. per annum salary; the sum of 52l. yearly, is bequeathed, by the pious donor for the use of this charity, who further gives a loaf of bread to each poor child every Sunday. The late rev. archdeacon Pomroy, minister of this parish, added six boys to the foundation, and gave 180l. to be put to interest for this use. In the alms-house are maintained eight poor people, 6 men and 2 women, who have a weekly allowance of 1s. 6d. each. They have also a suit of clothes every other year, a great coat, and other necessaries. The building is plain, and commodious for the purpose.

The quay, called Kyrle's-quay, on the east side of the north-gaol, was built.

Ulrica Eleonora, sister to Charles XII. elected queen, but she relinquished the crown to her husband, the

prince

prince of Hesse, who was chosen by the States, and mounted the throne on the same condition, with his royal consort.

Philip V. of Spain acceded to the terms prescribed by the quadruple alliance.

Seven thousand Swedes perished in a storm of snow, upon the mountains of Rudel and Tydel, in their march to attack Dromtheim.

1720 South-sea scheme in England began April 7; was at its height at the end of June, and quite sunk about September 29th, which ruined several hundred families.

A great earthquake in China.

The plague broke out at Marseilles, August 16th.

A charity sermon preached at all the churches in Dublin, for the poor weavers, by order of government, and the money gathered amounted to 1227l. 14s. 2d.h.

June 16th, happened the unfortunate accident at the four-courts, Dublin, at the trial of the two Mr. Brigantines, for killing a constable in golden-lane, whereby twenty were crushed to death, and several wounded, by their crowding out of the courts upon a false alarm of their being on fire.

The mardyke (commonly called the red-house-walk) first laid out by Edward Webber, esq; town-clerk.

St. Nicholas's church in Cork, began to be erected on the 19th of January.

Late lord Gerald de Courcy, was by his grace the duke of Grafton, presented to his majesty king George the First, when he had the honour to kiss his hand, and to assert his ancient privilege; and on the 22d of June 1727, he was presented by the lord Cartaret to his late majesty, king George II. by whom he was graciously received, had the honour of kissing his hand, and of being covered in his presence.

1721 Buttons and button-holes of cloth, prohibited by law.

Inoculation first tried on criminals.

St. Anne's

1722 St. Anne's church began to be built upon the old foundation where St. Mary Shandon stood, and it was determined to make it a distinct parish, on the demise or removal of the incumbent; it was erected by subscription.

John, duke of Marlborough, died June 16th.

Counsellor Layer hanged for treason, March 17th.

Captains Henry Ward and Francis Fitzgerald, were hanged and quartered at gallows-green, Cork, on Wednesday, April 18th, for enlisting men for the service of the Pretender; they were prosecuted by Maurice Hayes.

William Roe stood in the pillory on Saturday the 19th, and was severely whipt on Wednesday the 23d. of May, for repeating the following seditious words: *May king James the Third enjoy his own again!*

Daniel Murphy, on Saturday the 9th, and Patrick Sweeney, on Saturday the 16th of June, were executed at gallows-green, Cork, for enlisting men for the service of the Pretender, at the prosecution of Maurice Hayes; they were tried by a special commission.

This year Ryland and Keating were executed for the murder and robbery of Isaac Watkins, of Water-Park, esq; they both died innocent, as appeared by the confession of William Lyne, who was, at the same assizes, convicted of cow-stealing; he was tried by the same jury with Ryland and Keating, but being unwilling to criminate himself, permitted the blood of the two innocent men to be shed. Lyne declared on the gallows, that James Byrne and Michael Byrne, both brothers, himself and another man not then taken, were the only persons guilty of the said murder and robbery.— In about two years after, the two Byrnes were executed at gallows-green for another murder, and were remarkably impenitent at the time of their death.

1723 The ground on which St. Paul's church is built, was granted by the corporation to the late bishop Brown, on May 14th, and divine service was, for the first time, celebrated therein, by the reverend Edward Sampson, October 9th, 1726.

Protection of foreign ministers cancelled, Jan. 17th.

Bills of pains and penalties ordered against the bishop of Rochester, March 2d.

A patent for coining halfpence, granted to William Wood, esq; July 24th. Against this projector, Dean Swift appeared in the character of the Draper, exposed the designs of the coiner, and raised such a spirit as effectually banished him the kingdom.

Great fire at Stockholm, May 1st.

A severe edict in France against Protestants, May the 14th.

1724 An earthquake in Denmark.

A great eclipse of the sun, Monday May 12th.

The old custom-house being too small, was taken down, and the present one erected the next year.

Names of the Collectors of the Port of Cork, since King James.

Anno 1690 Sir James Cotter, knt.
1690 Christopher Carleton, esq; for king William.
1693 Arthur Bushe, esq;
1698 Warham Jemmat, esq;
1716 Henry Arkwright, esq;
1717 William Maynard, esq;
1734 Hugh Dickson, esq; and recorder of Cork.
1734 John Love, esq;
1734 Hugh Dickson, esq; again.
1738 Henry Hamilton, esq;
1743 Henry Cavendish, esq;
1746 Bellingham Boyle, esq;
1749 John Love, esq; again.
1750 Sir Richard Cox, bart.
1755 Hon. James O'Bryen.
1767 Hon. Joseph Lysaght.

Besides

EVENTS, 143

Befides a furveyor-general of the province, who commonly refides in this diftrict, and whofe falary is 300l, per annum, there are

A port-collector, at 150l. falary,
A collector of excife, at 100l. a year.
Two furveyors, one on the quay, and one in the ftores, 60l. each.
Three land-waiters, at 40l. each.
A riding furveyor, at 65l.
A walking furveyor on the out quays, 30l.
A ftore-keeper, 20l.
A tide-furveyor at Cove, 50l.
His deputy, 35l.
Surveyors at Crofs-haven and Paffage, 35l. each.
A door-keeper of the ftores, 20l.
Three coaft officers, at 35l. each.
Twenty-five tide-waiters, at 30l. each.
Eight boat-men at Cove, and five more at Cork, at 20l. each.
Six boatmen at Paffage, at 18l. each.
Two fcale porters, at 20l. each.
Twelve fupernumerary tide-waiters, at 5l. each.
Two furveyors of excife, at 65l. each.
In the whole diftrict 18 guagers, at 40l. each. And Two fupernumerary ones, at 30l. each.

1725 St. Finbarr's church taken down, and rebuilt in 1735.
Peter, emperor of Ruffia, died.
1726 John Ward, of Hackney, expelled the houfe of commons for forgery, May 16th.
The eaft end of Nicholas's church in Cork, greatly damaged by thunder and lightning, on Monday June 20th; fome of the books and cufhions were burnt.
Douglas factory began to be built.
1727 King George died in the 68th year of his age; and was fucceeded by his only fon, George II.

Ruffia,

Russia, formerly a dukedom, is now established as an empire.

The aberration of the fixed stars discovered and accounted for by doctor Bradley.

Sir Isaac Newton died March, 28th.

A large whale came on shore at Erris, in the county of Mayo; the jaw-bone was 22 feet long.

1728 Linen-hall, Dublin, opened.

There being a great scarcity of provisions this year in the city of Cork, a desperate mob arose, and broke open the cellars of Hugh Millerd, esq; mayor of Cork, and after doing a great deal of mischief, the army was called to suppress them, when a few shots were fired; Alice Murphy, who was looking out of her window, was unfortunately shot dead, and not one guilty person hurt.

1729 In a parliament held at the blue-coat hospital, Dublin, motion for a 21 years supplies negatived by a majority of one.

Foundation of the parliament-house in college-green laid.

The first burial with linen scarves at colonel Groves's funeral, in Dublin, October 15th.

The North and South chapels in Cork built; the south one was afterwards burnt.

So remarkable a fog in London, that several chairmen mistook their way in St. James's-Park, and fell with their fares into the canal; many persons fell into Fleet-ditch, and considerable damage was done on the Thames, Jan. 1st. in the evening.

A proposal was made in the house of commons, to set up a ballast-office in the city of Cork.

By Mr. Richard Fenton's account, who collected the duty on coals applied to the building the cathedral, Christ-church, and the work-house, there was received, from Nov. 1719, to November 1726, being 7 years, 1794l. and from the first Nov. to March the 3d, 1729l. being three years and five months, 999l. 14s. the duty being 1s. per tun, making each year communibus ann. 256l. 5s. 8d. by which

which computation, there feems to be about 6000
tuns of coals burned in this city yearly, amounting
to about 16 tuns and a half each day, and 500
tuns a month, which may be. fupplied by 150
fhips, being, one with another, 40 tuns; there
are alfo great quantities of turf confumed here.
1730 Brazil diamond mines difcovered.
The ancient city of Herculaneum difcovered.
Silver mines difcovered at Britany in France.
The judge, fheriff, and feveral other perfons died of
the gaol diftemper, at Blanford aflizes.
Hannah Snell, the female foldier, had a penfion fettled on her.
The dragon blown off the exchange of Cork.
1731 The heart of a man found at Waverly in Surry,
preferved 700 years in fpirits.
The bridge on Hammond's-marfh, leading to the
meeting-houfe, was erected; and on the fame
canal are feveral other fmall bridges.
A new bridewell erected in Cork, at the expence of
the city.
The Dublin fociety formed, and has continued to
maintain the precedence of its merit unrivalled.
Pragmatic fanction guarranteed, by which the fucceffion to the Auftrian hereditary dominions was
fecured to the heirs female of the emperor Charles
the Sixth, in cafe he fhould die without male
iffue.
Law pleadings ordered to be in Englifh.
This year there were 1,309,768 Roman catholics,
and 700,453 Proteftants in Ireland.
The fhambles and milk-market near the barrack in
Cork, built.
Timothy Croneen, for the murder and robbery of
Andrew St. Leger, efq; and his wife, was hanged
quartered and beheaded, at gallows-green, Cork,
the 25th day of January; he was tried by a fpecial
commiflion, and immediately after his conviction,
was put into a cart, and conveyed to the place of
execution; his head was afterwards fpiked on the
fouth-

south-gaol. Joan Condon, for the same murder, was burnt the Saturday following.

1732 Kouli Khan usurped the Persian throne, conquered the Mogul empire, and returned with two hundred millions sterling.

Several public-spirited gentlemen began the settlement of Georgia in North America.

May 29th and 30th, being Whit-Monday and Tuesday, the weavers, combers, and other persons belonging to the clothing business, made an elegant appearance through the streets of Cork, with a loom drawn by horses, exhibiting to public view, the practical part of their trade in all its various branches.

1733 The Jesuits expelled from Paraguay.

Sect called *Methodists* arose in England.

Excise scheme introduced into the house of commons, and opposed by every trading town in the kingdom. For one week in this year it amounted to 28,000l. In 1744, it was 3,754,072l. In the same year the malt distillery of London, was 450,000l. The revenue was 3,847,000l. in 1746.

1734 Forgery first punished with death in England.

Stock-jobbing forbid by parliament.

The prince of Orange married in London to the princess Royal, March 14th.

The French and their allies were successful in Italy.

The Spaniards made themselves masters of Naples and Sicily.

Count de Mortemar gained a complete victory over the Imperialists.

The forces of France and Piedmont, under old Marshal Villars and the king of Sardinia, took Milan and other important places.

The Marshal de Coigny, who succeeded to the command of the French army on the death of Villars, defeated the Imperialists, in which their general was killed; they were again defeated at Guastalla where the prince of Wirtemberg was slain; on this the emperor sued for peace.

Fifty

EVENTS.

Fifty sheriffs of London appointed in one day, 35 of whom paid their fines, July 2d.

Three tygers whelped in the tower of London, August 2d.

Mr. Ford, one of the fellows of Trinity-College, Dublin, was shot by one of the scholars.

Mrs. Harris, a Quaker, presented her majesty with two caps of uncommon fineness for the princess of Orange, as part of her child-bed linen, with verses in needle-work on them; that for a prince had the following lines:

As providence to glorious William *gave*
These happy nations, which he came to save;
Still may kind heaven with royal honours bless
His princely race, and send us large increase.

" May it please the Queen,
" A faithful subject of thine, and one of those
" called Quakers (a people who have distinguished
" themselves by their love to thy family) has been
" excited by the happy marriage of that amiable
" princess thy eldest daughter with the prince of
" Orange, to shew that the pleasing thoughts of
" it remained with her many days; I have, O
" queen! with my own hands (though I am
" more than 64 years of age) wrought this linen,
" which I have taken the liberty to present to thy
" royal hand; I beseech thee suffer thy grand-
" child to wear it, and may the Almighty, who
" has made thee mother of many children, make
" them and their children comforts to thee and
" to thy people. So prays thy humble but faith-
" ful subject, *Mary Harris*."

1735 Forty carcasses of beef were seized and burnt before the exchange of Cork, as not being fit for transportation.

Portland Isle had one hundred yards of its north end sunk into the sea, which did 4000l. damage to the pier, Dec. 20th.

The Derwentwater estate forfeited to the crown, in the

the year 1715, appointed for the support of Greenwich hospital.

1736 Captain Porteous having ordered his soldiers to fire upon the populace at an execution of a smuggler, was hanged by the mob at Edinburgh.
A transit of Mercury observed by Caffini.
Prince Eugene of Savoy, died April 10th.
War between the Empress and the Port.
General Lases reduced Azoph; the Count de Munich forced the lines of Prekop, took Banievary, and laid all Tartary waste by fire and sword. Next campaign, Munich entered the Ukraine, and invested Oczakow, which he carried, though defended by an army of 10,000 men.

1737 A dreadful hurricane at the mouth of the Ganges, October 10th.
The city of Venice made a free port.
Queen Carolina died November 20th.
Plays required to be licensed by the lord chamberlaine by parliament.

1738 Westminster-bridge, consisting of 15 arches, begun; finished in 1750, at the expence of 389,000l. which was defrayed by parliament.
The order of St. Januarius established at Naples.
The value of the gold coin reduced in Ireland, September 10th.
Gill-Abbey castle fell down, after standing 980 years.

1739 Letters of marque issued out in London against Spain July 21, and war declared Oct. 23.
The empire of Indostan ruined by Kouli Khan.
An intense frost in Britain.
Henry lord baron Santry, tried by his peers, and found guilty of stabbing a man, of which he died, April 27th.
The river Dee made navigable from Hertford to Ware, and so to London, 12. George II.
Lough-a-Drippel, near Dunmanway, did not freeze in the great frost of this year. The famous lake Nefs in Scotland, never freezes; but on the contrary, in the most violent frosts, great clouds and

steams

1739 steams arise from it. Rosemary, growing in gardens round it, stood the severest frosts; whereas a far less intemperate winter, killed all that grew in gardens situated in warmer places. On the top of a high mountain in Scotland, called Meal-Furvenny, four miles west of Lough-Ness, is a lake of cold fresh water, about 30 fathoms in length, and six broad, that could not be sounded with 100 fathoms of line; this water is also said never to freeze.

The river Lee was frozen up towards the end of this year, after which a great scarcity followed; so that wheat sold the ensuing summer for 2l. 2s. the kilderkin; and in two years after was sold for 6s. 6d. the kilderkin.

Augustus II. king of Poland, died in 1733; on this event, Staniflaus Leczinfks, whom Charles XII. had invested with the sovereignty in 1704, and whom Peter the Great had dethroned, now become father-in-law to Lewis XV. was a second time chosen king. But the emperor, assisted by the Russians, obliged the Poles to proceed to a new election. The elector of Saxony, son of the late king of Poland, who had married the emperor's neice, was raised to the throne, under the name of Augustus III. and Staniflaus, as formerly, was obliged to abandon his throne.

In 1734, France entered into an alliance with Spain and Sardinia, and war began in Italy.

The duke of Berwick passed the Rhine, reduced Fort-Kehl, and invested Phillipsburgh; and the Count de Belleisle conquered Trawback. Berwick was killed, but Phillipsburgh was taken nevertheless. The marquis d'Asfeld, who succeeded to the command of the French army, continued the operations in the fight of prince Eugene, and in spite of that experienced general, and the overflowings of the Rhine, the place was forced to surrender.

War was declared this year against Spain, and Admiral Haddock sent to cruize off their coast;

Vernon

Vernon to command in the West-Indies, who took Porto-Bello with only six ships and 240 soldiers. Anson was sent to ravage the coasts of Chili and Peru, and 27 sail of the line, with frigates, &c. sent to the West-Indies to act in consort with Vernon, and co-operate with Anson, by means of intelligence to be received across the Isthmus of Darien.

1740 Silesia taken by the king of Prussia.

Impressed seaman's bill.

Potatoes sold this year at 30s. the barrel.

The emperor Charles VI. died.

The king of Prussia offered to supply the queen of Hungary with money and troops, to protect her dominions, and place her husband on the throne, provided she would cede to him the lower Silesia, which she refused, and which produced three engagements, in which the Prussian monarch was victorious. When the court of Versailles heard of his success, they sent 50,000 troops towards the Danube, and 40,000 on the side of Westphalia, to keep in awe the elector of Hanover, and proposed an application to be made to the princes of the empire to concur in the destruction of the house of Austria, and to share its spoils.

The Corn-market of Cork built.

The summer after the hard frost, there was a large pit dug at the back of the green in Shandon church-yard, where several hundred indigent persons were buried for want of money to purchase graves for themselves.

The sixpenny houshold loaf this year, weighed but two pound thirteen ounces.

Timothy Hurly, Honora Hurly his wife, Timothy Hurly his son, Maurice Filihy his son-in-law, Cornelius Fowloe, Michael Shinnick and Mary Bradeen, were executed at gallows-green, Easter-Saturday, April 5th, for stealing a piece of linen-cloth out of the dwelling-house of John Terry, esq; one of the sheriffs of the city of Cork. Cornelius

nelius Fowloe, declared on the gallows, a few moments before he was launched into eternity, that if he had his liberty, he would steal the shirt and blanket, pointing to them where they were drying on a bush oppofite the gallows, and juft before his face, without being difcovered, notwithftanding the multitude of fpectators then in his prefence.

1741 The cuftom-houfe of Limerick burnt, October 2d.

The Superb man of war, brought into Kinfale a Caracca fhip, worth 200,000l. Dec. 25th.

The whole town of Omagh in Ireland, confumed by fire, except the church and four houfes, May the 4th.

In the dead of the night John Bodkin, with fome ruffians entered into his father Oliver Bodkin's houfe, about three miles from Tuam, murdered him, his wife, and fon, with 3 maid fervants and 4 men.

The count de Belleifle negociated a treaty between Lewis XV. and Frederick III. in which it was ftipulated, that the elector of Bavaria, together with the Imperial Crown, fhould poffefs Bohemia, Upper Auftria, and the Tyrolefe; that Auguftus the Third fhould have Moravia, and Upper-Silefia, and his Pruffian majefty Lower Silefia, the town of Neifs, and county of Glatz.

The elector of Bavaria appointed by Lewis general of his army, with Belleifle and Broglio to act under him.

The parliament of England granted 300,000l. as a fupply to the queen of Hungary.

The elector, joined with the French forces, furprifed the city of Paffau, and entered Upper Auftria with 70,000 men, took poffeffion of Lintz, advanced within a few leagues of Vienna, and fent a fummons to the governor to furrender the place. The queen left it in the care of her hufband, and brave generals, and retired to Grefbery, where fhe affembled the States, and addreffed them as follows :—

" Abandoned

1741 "Abandoned by my friends, perfecuted by my enemies, and attacked by my neareft relations, I have no refource but in your fidelity and valour. On you alone I depend for relief; and into your hands I commit, with confidence, the fon of your fovereign, and my juft caufe." The Palatines drew their fwords, and cried, "We will die for our king, Maria Therefa!" All were inftantly in arms; fix armies were immediately formed, and the Elector was induced to moderate his ideas, and march into Bohemia, where being joined by 20,000 Saxons, he laid fiege to Prague, which was taken by the gallantry of count Saxe, natural fon of Auguftus II. of Poland, who had entered into the French fervice.

The elector of Bavaria was crowned king of Bohemia at Prague, proceeded to Frankfort, where he was elected Emperor, under the name of Charles the Seventh.

The right rev. the lord bifhop of C'ogher, has given us the following relation, in the Philofophical Tranfactions, N°. 461, page. 813, Aug. 1741.

"His lordfhip met with a man at Innifhannon, about 70 years of age, who, out of gratitude for a charity he had given him, fhewed him a curiofity, which was that of his breafts, with which he affirmed, he had once given fuck to a child of his own: his wife, he faid, died when the child was about two months old; the child crying exceedingly while it was in bed with him, he gave it his breaft to fuck, only with an expectation to keep it quiet; but behold, he found that the child, in time, extracted milk; and he affirmed, that he had milk enough afterwards to rear the child. His breafts were very large for a man, and his nipple larger than is common in women."

1742 Firft fhips with Irifh coals arrived in Dublin, from Newry.

A letter

1742 A letter from admiral Matthews gave an account, that a French man of war paſſing in ſight of the fleet, and refuſing to pay the compliment to the Britiſh flag, the admiral fired at him, to bring him to, but the commander perſiſting in his obſtinacy, a man of war was ordered out to force him to good manners, who, pouring a broadſide into him, ſunk him directly.

Sweden declared war againſt Ruſſia, to prevent the empreſs Elizabeth (daughter to Peter the Great) from aiding her ſiſter ſovereign.

The Engliſh nation eſpouſed the cauſe of the queen of Hungary, and liberal ſubſcriptions were opened by private individuals, for the ſupport of Maria Thereſa. The parliament voted her 50,000l. augmented the land forces to 62,000, ſent 16,000 men under the earl of Stair, to make diverſions in her favour, and ordered them to be joined by 6000 Heſſians, and 16,000 Hanoverians.

e The new-created emperor loſt Lintz on the day of his creation, though defended by 10,000 French; the Auſtrians diſlodged them from all their ſtrong holds, entered the emperor's dominions, defeated Thoring at Memberg, and took Munich the capital, while prince Charles of Lorraine, with 30,000 infantry, and 18,000 cavalry, drove the Pruſſians out of Moravia and Olmentz, which they had taken.

The Auſtrians now turned their thoughts to attacking Belleiſle and Broglio, but the Pruſſian monarch being reinforced with 30,000, returned to aſſiſt his allies. The armies met and fought, but neither could be ſaid to have conquered.

The king of Pruſſia began to ſicken of ſuch bloody engagements, and to doubt the ſincerity of the French. He concluded an advantageous peace with the queen of Hungary. Auguſtus III. did the ſame.

The French offered to evacuate Prague, &c. provided they were allowed their arms, &c. which the queen would

1742 would not confent to. Maillebois was fent to their aid with 42,000 men; in his march he joined a reinforcement of 30,000 under count Saxe, and entered Bohemia without refiftance.

Belleifle and Broglio were befieged by prince Charles at Prague, who changed it to a blockade, left the care of it to 18,000 men, under the command of Feftitz, and marched to oppofe Maillebois. Mean while, Belleifle and Broglio formed the defign of joining Maillebois, and Feftitz being too weak to oppofe them, they left Prague, and marched to Lentmaritz. Lorraine drove Maillebois to the Palatinate, while prince Lobkowitz obliged Belleifle and Broglio again to take refuge in Prague; the fiege of which was refumed, but Broglio made his efcape in the difguife of a courier, and took the command of Maillebois's army. Belleifle out-manouvered the Auftrian general, and efcaped from Prague.

As admiral Haddock with 14 fhips of the line, was making ready to engage a Spanifh fleet of 12 fail and 200 tranfports, a French fleet ftood in between the two hoftile fleets with a flag of truce. The French and Spaniards being engaged in a joint-expedition, the French admiral was under the neceffity of acting in confort with his mafter allies.

Admiral Leftock fent commodore Martin into the Bay of Naples, to bombard that city, unlefs the king would withdraw his troops, and fign a promife that they fhould not act in conjunction with Spain during the war. The king was afraid, and fent an ambiguous anfwer. The commodore hung his watch to the flag-ftaff, and faid he fhould only wait an hour, that his orders were abfolute; on which the king immediately figned the promife.

1743 The battle of Dettingen, won by the Englifh and allies in favour of the queen of Hungary.

A dreadful plague in Sicily.

Seventeen thoufand geneva fhops abolifhed in England.

Handker-

1743 Handkerchiefs firſt manufactured at Paiſley, in Scotland, when 15,886l. worth were made; in 1784, the manufacture yielded above 164,385l.
The exports from Cork were, 86,951 barrels of beef, 19,256 barrels of pork; 83,844 cwt. of butter; 8,586 tanned hides; 37,509 raw hides; 16,054 cwt. of tallow; and 420 ſtone of wool.
Admiral Anſon took an Acapulco ſhip, laden with treaſure to the amount of 300,000l. beſides many other valuable commodities.
Prince Charles of Lorraine, defeated the Imperialiſts at Brenau.
Prince Lobkowitz drove the French from all their poſts in the upper Palatinate. They obliged Broglio to abandon his ſtrong camp; after which, being joined by 12000. under count Saxe, yet did he not think proper to hazard an engagement. He retreated before prince Charles to Hailbrou. The emperor finding himſelf abandoned by his allies, and ſtript of his dominions, took refuge in Frankfort, where he lived in indigence and obſcurity.
The king of Great Britain, and his ſecond ſon, the duke of Cumberland, with lord Cartaret, arrived at the camp of the allies, where he found his army 41,000 ſtrong, eager for battle, and in want of proviſion. A battle commenced The French cavalry, led by the nobility, marched on in deſperation; the Britiſh infantry opened their lines, and let them paſs, then cloſed them, and cut them to pieces. Terror ſeized the French army, every one crying " Save himſelf, who can."
In the above bloody, but deciſive engagement, ſir Robert Rich's regiment having loſt their ſtandard, a private man rode into a ſquadron of French horſe, ſword in hand, and retook it, for which the king conferred on him the honour of Knight Baronet.
Captain Tucker took a Spaniſh regiſter ſhip, worth 100,000l.
400 houſes burned at Crediton, near Exeter.

His

1743 His majesty's ship, Monmouth, brought in two prizes to the Downs, one of which was a Spanish register ship, worth 150,000l. besides 66 tons of quicksilver.

Letters patent passed, for erecting within the city and liberties of Cork, one guild or fraternity of the arts and mysteries of brewers and malsters. Alderman Robert Atkins was thereby appointed first master; Mr. William Clarke and Mr. Matthias Smyth, first wardens.

When the Fame galley, captain Saunderland (one of the Jamaica fleet that were in the dreadful hurricane) foundered at sea, all the crew perished except one man, who took hold of one of the hen-coops, and kept his head above water 30 hours, when he was providentially seen and taken up by captain Blackburn, of the Queen of Hungary.

1744 War declared against France.

Commodore Anson returned from his voyage round the world.

Admiral Balchen, in the victory man of war, lost in October.

This summer, the sixpenny household loaf in Cork, weighed 14lb. 6oz.

The first division of the Pretender's army, consisting of 7000 French troops, sailed from France, while M. de Roquafeille, with 20 ships of the line, sailed exultingly up the British channel to protect the transports and cover the landing of the troops; but a storm dispersed them, and sir John Norris, in a British fleet, obliged the French to make the best of their way to Brest.

Brest magazine, 400 yards long, was destroyed by fire, to the value of 7,000,000l. in stores, besides the building, January 19th.

The Victory man of war lost in a storm.

There were exported this year from Cork, 118,006 barrels of beef; 37,852 cwt. of butter; 3,873 tanned hides; 50,850 raw ditto; 19,289 cwt. of tallow, and 367 stone of wool.

The

EVENTS.

1744 The combined fleets of France and Spain, defeated by admiral Matthews; Lestock standing aloof with his squadron.

The prince of Conti, with 30,000, joined Don Phillip, and passed the Var: the whole county of Nice submitted to them; attacked the strong post of Chateau Dauphine, where the king of Sardinia was defeated: in this action, the French and Spaniards had the boldness to clamber up rocks of an incredible height, mounted with cannon, and to pass through the embrasures when the guns recoiled. Don Philip invested the strong town of Coni, and the king of Sardinia being reinforced with 10,000 Austrians, went to its relief, attacked the French and Spaniards, but was obliged to retire with the loss of 5000; however, Coni was reinforced, and Don Philip and the prince de Conti, raised the siege.

Count Brown with 6000 Austrians, surprized Velitri in the night, and seized a great booty; the duke of Modena, and the king of the Two Sicilies, with difficulty escaped.

The king of France put himself at the head of his army, consisting of 120,000 men; the duke de Noailles and marechal Saxe acted under him, and carried every thing before them; Menin, Ypres, Fort-Knocke, and Furnes, surrendered; and the king entered Dunkirk in triumph.

Prince Charles of Lorraine, passed the Rhine, and entered Alsace with 60,000 men; the king dispatched de Noailles with 40,000 picked men, to join de Coigni, and himself followed with a farther reinforcement; and Saxe, who was left to command, prevented the allied army from gaining any advantage during the campaign.

Prince Charles took Weissenburg, and laid lower Alsace under contribution.

The king of France was seized with a fever at Metz.

The king of Prussia entered Bohemia.

Charles repassed the Rhine in sight of a much larger army,

army, and went to the relief of that kingdom. Lewis, after his recovery, laid siege to Friburg, which he reduced. The king of Prussia made himself master of Prague, Tabor, and all Bohemia, to the east of the Moldaw. Prince Charles being reinforced, obliged him to evacuate his conquests, with the loss of 30,000 men, with all their heavy baggage, artillery and waggons, loaded with provisions and plunder.

The Imperial general, joined by a body of French, drove the Austrians out of Bohemia; and Charles the Seventh once more got possession of his capital; but the rapid progress of prince Charles of Lorraine, filled him with apprehensions, when death came to his relief.

October 20th, A dreadful storm happened at Jamaica, which did considerable damage to the shipping; out of eight king's ships, and ninety-six merchant men, lying at Port-Royal, only his majesty's ship Rippon, rode it out, and she without masts.

1745 Dec. 21st, His majesty's ship Rose, of 20 guns, captain Frankland, after a most unequal fight, took a very large Spanish ship containing 310,000 pieces of eight, and 5000 ounces of gold. The engagement lasted five hours, during which time the two ships were three times aboard of each other. The prize was full of soldiers and sailors, had near 100 killed; the Rose had only 177 men, including officers and boys, five of which were killed, and twelve wounded.

The exports from Cork this year were, 73,594 barrels of beef; 70,620 cwt. of butter; 5,361 tanned hides; 27,578 raw ditto; 18,852 cwt. of tallow; and 1100 stone of wool.

Dean Swift died, and left 11,000l. to build St. Patrick's hospital, for lunatics and ideots.

The Pembroke man of war, a 60 gun ship, lately rebuilt and rigged at Chatham, having been ordered from thence to Black Stakes to take in her guns, overset as she was going down the river,

and

1745 and upwards of 100 of her crew drowned, with seven officers and many women that went aboard her either out of curiosity, or upon business. She has since been weighed, and upwards of eighty dead bodies were taken out of her. The following melancholy circumstance (among many others) is attested by those who had the good fortune to be saved, viz. One of the officers, as soon as the ship overset, swam to the assistance of his wife, whom he saw floating, and bid her hold fast by him, and doubted not they should reach the shore; which he had pretty near accomplished, when a chest or beureau which had floated off the ship's deck, struck against her head so violently, that she let go her hold, and was immediately drowned, though her husband endeavoured at the extreme hazard of his own life, to lay hold on her again.

A sad accident happened at the royal foundery at Woolwich; where an old bomb-shell, which had some days before been landed from on board one of the tenders, and whose charge had not been drawn, took fire, and bursting, wounded six of the matrosses in so terrible a manner, that two of them died; the third had both his legs and his right arm cut off.

Copy of a letter from the lords of the admiralty to the commissioners of the navy.

" *Gentlemen,*

" His majesty having been pleased in council to
" sign an order, desiring and directing us to sign
" a bill on you, for paying unto sir Andrew
" Fountain, knt. warden of his majesty's mint,
" the sum of 10*l*. for enabling him to provide a
" medal and chain of that value for Richard
" Hornby, master of the ship Wrightson and Isa-
" bella, as a reward to him for his good service,
" in not only defending the said ship, whose crew
" consisted but of five men and three boys, from
" a French privateer of 75 men, but also by firing
" a shot in the stern of the privateer, whereby she

blew

1745 "blew up, and all her crew perished; and as an
"encouragement to others under the like circum-
"stances, to exert themselves in the defence of
"their ships, and the destruction of the enemy;
"and you are likewise to pay a bounty of 5l. to
"each of the five men, and 40s. to each of the
"three boys belonging to the said ship."

The lords of the regency offered 30,000l. reward for apprehending the eldest son of the Pretender, who it is supposed is on his way to the British dominions. Shortly after which they received intelligence that he landed at Lochaber.

Don Phillip and Maillebois, with a powerful army, obliged his Sardinian majesty and Schulenberg to retire beyond the Tanaro.

Count de Gages took Tortona, while the duke of Modena took Parme and Placentia.

The city of Parie was taken by assault, and Milan surrendered.

Don Phillip passed the Tanaro, compelled the combined armies to take shelter behind the Po. He reduced Valenza, Casal, Asti, Gabrano, and Veime, only 20 miles from Turin. The king of Sardinia was so apprehensive, that he ordered the army within the cannon, and the pavement of the streets to be taken up; but Don Phillip closed the campaign with a triumphal entry into Milan.

In the beginning of the month of April, Armagh, Omagh, the county Tyrone, and the city of Derry, were in the utmost distress from a mortality among the cattle, occasioned by rotten hay and straw. Thousands were obliged to draw home these rotten dead carcasses to eat. A humane gentleman offered 500l. if five others would give the same sum each, to send to England and Scotland for grain and oat-meal; but they were not to be found. A young nobleman gave 100l. another gentleman 100l. which with the above 500l. making 1,600l. were laid out in the manner proposed.

Louisburg

1745 Louisburg taken by the English, June 17th. Given up to the French in 1749; retaken July 22d. 1758. Cape Breton taken.

Cambricks from France prohibited;—re-admitted in 1786.

The Duke and Prince Frederick privateers, brought in two French prizes into Kinsale, worth nearly 1,000,000 sterling; the proprietors made an offer of the same to the king, to dispose of as he thought proper in prosecuting the war, which his majesty accepted of.

The admirals and captains of the navy agreed to support a regiment out of their salaries.

The lord lieutenant of Ireland issued a proclamation, offering a reward of 50,000l. for the Pretender, dead or alive, if he landed, or attempted to land on the coast.

Charles VII. died, and was succeeded by his son Joseph, only 17 years of age, who wisely concluded a treaty of peace (through the mediation of his Britannic majesty) with the queen of Hungary. By this treaty she agreed to recognize the Imperial dignity, and to put the son in possession of all his father's dominions.

The king of Prussia gained two bloody victories over the Austrians, under the prince of Lorraine, one near Fridburg, the other at Slandentz; he invaded Saxony, and made himself master of Dresden.

A treaty of peace concluded between Augustus III. and the king of Prussia.

Marshal Saxe (under whom de Noailles condescended to act) with 76,000 men invested Tournay; the king and dauphin animated the army with their presence, and though the allied army consisted of only 53,000 men, under the duke of Cumberland, a brave but inexperienced young prince; the Austrians, by old count Konigseg, and the Dutch by the prince of Waldeck, as young and inexperienced as the duke of Cumberland.

Marshal Saxe, who to a natural genius for war, joined

1745 joined to a knowledge of the military art, was no sooner informed of the purpose of the confederates, than he made the most masterly dispositions for receiving them. The French army was posted on a rising ground, with the village of Antoine, near the Escaut, on its right, the wood of Barry on its left, and in front the village of Fontenoy. In the wood, and at both these villages, were erected formidable batteries of heavy cannon, and the intermediate space was farther defended by strong redoubts. The confederates, however, who had but imperfectly reconnoitered the situation of the enemy, rashly persisted in their resolution of hazarding an attack. Nor were the French without their apprehensions of its consequences, from the known valour of the British troops. The bridge of Colonne, over which the king had passed the Escaut, was accordingly fortified by entrenchments, and occupied by a stout body of reserve, in order to secure him a retreat, if necessary. And to this danger he must have been exposed, had the British troops been properly supported, and the duke of Cumberland's orders duly executed.

The allies were in motion by two o'clock in the morning, and the canonading began as soon as it was light. By nine both armies were engaged, and the action lasted till three in the afternoon. Never was there a more desperate or gallant attack than that made by the British infantry, commanded by the duke of Cumberland in person, assisted by sir John Ligonier. Though the fire from the enemy's batteries was so heavy, that it swept off whole ranks at a single discharge, they continued to advance, as if they had been invulnerable, and drove the French infantry before their lines. The French cavalry in vain endeavoured to stop their progress. Forming themselves into a column, they bore down every thing before them, and baffled every effort to put them into disorder. The village of

Antoine

1745 Antoine was evacuated; and marefhal Saxe, concluding that all was loft, fent advice to the king to provide for his fafety, by repaffing the bridge of Colonne. But Lewis XV, who did not want perfonal courage, fenfible that fuch a ftep would give a decided victory to the allies, refufed to quit his poft. His firmnefs faved his army from ruin and difgrace.

Afhamed to defert their fovereign, the French infantry returned to the charge; the cavalry renewed their efforts; and other circumftances contributed to give a turn to the battle. The Dutch, under the prince Waldeck, having failed in an attack upon the village of Fontenoy, which valour might have rendered fuccefsful, had fhamefully left the field. An Englifh and Hanoverian detachment, under brigadier Ingoldfby, had alfo mifcarried, through miftake, in a practicable attempt to take poffeffion of a redoubt at the corner of the wood of Barry, and immediately oppofite Fontenoy; fo that the Britifh cavalry, by the crofs fire of the enemy's cannon, were prevented from coming up to the fupport of the infantry. This victorious body, now affailed on all fides, fatigued with inceffant firing, and galled by fome field-pieces unexpectedly planted in front, was therefore obliged to retire with the lofs of feven thoufand men, after having fucceffively routed almoft every regiment in the French army. The lofs of the Hanoverians, who behaved well, was alfo very great, confidering their numbers, but that of the Dutch and Auftrians inconfiderable.

The French had near ten thoufand men killed, and among thefe a number of perfons of diftinction, yet was their joy at their good fortune extravagantly great. Their exultation, in the hour of triumph, feemed to bear a proportion to the danger they had been in of a defeat. The princes of the blood embraced each other on the field of battle. And diffolved in tears of mutual congratulation.

lation. They had, indeed, much reason to be satisfied with their victory, which was followed by the most important consequences. Though the duke of Cumberland had led off his troops in good order, and without losing either colours or standards, the allies were never afterwards able, during the campaign, to face the enemy; but lay entrenched, between Antwerp and Bruffels, while marefchal Saxe and count Louendhal reduced, by stratagem or force, Tournay, Oudenarde, Ath, Dendermond, Ghent, Oftend, Newport, and every other fortified place in Auftrian Flanders.

"All the regiments," fays Voltaire, who is very accurate in his account of this battle, "pre-
"fented themfelves, one after the other; and the
"Englifh column, facing them on all fides, re-
"pulfed every regiment that advanced. From
"the moment the French and Swifs guards were
"routed (adds he) there was nothing but afto-
"nifhment and confufion throughout the French
"army. Marefchal Saxe ordered the cavalry to
"fall upon the Englifh column; but their efforts
"were attended with little effect againft a body
"of infantry fo united, fo difciplined, and fo in-
"trepid. If the Dutch (continues he) had paffed
"between the redoubts that lay between Fontenoy
"and Antoine; if they had given proper affift-
"ance to the Englifh, no refource had been left
"for the French; not even a retreat perhaps for
"the king and the dauphin."

The Pretender failed from France, under convoy of a 64, laden with arms and ammunition, which was attacked by the Lion of 58 guns, and obliged to return to Breft. The Pretender landed at Lochaber, was joined by about 3000 men, and proceeded to Edinburgh, which was to be furrendered to him the next day, but fome of his Highland troops attacked in the night, and took poffeffion; the caftle held out. Charles, to avoid the fire from the caftle, retired to Holywood houfe; here

he

1745 he kept a court, and had his father proclaimed at the Crofs of Edinburgh. General Cope landed at Dunbar, where he was reinforced, and proceeded towards the capital, with near 4000 horfe and foot, but hearing that the enemy was on their march to give him battle, he pitched his camp near Prefton-Pans, and early in the morning about 3000 undifciplined and half-armed Highlanders, advanced in hoftile array. Charles gave the word of command, and drawing his fword, threw away the fcabbard; they rufhed on like demons, regardlefs of the artillery. The king's troops were routed; 500 were killed, and 1500 made prifoners; the military cheft, cannon, colours, camp, equipage and baggage, fell into the rebels hands. Charles returned to Holywood houfe, where he was joined by many noblemen and gentlemen; and after fome time, marched into England with 6000 men, and took Carlifle. On hearing this, the French projected an invafion; but admiral Vernon was fo active, as to prevent it. Charles then proceeded to Manchefter, where he fet up his head-quarters, and was furprifed at not being able to raife more than 200 men; on hearing that two royal armies were marching towards him, a council was called, and he determined to proceed through Liverpool and Chefter into Wales, but learning afterwards that thefe two towns were fecured, and the bridges over the Merfey broken down, he turned off, and unexpectedly entered Derby, where his father was proclaimed. A camp was formed in Finchley-common, where George II. took the field; the Pretender held a council of war, which determined him to march back to Scotland; in their way, the rear of his army, under lord George Murray, was attacked by the duke of Cumberland, the duke was repulfed, and Murray proceeded after the Pretender, who augmented the garrifon of Carlifle, and pafsed into Scotland. The duke of Cumberland being reinforced,

reinforced, retook Carlisle. Soon after Charles left Edinburgh, Glasgow and other towns raised troops for their own defence; and "*Kirk* and *King*," was the only cry.

The majority of the people beyond the Tay, were for the Pretender.

Spain sent money, and France troops, with a promise of more.

Lord Lewis Gordon routed the lairds of Macleod and Monro, and obliged them to pass the Spey.

The society of True Blues first assembled in Cork.

1746 British Linen Company erected.

Lima destroyed by an earthquake.

The Boyne privateer of Dublin, brought into Cork a prize of four hundred tuns, computed at 20,000l. value, Jan. 21.

The Pretender severely fleeced Glasgow for its loyalty, and being joined by the French troops, and those under Lovat and Gordon, invested Stirling, which surrendered, but the castle held out. General Hawley was sent to its relief; the rebels repulsed him with great loss, and Charles returned to take Stirling castle. The duke of Cumberland marched to its relief with 14,000 men, on which the rebels raised the siege, and proceeded northwards; in their way they took Inverness, Fort-George, and Fort-Augustus, and obliged the earl of Loudon to take refuge in the Isle of Spey. The duke of Cumberland being joined by 6000 Hessians, passed the Spey, and gained a complete victory over the rebels at Culloden. Lovat advised him to rally his troops, and though 2000 Highlanders, and a body of Lowlanders, attended to know his commands; though a ship arrived from France with 40,000l. and 1000 men came to his relief, he desired them all to disperse, and wandered for five months a wretched fugitive, almost destitute of the necessaries of life, when he embarked in a vessel for France. On his arrival he was caressed; but when the court of Versailles found he could be of no farther use, he was ordered to quit the kingdom; and on his refusal, was seized, pinioned and conducted to the Frontiers.

The

The heroic attachment of a gallant youth, whose name is said to have been Mackenzie, contributed greatly to the escape of the Pretender. About the 20th of July, when Charles had fled for safety to the top of the mountain of Mamnyncallum, in Lochaber, the king's troops surprised a party of his followers in a hut, on the side of the mountain, and obliged them to surrender, after an obstinate resistance. One young man, however, made his escape. The prisoners assured the commanding officer that this was the Pretender. Animated by the prospect of an immense reward, the soldiers eagerly pursued, and at last overtook the fugitive. They desired him to submit, as resistance would be ineffectual, and intimated that they knew who he was. He seemed to acquiesce in their mistake, but refused quarter, and died with his sword in his hand, exclaiming as he fell, "You have killed your prince!"—Independent of these generous expressions, the person slain resembled so much, in all respects, the description of the Pretender given to the army, that an end was immediately put to farther pursuit; and although government pretended to discredit the report, a general belief of the Pretender's death prevailed, and little search was henceforth made after him. An example of such truly noble and disinterested affection, so glorious a self-sacrifice for the safety of another, is scarcely to be met with in the annals of mankind.

Mons, reckoned the strongest town in the world, held out only a few weeks. St. Guislain and Charleroy, were obliged to submit. Mareschal Saxe reduced Dinant, while Louendhal took Huy. The allied army attacked Saxe, but after a desperate engagement, was repulsed by the enemy's cannon, with the loss of 5000 men. The French lost double the number.

Lewis XIV. concluded a peace with the king of Sardinia.

The king of Sardinia made himself master of Anty, one of the strongest places in Italy.

The confederate army drove Maillebois from Nevi; ravaged the Cremonese, and took Lodi, Guastalla, Parme, and other places.

Maillebois

1746 Maillebois formed a junction with the Spanish troops and attacked St. Lazaro, but was repulsed with the loss of 6000 killed, and as many wounded.

Phillip V. of Spain, died.

Maillebois, in his retreat, was attacked by the king of Sardinia at Rotto Fredo, and suftained a fevere lofs.

Placentia furrendered.

Genoa furrendered.

Count Brown entered Provence with 50,000 men, and advanced to Dragninan.

Baron Roth invested Antibes, which was at the fame time bombarded by a British squadron under admiral Medley, but the Marefchal de Belleisle obliged the Auftrian general to relinquish his ideas.

The army destined for Quebec, being detained too long, made a descent on Port L'Orient, without effect.

One hundred sail of the line, 2 artillery ships, and 56 transports, with 3,500 men, and ammunition; also 40,000 stand of arms for the Canadians and Indians, failed from France for the recovery of Cape Breton, but through sickness and distress of weather, did nothing.

France was desirous of peace, but so insolent in her demands, that the States-General propofed to augment their forces in the Netherlands to 40,000, England to supply the same, and the Emprefs 60,000. Befides these, an army of 90,000 Auftrians and Piedmontefe, was to enter Provence, while a smaller body should keep the king of Naples in awe.

France ordered 150,000 to affemble in the Netherlands under Saxe, to whom he gave the title of Marefchal de Camp Generale, which had been conferred on the famous Turenne.

The Spanish army was confiderably augmented; and 60,000 French were appointed to act in Provence;—a final trial of ftrength feemed refolved on by all parties.

The following inftance of true and loyal patriotifm, deferves to be recorded:—As foon as the young Pretender came to Glafgow, he fent for the provoft, and demanded of him the names of those that had fubfcribed for raifing troops againft him, threatening to hang him immediately

EVENTS.

1746 in cafe of a refufal; upon which the provoft bravely and boldly replied, he would not give up the name of any one perfon in the town; but that he himfelf had fubfcribed a greater fum than any other perfon, as he thought it his duty; and that he feared not to die in fuch a caufe.

The Dublin privateer arrived in the bay, and brought in a very rich Spanifh prize.

The Nottingham man of war took the Mars of 64 guns, and 550 men, after an engagement of two hours, and brought her into Plymouth.

A fleet of merchantmen from Barbadoes and the Leeward Iflands, under convoy of the Severn and Woolwich men of war, fell in with the Terrible and Neptune, two French men of war; which took three or four of them, and chacing the Severn and Woolwich, took the former, but the latter efcaped, and got into Lifbon.

Fort St. George in the Eaft-Indies, feized by the French; reftored in 1780.

Admirals Matthews and Leftock, fuffered the French and Spanifh fquadrons to efcape.

Highland drefs forbid in Scotland; reftored in 1782.

The militia of Cork confifted of 3000 foot, and 200 horfe; alfo an independent company, commanded by colonel Henry Cavendifh, compofed of one hundred gentlemen, extremely well difciplined.

1747 Kouli Khan murdered.

A bottle that held two hogfheads, blown at Leith, in Scotland, January 7th.

Lord Lovat beheaded at Tower-hill for high-treafon, April 9th.

The clanfhip of Scotland entirely fubverted, and the liberty of Englifhmen given them.

A fire in the city of Mofcow, which confumed 5000 houfes, June 1ft.

The town of Mullingar in the county of Weftmeath, almoft confumed by fire, July 29th.

The allied armies took the field in March; lay inactive fix weeks, and were deftitute of forage, &c. while

P Saxe

The Fitzroy and Knowles privateers, of Antigua, with only 185 men, took the island of St. Bartholomew, and made 400 white people prisoners.

1748 The peace of Aix-la-Chapelle, by which a restitution of all places taken during the war was to be made on all sides.

The gaol of Kinsale took fire, and 54 prisoners, (chiefly Spanish) perished.

The river Teviot stopped running, and its channel became dry, leaving fishes, &c. on dry ground; and in nine hours began to flow again in its regular way.

On February 19th, the river Kirtle did the same for six hours; and on February 23d, the river Eske stopped for the same time: this last river is as rapid as most in England.

The French had near 50 merchantmen and 7 privateers taken, in the West Indies.

A terrible fire broke out in Exchange-Alley, Cornhill, which spread three different ways, and consumed 100 houses.

His majesty's letter patent passed the great seal, granting to the corporation of the city of Cork, two fairs to be held annually, in or near the Lough, in the South liberties, on the Tuesday and Wednesday next after the 25th of March, and the 15th of August.

The magistrates of the city of Cork, opened a work-house to receive all foundlings, beggars, &c. pursuant to a late act of parliament.

Captain Coates, with four sail of the line, captured three Spanish register ships, and two others, in the face of nine Spanish sail of the line.

A waggon load of money was brought from Dover for the use of the merchants, to the bank, guarded by soldiers.

A poor woman, in the earl of Meath's liberty, aged 65 years, passed a stone of four ounces and half weight, without assistance, of which she had been indisposed above six years.

At the chriſtening of a child of ſir Nicholas Hacket Carew's, at Beddington, Surry, the nurſe was ſo intoxicated, that after ſhe had undreſſed the child, inſtead of laying it in the cradle, ſhe put it behind a large fire, which burnt it to death in a few minutes. She was examined before a magiſtrate, and ſaid ſhe was quite ſtupid and ſenſeleſs, ſo that ſhe took the child for a log of wood; on which ſhe was diſcharged.

Art of fixing crayons diſcovered.

The ſteeple of Chriſt church ſunk ſo much at one ſide, that it was taken down as low as the roof of the church.

In the ſummer of this year, a ſhower fell in and about the town of Doneraile, of a yellowiſh ſubſtance, reſembling brimſtone, and had a ſulphurous ſmell; it lay but thin on the ground, and ſoon diſſolved.

On Monday June 18th, about four of the clock in the afternoon, happened the moſt violent ſtorm of hail that was known in the memory of man, attended with lightning and thunder, which held above a quarter of an hour; ſeveral hail-ſtones meaſured five inches ſquare, and others had five or ſix forks from the main body, of an inch long each, which broke ſeveral windows, and did other conſiderable damages in and about Cork.

Admiral Boſcawen failed in attempting to reduce Pondicherry, and Admiral Knowles in an attack upon St. Jago de Cuba.

Admiral Knowles took Port-Louis, demoliſhed the fortifications, and defeated a Spaniſh ſquadron of equal force, and took one ſhip of the line.

1749 The intereſt on the Britiſh funds reduced to Three per Cent.

Britiſh herring-fiſhery incorporated.

The colony of Nova Scotia founded.

Dublin Society incorporated.

Spire erected on St. Patrick's ſteeple, Dublin.

A general peace proclaimed at Dublin, Feb. 17th.

EVENTS.

1749 The count de la Galliſſoniere, governor of Canada, committed the firſt hoſtilities in Nova Scotia.

The chevalier de la Corne and father Loutre, defeated major Lawrence, near the mouth of St. John's river.

Captain Rous, in the ſloop Albany, took a French ſhip laden with ſtores, and carried her into Hallifax.

Four Engliſh veſſels were ſeized in the harbour of Louiſbourg.

Mr. Charles Lucas, of the city of Dublin apothecary, was voted an enemy to his country, by the hon. houſe of commons, and to be committed to Newgate, Monday Oct. 16th.

Dennis Dunn executed near broad-lane, Cork, on Saturday April 15th, for enliſting John M'Fall to be a ſerjeant in the French army.

A conſiderable body of locuſts overſpread a great part of Bavaria; a great ſwarm paſſed through Aichach in three columns, each of which was 300 paces in breadth, and in the whole took up three hours in their paſſage;—took its flight to Blumenthal, darkening the air to ſuch a degree that one could not ſee the ſky. They were ſeen in Ingolſtadt, Neubourg, Swabia, and Franconia.

Mr. Richard Meade of Bantry, to entitle him to a premium given by the Rev. doctor Madden, fully proved to the Dublin ſociety, that he had within the year, catched and cured 380,800 fiſh of different kinds, ſix ſcore to the hundred; and that this was no caſual thing, is evident; as Mr. James Spray of the ſame place, catched and cured 482,500 herrings, and 231 barrels of ſprats, the preceding year.—If private adventurers with ſmall funds, are able to do ſo much, what may we not reaſonably expect, if a ſufficient ſtock was raiſed to eſtabliſh a general fiſhery on our coaſts?

Spain, Portugal, and Italy, was the market for the above.

It was computed that in the city and liberties of Dublin,

Dublin, there were two thousand ale-houses, three hundred taverns, and twelve hundred brandy shops.

1750 Earthquake in England.

Jan. 20, A bell was found in Killarney Lough, the circumference whereof is as big as a table that will hold eight people to dine at; the clapper was quite eaten with rust, it had been so long in the water; and they are now making a steeple for it in Killarney.

In the Old-Bailey sessions-house, the lord mayor, one alderman, two judges, the greatest part of the jury, and a number of spectators, caught the gaol distemper, and died.

Robert Long, born in Bandon, both deaf and dumb, did, by his own industry, with very little assistance from any master, acquire a considerable knowledge of some branches of the mathematics. He had a perfect knowledge of the principles of geography, and could calculate eclipses. He made both globes, and drew the map and constellations himself. He could survey and guage, and also read as far as words signify the names of things, or what the grammarians call nouns; but he seemed to have no notion of the other parts of speech. A wheel barometer of his making, and also some tables of his, for calculating the motions of the planets, have been shewn. This year he was living in Mallow, about thirty-seven years of age, married, and had children.

Doctor Lyne, an Irish physician, who died some years ago, of the small pox, aged eighty-five, lived at a place called Arloom, in the half barony of Bear, in this county. It was remarkable, that for fifty years together, no body died out of his house, though he always had a numerous family. His house was built in an odd manner; every window had another opposite to it, none of which he ever suffered to be shut or glazed, but were continually kept open, without any defence against the weather.

ther. The room the doctor lay in had four windows, two open on each fide his bed. Upon his death, his fon glazed all the windows; fince which time, there were feveral buried out of the houfe.

Spanifh gold prohibited in Ireland, October 19th.

One Jane Smith, a fifherman's wife, in the town of Kinfale, was brought to bed of four boys, all well and likely to live; they were baptized by the names of George, Frederick, William, and Edward.

October 28th, Mr. Rowe, an eminent painter, in Aungier-ftreet, Dublin, went to bed in very good health, and about five o'clock in the morning, he ftarted out of his fleep, and ftruck his wife with his elbow (by accident) when fhe cried out, You have killed me! he replied, I am dead myfelf; and never fpoke more.

1751 Frederick, prince of Wales, father to his prefent majefty, died.

Antiquarian fociety at London, incorporated.

M. de Villiers obliged the Englifh Ohio company to leave the banks of that river.

Mr. Clive (who went out to the Eaft Indies as a writer) with 130 European foldiers, took Arcot, and was afterwards befieged there by a numerous army of French and Indians, under Chund Saib; but by his courage and conduct, he repelled all the efforts of the affailants, and obliged them to raife the fiege. Soon after he received a reinforcement, purfued the enemy as far as the Plains of Arani, and gained a complete victory; and after a variety of bloody battles, the French and their allies, were totally defeated at Trichionopoli.

1752 The New Stile introduced into Great Britain; the 3d of September being counted the 14th.

Places of interment about London licenfed.

Thomas Hierlihy, for enlifting William Towers and Thomas Dove, to ferve the French king; William Fitzgerald and Thomas Fitzgerald, brothers, for robbing William Keating on the highway, of fix fhillings in money, were executed near Broad-lane,

Cork

Cork, on Saturday April 4th. It is worthy of remark, that whilst William Fitzgerald was on his trial in the city court, his brother Thomas (who was accused of the robbery, but not taken) being conscious of his own innocence, carried a quart of ale into the open court, and reached it to his brother in the dock; he was immediately seized, tried by the same jury, found guilty, and executed with his brother.

Dennis M'Carthy was executed on Monday May 4th, for enlisting men for the French king's service.

1753 The British museum erected at Montague-house.

Society of arts, manufactures, and commerce instituted in London.

Marriage act passed.

The Jews naturalized by parliament, but the act was afterwards repealed.

Colonel Washington sets out on his remarkable journey to Lake Erie, October 14th.

Matthew Callaghane, aged eighteen years, was capitally convicted in the city-court, Cork, April 17th, for the robbery of captain Capel at Glanmire; as soon as he received sentence of death, he leaped out of the dock with his bolts on, made his escape out of the court, but was retaken the same day, and hanged at the corner of Broadlane. Since this transaction happened, the dock in the city court has been made higher.

April 19th, Francis Taylor was buried in Peter's-churchyard, and the next morning was found sitting up in the grave, his cap and shroud tore to pieces, the coffin broke, one of his shoulders much mangled, one of his hands full of clay, and blood running from his eyes. A melancholy instance of the fatal consequences of a too precipitate interment.

Three men and a child of nine years old, were burnt to death in a house in Bowling-green lane, May 2d.

1754 A dreadful eruption of Mount Ætna.

The Dey of Algiers assassinated by a soldier, Dec. 11.

A great

EVENTS.

A dreadful earthquake at Conftantinople, Cairo, &c. September 2d.

M. de Contrecoeur deftroyed Logg's-Town in April, and obliged captain Trent to abandon Fort Monongahela, fituated on the forks of that river.

May 24th, Wafhington defeated a detachment of Contrecoeur's, commanded by Tounonville.

June 12th, Contrecoeur took poffeffion of the outlines of a fort planned by the Englifh, and when finifhed, called it Fort-du-Quefne.

June 20th, The forts Beau-fejour and Bay-Verte, reduced.

July 3d, Villiers obliged Wafhington to capitulate in Fort-Neceffity.

March 12th, Admiral Watfon, with fix men of war, arrived in Kinfale.

March 25th, Colonel Aldercron's regiment embarked for the Eaft Indies.

July 3d, Colonel O'Brien appointed collector of the city of Cork.

Auguft 18th, Samuel Levy, a Jew, was baptized in Peter's church, by the bifhop of Cork.

1755 Quito in Peru, deftroyed by an earthquake, April the 28th.

Lifbon deftroyed by an earthquake, Nov. 1ft.

Amethifts difcovered at Kerry, in Ireland.

Extract of a letter from Peake, in the parifh of Aghabulloge, and county of Cork; wrote by the rev. Marmaduke Cox, in March 1755.

"Laft Thurfday, as fome labourers were mak-
"ing a ditch, to enclofe a potatoe-garden, one of
"them dropt his fpade into a deep hole, which
"obliged him to open the earth, to get out his
"fpade, where he found a paffage into fifteen,
"fome fay feventeen, very large fubterraneous
"rooms, or caverns; in one of which, by efti-
"mation, were above five hundred fkeletons; and
"in another, five fkeletons, all entire, and laid
"at a diftance of about a foot from each other.
"I exa-

1755 "I examined one of the skulls, and found it more
"perfect, and clean, than any boiling, or chirur-
"gical art could prepare it; the teeth very regu-
"lar and distinct; but upon being exposed to the
"air, it opened, and mouldered to pieces. The
"bones were of a pale reddish, or brick-colour;
"some others of them appeared, as if they were
"burned. The country people flocked in so fast,
"on hearing of this antique place, that they trod
"the bones into powder, they being quite desti-
"tute of oil or substance; for they were, indeed,
"as the shadow of bones. *Pulvis & umbra Su-*
"*mus!*

"'Tis imagined, there must be another passage
"to these subterraneous chambers, from a Danish
"fort, about one hundred and fifty yards from
"the present entrance, this being very narrow.
"The rooms are about five feet high. There are
"other chambers that are not got into; the en-
"trance being defended by very large stones, laid
"in the doors, which cannot easily be removed.

"Whether they were the habitation of the
"Aborigines Irish, or contrived by the Danes,
"about the year 800 or 900, the curious may
"judge.

"There was a beautiful carved wood comb and
"comb-case, found in one of the rooms; but the
"air mouldered it into dust.

"'Tis supposed, if an entrance can be made
"into these chambers, defended by the stones,
"that some curiosities will be found, that will give
"further light into this affair; for one part of
"these caverns was their dwelling, and the other
"part the repository of their dead."

Two French ships of the line taken by part of admiral Boscawen's squadron, on the Banks of Newfoundland.

The Terrible, one of the French ships taken in the
last war, was cleared and sheathed at Portsmouth
in eight hours and three quarters, by torch and
candle-

1755 candle-light; she is of 74 guns, and takes more sheathing board than any of our first rates.

Mr. Richard Forsbrork, a bag-weaver, was buried at Birmingham; the directions for his funeral was duly observed, viz.—That half-a-crown in queen Anne's coin should be given to each bearer; 20s. to his spinners; 13s. 6d. to the ringers for ringing a peal; that 240 quarts of the best ale should be drank; three songs sung, and a battle fought between two cocks. He left many legacies to persons who were to attend his funeral; but if they shed a tear, they were not entitled to their legacies.

Christina Michelot, daughter of a vine-dresser at Pomard, lived from the age of ten, till fourteen, on water alone.

William James had his leg cut off in the Liverpool infirmary, without the loss of blood.

June 10th, The Alcide and Lys French ships of war, taken by admiral Boscawen; which may be justly deemed the commencement of hostilities in Europe.

July 9th, General Braddock's army defeated, and himself killed, near Fort du Quesne.

Dennis Sheehan, taylor, executed at gallows-green, for the murder of his aunt, near Macromp; he afterwards came to life, and made his escape.

June 2d, The marquis of Harrington, lord lieutenant of Ireland, landed in Cork.

Saturday, Nov. 1st. A violent shock of an earthquake felt in Cork, at 36 minutes past nine in the morning, but no damage happened.

October 23d, The first market-jury sworn in Cork, by John Reilly, esq; mayor.

The jury.—Robert Travers, esq;
   Noblet Phillips, burgess.
   Usher Philpott, burgess.
   James Chatterton, burgess.
   John Webb, burgess.
   John Swete, burgess.
   John Wrixon, burgess.

Stephen

Stephen Denroche, burgefs
Kevan Izod, burgefs
Nathaniel Lavit, merchant
Samuel Perry, merchant.
Peter Laulhe, merchant.
Paul Maylor, merchant.
Peter Ardouin, merchant.
Wm. Rickotts, merchant.
Andrew Franklin, gent.
John Deyos, merchant.
Stearne Tuckey, gent.
Robert Lane, merchant.
Francis Gray, merchant.
William Finch, merchant.
John Skeyes, merchant.

1756 One hundred and forty-fix Englifhmen were confined in the black hole at Calcutta in the Eaft Indies, by order of the nabob, and 123 found dead next morning.

Marine fociety eftablifhed at London.

The king of Pruffia commenced hoftilities in the month of Auguft in Saxony. Defeated the Auftrians at Lo.

May 18, Great Britain declared war againft France.

May 20, An engagement between admirals Byng and Galliffoniere, off Minorca.

June 29, Fort St. Philip, in Minorca, commanded by general Blakeney, furrendered to the French under the command of marfhal Richlieu.

Auguft 14, Fort Ofwego taken by the French.

Hanoverian troops arrived in England, Aug. 14th.

John Lott, taylor, for highway robbery on Bottle-hill road, and Patrick Croncen, for enlifting men for the French king, were executed at gallows-green, the 1ft of May. Lott afterwards came to life, and made his efcape.

William Taylor, John Walton, and John Geale, three foldiers belonging to general O'Farrel's regiment, were executed at gallows-green, the 2d. of October, for committing a rape on the body of

Anne

Anne Dunn, at Friar's-Walk, and robbing her of wearing-apparel; the whole regiment under arms, surrounded the gallows at the time of execution.

The Fox-hunter privateer, captain Townsend, sailed from Cove on a cruize, and was never after heard of, August 7th.

October 28th, The Blakeney privateer brought a prize into Cove.

The grand Canal commenced, under the direction of parliament and the navigation board; but so little progress was made in it, that the legiflature held out encouragement to private subscribers; and in 1772, 100,000l. was subscribed towards the finishing of it, which was completed from Dublin to Monastereven, in 1786.

Minorca surrendered to the French.

Mr. Pitt appointed chancellor of the exchequer.

1757 Francis Damien stabbed the king of France with a penknife: every refinement in cruelty, that human invention could suggest, were used to extort his reasons; he maintained a sullen silence in the midst of the most exquisite torments; or expressed his agony only in frantic ravings. His judges, tired with his obstinacy, at last thought proper to terminate his sufferings by a death shocking to humanity; which, although the act of a people who pride themselves on civility and refinement, might fill the hearts of Savages with horror. One of his hands was burnt in liquid flaming sulphur; his thighs, legs, and arms were torn with red hot pincers; boiling oil, melted lead, rosin, and sulphur, were poured into the wounds; and to complete the awful catastrophe, tight ligatures being bound round his limbs, he was torn to pieces by young and vigorous horses.

A vein of coals was discovered at Ballintoy, which has been wrought with such effect, as to supply the salt-works there, at Portrush, and Coleraine.

1757 The king of Pruffia beat the Auftrians at Lowofitz, where about 6000 were killed on each fide.

The Saxon army furrendered to the king of Pruffia, who made himfelf mafter of Drefden.

The French made themfelves mafters of Cleves, Meurs, Guelders, the town of Embden, and whatever elfe belonged to the Pruffians in Eaft-Friefland.

The famous battle of Prague, in which the Pruffians were victorious, but loft 3000 killed, befides 6000 wounded, with 397 officers; the Auftrians loft about 12,000.

Frederick befieged Prague, but was obliged to draw off part of his army to attack prince Ferdinand at Kolan, and was defeated; the lofs was nearly equal on both fides; about 20,000 were left dead.

The Ruffians took Memel, and defeated the Pruffians again near Norkitten.

The duke of Cumberland was defeated at Haftenbeck, by marefhal d'Etrees, and afterwards was obliged to take refuge under the cannon of Stade, and to fign the fingular convention of Clofter-Seven, Sept. 8th.

Colonel Clive and admiral Watfon took Calcutta, and Hughly (a place of great trade) and entirely defeated Sulajud Dowla, with 10,000 men.

The admirals Watfon and Pococke, with captain Clive, took Chandenagore, which was defended with 183 cannon.

Colonel Clive defeated the Subah's army of 20,000 men, and took his artillery and baggage.

The king of Pruffia defeated the French and Imperialifts at Rofback, with the lofs of only 300 men; the combined army loft 9000 men, with eleven general officers, and 300 of inferior rank.

The Auftrians took Schweidnitz and Breflaw.

The king of Pruffia defeated the Auftrian army of 80,000 at Luthen, with 36,000; the Auftrian army loft 6000; the Pruffians took 20,000 prifoners, 3000 waggons, and 200 pieces of cannon, &c.

1757 He then took Breslaw, and made 17,000 men prisoners.

Fort-William taken by the English.

On the 31st of March, the duke of Bedford, lord lieutenant of Ireland, obtained the king's letter for 20,000l. to be laid out as his Grace should think the most likely to afford the most speedy and effectual relief to his majesty's poor subjects of this kingdom.

The lying-in hospital opened by doctor Mosse.

The king of Prussia invaded Bohemia. Defeated the Austrians at Reichenberg, April 21st.

December 23d, Captain William Death, of the Terrible privateer of London, killed in an engagement with the Vengeance privateer of St. Maloes. The annals of mankind cannot shew an effort of more desperate courage, than was exerted under the command of the said captain Death. He had, in the beginning of his cruize, made prize of a rich merchant ship, and with this was returning home to England in triumph, when he had the misfortune to fall in with the Vengeance privateer, much his superior in force; he having but twenty-six guns, the enemy thirty-six, and a proportionable number of men. The Terrible's prize was soon taken, and converted against her; but though so unequally matched, captain Death maintained a furious engagement. The French commander and his second were killed, with two-thirds of his company; but much more dreadful was the slaughter on board the Terrible. When the enemy boarded it, they only found a scene of slaughter, silence, and desolation. Of two hundred men, only sixteen were found remaining, and the ship itself so shattered, as scarcely to be kept above water. The following are the remarkable names of the officers: captain Death, lieutenants Spirit and Ghost, boatswain Butcher, and quarter-master Debble. She was launched out of Execution-dock in London.

1758 The duke of Brunswick obliged the French to evacuate Otterberg, Bremen, and Verden; also the town and castle of Hoya on the Weser.

Prince Ferdinand recovered the city of Minden, and took 4000 prisoners.

Commodore Holmes obliged the French to abandon Embden.

M. de Chevert with 12000 men, attacked baron Imhoff, and was repulsed with great slaughter.

The king of Prussia took the Austrian garrison of Schweidnitz.

Mareshal Daun defeated the king of Prussia at Kitlitz, killed mareshal Keith and prince Francis, and 7000 men; the Austrians lost the same number.

Admiral Osborn took the Foudroyant of 80 guns, and the Orphee of 64 guns.

Admiral Hawke dispersed and drove on shore five ships of the line, 6 frigates, and 40 transports, having on board 3000 troops.

Captain Dennis, in the Dorsetshire, took the Reasonable, a French ship of the line.

Admiral Hawke destroyed the shipping in Concalle-Bay.

Lord Howe and general Bligh, took Cherburg, demolished the Mole, and took 21 pieces of cannon, which were triumphantly carried through London, and lodged in the tower. They afterwards landed at St. Cas, but were obliged to re-imbark in a great hurry, with the loss of 500 men.

General Amherst, with 14,000 men, and admiral Boscawen with 157 sail, arrived before Louisburg. General Wolfe took the light-house battery; three French ships of the line were burnt; 600 seamen in boats, under the captains Laforey and Balfour, boarded the remaining two ships of the line, destroyed one which was aground, and towed off the other in triumph; on which Louisburg surrendered.

General

1758 General Abercrombie defeated at Crown-Point, in which battle lord Howe was killed.
General Forbes took Fort du Quefne, which he called Fort-Pitt.
Commodore Keppel took Fort-Louis and Goree.
Feb. 18th, A master of an English merchantman, trading up the river St. Lawrence, was taken prisoner, and detained near three years, by M. Montcalm, who would not admit of any exchange for him on account of his very accurate knowledge of all the coast, and particularly the strength and foundings of Quebec and Louisburg. It was therefore determined to send him to Old France in the next packet boat, there to be confined till the end of the war. In the voyage he was admitted into the cabbin, where he observed one day, that they bundled up the packet and put it into a canvas bag, having previously made it ready to be thrown overboard upon any danger of being taken. They were constrained to put into Vigo for provisions, and also to gain intelligence of the strength of the English in those seas; there they found an English man of war at anchor. One night taking the opportunity (all but the watch being asleep) the prisoner took the packet out of the bag, and having fixed it in his mouth, silently let himself down the ship's side, and floated on his back unto the wake of the English man of war, where, calling for assistance, he was immediately taken on board, with the packet. The captain received him with great kindness, transcribed the packet, and immediately sent him post over land to Lisbon, with the copy of it. From Lisbon he was brought to Falmouth in a sloop of war, and immediately set out post for London, where he was examined by proper persons in the administration, and rewarded with a present supply; and by his own desire was sent to Portsmouth, to go out on board admiral Boscawen's own ship, upon the present expedition to North America.

1758. April 13th, the Prince George man of war, of 80 guns, commanded by admiral Broderick, took fire off Lisbon, and out of 745 men that were on board, 485 were lost.

March 13th, Miss Bab. Wyndham, of Salisbury, a maiden lady of ample fortune, remitted 2000l. as a present to the king of Prussia.

April 21st. A terrible fire in Barbadoes, which consumed 120 houses.

June 1st. Florence Hervey, M. D. was tried in the court of king's-bench for high treason, for holding a secret correspondence with the French. He was found guilty and condemned, but afterwards reprieved, and in September 1759, received a free pardon.

Nov. 22d, The Dublin Trader, captain White, from Parkgate, lost; she had on board for the linen merchants in Ireland, 70,000l. in money, 80,000 in goods, and above sixty passengers, among whom were the earl of Drogheda and his second son, with several other persons of fortune.

November. 28th, Doctor Shebbeare, for a libellous pamphlet, received sentence to stand in the pillory, and to be confined for three years.

Doctor Baldwin, after governing the college of Dublin forty-two years, died, aged upwards of ninety. By his will he bequeathed to the college, in real and personal property, to the amount of near 100,000l. Doctor Gilbert enriched the library by a bequest of his books, 12000 volumes, chosen by himself in a long course of years for this purpose, without regard to expence.

The statue of George II. in brass, erected in Stephen's-Green, Dublin.

Prince Ferdinand obliged the count de Clermont to retire under the cannon of Cologne, with the loss of 7000 men.

The king of Prussia defeated the Russians, who lost 15,000 men, the Prussians only 10,000.

The duke de Broglio defeated the Hessian army, near

1758 near Sangushausen, which gave the French the command of the Weser.

Senegal taken by the British, May 1st.

January 10th, The Hussar frigate, of 28 guns and 220 men, brought the Vengeance privateer of St. Maloes, of 36 guns and 400 men, into Kinsale. The Hussar had nine men killed and nine wounded; the Vengeance lost 170 men killed and wounded. This was the privateer which engaged capt. Death, of the Terrible.

July 8th, This day the greatest part of the crew belonging to the City of Cork privateer, lying at Cove, confined their officers to the cabbin, and forced from the side a lighter, that had brought provisions for their use, and endeavoured to get ashore, but some on board (well affected to the owners) made a signal of distress to a man of war that lay near them, upon which them an of war manned her long boat and pursued them; at whom the privateer's men fired, which was returned; this being perceived on board the man of war, they loaded two of their great guns with small shot, which they let fly at the lighter, killed two men, and wounded some others, after which they readily pressed the remainder.

Sept. 2d. Captain Cole's vessel foundered under the Giant's Stairs, below Passage.

October 26th, Seven East-Indiamen arrived at Cove, under convoy of the Colchester of 50 guns.

Four East-Indiamen also arrived in Kinsale, with the remains of colonel Aldercron's regiment on board, and landed at the custom-house quay.

This year an attempt was made to assassinate the king of Portugal, on Sunday night the 3d of September, when Antony Alvares Ferreira, and Joseph de Policarp de Azevedo, lay in wait for his majesty, who was then in his carriage returning from a private visit, and fired two shots at his majesty's person, from blunderbusses loaded with powder and slugs, six of which lodged in his majesty's body,

body, which wounded and dilacerated from the right shoulder along the arm, and down to the elbow on the outside, and also on the inner part of the same, and proceeded so far as to offend the breast; but the slugs were extracted, and his majesty recovered.

1759 January 18th, Joseph Mascarenhas, duke of Aveiro; Francis Assizes, marquis of Tavora; lady Elenor, marchioness of Tavora; Lewis Bernard, marquis of Tavora; Don Jerome, Count of Attouguia, Joseph-Maria, of Tavora, adjutant of the military orders of the marquis his father; Blaize-Joseph Romeiro, corporal in the command or company under the direction of the criminals; John Michael, attending page to Joseph duke of Aveiro; Emanuel Alvares Ferreira, keeper of the wardrobe to the said duke of Aveiro, and Antonio Alvares Ferreira (one of the two criminals who fired the shots) were executed in the following manner, for attempting to kill the king of Portugal. Joseph, duke of Aveira, was broken on the wheel, by the rupture of eight bones of his legs and arms, was then burnt alive with the scaffold on which he was executed, till all were reduced into ashes, which were then thrown into the sea, that there may be no more notice taken of him or his memory; his estate confiscated to the use of the crown, being divested of all his honours and titles previous to his execution; his house demolished and rent in pieces, reduced to ashes, and covered with salt, in order to obliterate every remembrance of his name. Antonio Alvares Ferreira, and Joseph de Policarp de Azevedo, who fired at his majesty, the latter having made his escape, the former was burnt alive, and his ashes thrown into the sea. Lady Tavora had her head severed from her body, being afterwards burnt to ashes, and thrown into the sea. The rest of the criminals suffered the same death as the duke of Aveiro.

Balbec

1759 Balbec and Tripoli destroyed by an earthquake; December 5th.
General Wolfe was killed in the battle of Quebec, which was gained by the British.
The Prussians destroyed the Russian magazines in Poland, took Anclem and Demen, and laid Bohemia under contribution.
The duke de Broglio took Retberg, Minden, and Munster.
Prince Ferdinand defeated Broglio at Minden, and had the British and Hanoverian cavalry under lord George Sackville; come to his assistance when required, the French army would have been utterly destroyed; after which he took Munster, and obliged the French to evacuate Westphalia.
The king of Prussia with 50,000, repulsed the Russians with 90,000 at Cunersdorf, but was defeated with the loss of 16,000, the combined army 14,000. On repulsing the Russians, the king of Prussia wrote the following note to his queen, without waiting for the final event. " We have " driven the Russians from their entrenchments : " expect within two hours to hear of a glorious " victory." After his defeat, he wrote another laconic note to her : " Remove from Berlin with " the royal family : let the archieves be carried " to Potsdam : the town may make conditions " with the enemy."
General Finck, with 2,000 men, surrendered to Mareshal Daun.
M. de Lally invaded Madrass, but was obliged to raise the siege.
Colonel Coote reduced Wandewash, and defeated M. de Lally, who attempted to recover the Settlement with 13000 men.
Admiral Pocock defeated the French squadron under M. d'Ache.
Surat taken from the Dutch, for interfering in the affairs of Bengal.
Admiral Rodney successfully bombarded Havre-de-Grace. Admiral

1759 Adm. Hawke blocked up Conflans in the harbour of Brest.
 Boscawen defeated the French fleet, and took two ships of the line, and destroyed two more.
 Admiral Hawke attacked Conflans; he ordered his own ship to be laid alongside the French admiral, called the Soleiel Royale; the Thesee a 74 threw herself between the two admirals; one broadside from the Royal George, sent her to the bottom; the Superbe shared the same fate; the Formidable struck her colours; the Soleiel Royale drove on shore, and was burnt by her own people; the Hero burnt by the British, and the Juste sunk at the mouth of the Loire. The English lost two ships of the line in a gale of wind, after the action, but the crews and part of the stores were saved.
 Captain Harvey, in the Monmouth, and captain Clements, in the Pallas frigate, watching the French fleet in Brest, saw four ships coming down, and come to close to the forts of Conquet, notwithstanding four forts and a battery played on the Monmouth and Pallas, which with difficulty worked up, yet they brought out the four ships in sight of the French fleet of 20 ships of the line. The Monmouth and Pallas kept a continual fire on the forts, and drove the French from their guns several times.
 Captain Bently, of the Waspight, knighted for his bravery in engaging two ships of M. de la Clue's squadron for some time.
 Guadaloupe taken by the British, May 1st.
 April 11th, London bridge (a temporary one) burnt and totally destroyed.
 April 26th, Marigalante, Grenada, and St. Martin, taken by captain Cooke, by virtue of a commission from sir Charles Hardy, at the head of a number of privateers, who put themselves under his command.

July

EVENTS.

1759 July 23d, The Pruffian general Wadel, defeated at Zullichau, by the count de Soltikoff, the Ruffian general.

July 25th, Fort Niagara, in America, taken by general Johnson.

July 28th, Ticonderoga taken by general Amherſt.

Auguſt 3d, Leipſic taken by the army of the Empire.

December 4th, A Pruffian detachment under general Durecke, defeated at Meiſſen by the Auſtrians, in which engagement general Durecke was wounded and taken priſoner.

March 16th, William Parks and Chriſtopher Collis, eſqrs. city ſheriffs, with the ſub-corporations, conſiſting of the maſter and wardens of the reſpective trades, aſſembled at the Lough of Cork, elegantly mounted on horſeback, where they formed according to ſeniority, and rode ſeveral miles out of town to meet John Swete, eſq; mayor of Cork, who was then on his return from Dublin, where he had been ſome time, in conſequence of an order from the ſuperior court, relative to quarterage.

July 5th, General Folliot's regiment (commonly called the Royal Iriſh) encamped at Balliphehane, and did not break up till October 17th. The city militia did duty in their abſence.

Sept. 25th & 26th, The mayor, ſheriffs, maſters and wardens of the ſeveral trades, perambulated the city-franchiſes.

Feb. 28th, Suſannah Hannokes, an elderly woman of Windgrove, near Ayleſbury, was accuſed by a neighbour for bewitching her ſpinning-wheel, ſo that ſhe could not make it go round, and offered to make oath of it before a magiſtrate; on which the huſband, in order to juſtify his wife, inſiſted upon her being tried by the church bible, and that the accuſer ſhould be preſent: accordingly ſhe was conducted to the pariſh church, where ſhe was ſtript of all her cloaths to her ſhift and under coats, and weighed againſt the bible;

where,

where, to the no small mortification of her accuser, she outweighed, and was honourably acquitted of the charge.

May 21st, Died, Mr. James Sheile, farmer, of Knocktopher, in the county of Kilkenny, aged 136 years.

June 11th, The earl of Belvidere obtained a verdict in the court of king's-bench, Dublin, against Thomas Rochfort, esq; his brother, for 20,000l. damages, besides costs, for criminal conversation with his lordship's lady. This transaction happened about fifteen years since.

June 26th, Early in the morning, Jenison Shaftoe, esq; started against Time, to ride fifty miles in two hours; in the course of which he used ten horses, and did it in eleven minutes and two seconds less time than prescribed by the articles, to the astonishment of all present.

Prince Edward appointed to the command of the Phœnix of 44 guns.

Donald Cameron, of Kinnicklabar, in Rannach, Scotland, died aged 130.

August 5th, A most daring robbery was committed at Limerick; two men entered the custom-house, one of whom presented a pistol to the clerk's breast, while the other robbed the house of 1800l. in cash, and afterwards made their escape, locking up the clerk in one of the offices, though two centinels were standing at the door.

Sept. 22d, An eminent London merchant rode four horses at Royston in Hertfordshire, for a wager of thirteen hundred guineas; he was to go forty miles in two hours, and performed it in one hour and forty-nine minutes. Bets to the amount of several thousands were depending.

October 2d, The Friendship, captain Brest, from Cork to Hallifax, was taken by a French privateer, who took out the master, and all the crew except the mate and a boy, and put eight Frenchmen on board; but after several days possession, the

the mate watched his opportunity, seized the arms, and without putting one man to death, secured as many of them as it was prudent to do for his own safety, and by the affistance of the boy, brought the ship safe into Pool harbour.

December 18th, William Andrew Horne, esq; of Butterly-Hall, in Derbyshire, aged 74, was executed at Nottingham for the murder of a child only three days old, thirty-five years before. The only prosecutor was his brother, who was privy to this long-concealed murder, and was at laſt induced to discover it, partly from uneafinefs of mind, and partly from the cruel treatment he received from Mr. Horne.

1760 Thurot landed at Carrickfergus, and pillaged the town; after he put to sea, captain Elliot in the Æolus of 36 guns, and the Pallas and Brilliant, of 32 guns each, came up with him, and after a bloody engagement, took him and his squadron.

Three of the principal banking houſes in Dublin stopped payment, and the remaining three discounted no paper, and in fact, did no busineſs. Public and private credit, that had been drooping since the year 1754, had now fallen prostrate. At a general meeting of the merchants of Dublin, with several members of the house of commons, the inability of the former to carry on business, was univerſally acknowledged; not from the want of capital, but from the stoppage of all paper circulation, and the refusal of the remaining bankers to difcount the bills even of the firſt houfes. The merchants and traders of Dublin petitioned the houfe of commons, that they ſhould engage, to the firſt of May 1762, for each of the then ſubſiſting banks in Dublin, to the amount of 50,000l. for each bank; and that an addreſs be preſented to the lord lieutenant, to thank his grace for having given directions that bankers notes ſhould be received as caſh from the ſeveral ſubſcribers to the loan, and that he would be pleaſed to give directions that their notes ſhould be taken as caſh in all

R payments

1760 payments at the treasury, and by the several collectors for the city and county of Dublin.

The allied armies under the Hereditary Prince, defeated by the French; in a few days afterwards, he defeated them, and took the commander in chief (M. Glanbitz) 177 officers, 2282 privates prisoners, besides killing a great number, and taking all their artillery and baggage.

Prince Ferdinand defeated the French at Warbourg, but was defeated by M. de Castris, at Campen, and lost 2000 men.

The Prussians defeated at Glatz; their general and 4000 men killed, the remaining army of 7000, threw down their arms, and surrendered to M. Laudohn.

The king of Prussia defeated the Austrians, and killed 8000 men, and obliged mareshal Daun to raise the siege of Schweidnitz.

The allied armies took Berlin. Leipsic, Torgau, and Wirtemberg successively surrendered to the Imperialists.

The French laid Halberstadt under contribution; the Swedes ravaged Pomerania; and the Russians invested Colburg by sea and land.

The king of Prussia, with 50,000 men, finding his affairs desperate, came up to mareshal Daun with 80,000, strongly posted; and having made the disposition for the attack, he divided his army into three divisions, and ordered his troops to be informed that he was determined to conquer or die; they answered, "That they would die, or conquer with him." Having disposed his army, he led on the center, and was received by a discharge from 200 pieces of cannon; after a vigorous attack, he was repulsed with great slaughter; and after being three times led on, and as often obliged to give ground, the king ordered his cavalry to advance, but they were soon forced to retire, and victory seemed ready to declare in favour of the Austrians, when the left division under general Zhethin,

1760 Zhethin, attacked the Auſtrians in the rear; the Pruſſian infantry returned once more to the charge, the cavalry followed their example, and totally routed the Auſtrians; 10,000 were killed on each ſide; 8,000 Auſtrians, among whom were four generals, were made priſoners, and mareſhal Daun was wounded. Night coming on, prevented many more being taken. The king of Pruſſia recovered all Saxony, except Dreſden.

Laudohn abruptly raiſed the ſiege of Cafel, and the Pruſſians raiſed the ſiege of Pomerania.

General Murray marched out of Quebec, and with 3000 men engaged M. de Levi with ten battalions of regular French troops, 6000 Canadian militia, and a body of Indians, but being out flanked, retired with the loſs of 1000 men; the French loſt 2000 men.

The Ramillies of 90 guns, was loſt on a rock called Bolthead, near Plymouth; only one midſhipman and 25 ſailors were ſaved, and above ſeven hundred periſhed, Feb. 15th.

A huntſman near Torrington, in Devonſhire, was devoured by his own hounds.

Earl Ferrers was tried by his peers, and found guilty of the murder of Mr. Johnſon, his ſteward, and was executed May 5th.

Lord George Sackville was tried by a court-martial, and pronounced unfit to ſerve his majeſty in any military capacity whatſoever; and his majeſty ordered his name to be ſtruck out of the liſt of privy counſellors.

The tower of a church at Peterſburg, which had been newly built, fell down, and more than 500 people were either killed or maimed.

Died, John Turner, who lived miſerably in a garret in St. Giles's; under his arms were found two bags, containing 136l.

Sept. 14th, was married at Clonmell, Patrick O'Neill, aged 113, to his ſeventh wife; he was born in 1647,

1647, and enlisted for a dragoon in the 17th year of Charles the Second, and continued serving their successive majesties till 1746, when he was discharged, having been in all the battles, &c. with king William and the duke of Marlborough. He is now in perfect health, of sound understanding, and walks without a stick.

At Berne, in Switzerland, a girl of nine years old was delivered of a child.

There has been lately discovered in Italy a new nation, which has subsisted there for many hundred years. These people live in several vilages in the mountains, lying north of Verona and Vicenza, and speak a language of their own, which hitherto was thought a corrupt German, but upon a closer enquiry is found to be pure Danish. Segnior Marco Pezzo, has written a very learned dissertation, to prove that these people are a remnant of the Cimbrians, defeated by Caius Marius.

A horse belonging to Mr. William Cross, in Boggs, near Hamilton, was grazing in a field until four o'clock in the afternoon, when he was observed to give over eating; from that time his neck swelled excessively, until the fourth day, when he died. To satisfy the owner's curiosity, his neck was opened, and a large adder was found in his throat, and the parts all around mortified.

It is remarkable that five sons of the earl of Banbury have suffered in action, within these few months past. Lord Wallingford, the eldest, having received a wound at Carrickfergus; the second wounded at the taking of Guadaloupe; the third, a lieutenant Knolles, of the Beddeford man of war, was killed in a late engagement with two French frigates off Lisbon, and the fourth and fifth, much wounded at Minden.

The thanks of the governors of the workhouse of Dublin, were presented to lady Arabella Denny, for her unremitting attention to the foundling children, but particularly for a clock, lately put
up

1760 up at her ladyship's expence, in the nursery, with the following inscription. "For the benefit of in-
"fants protected by this hospital, lady Arabella
"Denny presents this clock, to mark, that as
"children reared by the spoon, must have but a
"small quantity of food at a time, it must be of-
"fered frequently; for which purpose this clock
"strikes every twenty minutes, at which notice,
"all the infants that are not asleep, must be dis-
"creetly fed."

An Algerine zebeque of 20 guns, was driven on shore near Penzance in Cornwall, and entirely lost; 150 of the crew got on shore, which greatly alarmed the country people. It is twenty-four years since an Algerine cruizer was in any port in England.

France was so distressed in her finances, that the nobility and gentry, following the example of the king, threw their plate into the public treasury, in order to support the war in Germany.

King George II. died October 25th, in the 77th year of his age, and was succeeded by his present majesty, who, on the 8th of September, 1761, married the princess Charlotte of Mecklenburg Strelitz. Crowned 22d.

Blackfriars bridge, consisting of nine arches, begun; finished 1770, at the expence of 152,840l. to be discharged by a toll.

A transit of Venus over the sun, June 6th.

Earthquakes in Syria, October 13th.

Timmary, on the coast of Coromandel, retaken by the English.

The English took Arcott on the same coast.

The French took Marpurg by capitulation.

A terrible fire happened in the rope-house at Portsmouth, which did 100,000l. damage.

The castle of Dillenbourg surrendered to the French by capitulation.

The French and Saxons took Gottingen.

The French took Zingenhayn by capitulation.

Montreal

1760 Montreal and all Canada, surrendered to the English by capitulation.

The count of Lusatia defeated general Wangenheim, at Dramsfeld.

The town and castle of Cleves, surrendered by capitulation to the allies.

The city of Wirtemberg surrendered to the Imperialists by capitulation.

Wirtemberg evacuated by the Imperialists.

November 18th, The sessions of parliament opened by his present majesty, with a most gracious speech from the throne.

Three thousand Prussian hussars took Rostock.

July 21st, the new theatre in George's-street, Cork, opened.

November 4th, George III. proclaimed king in Cork, The Royal Scotch, Handasyde's, and Bagshaw's regiments lined the streets, whilst the mayor, corporation, and city regalia, attended by lieutenant-governor Molesworth, paraded the town.

The town of Malta was surprised the 6th ult. at the near approach of a large ship of Turkish construction; having a white flag, with a crucifix at her mizzen top, and a Turkish pendant embroidered with gold, that reached to the very sea. Boats were immediately sent off, who were informed, that it was a ship of the grand signior's, commanded by his admiral, and called the Ottoman Crown; that she sailed the second of last June, with two frigates, five galleys, and other small vessels from the Dardanelles; that the above-mentioned admiral had been with this ship only to Smyrna, Scio, and Trio, and at length anchored in the channel of Strangie, when he and his retinue to the number of 300 persons went on shore. The whole ship's complement was 700 men, but 400 being on shore the 19th of Sept. the remaining 300 were attacked and overpowered by 70 christian slaves, armed only with a knife each; part being killed, part obliged to jump overboard, and the rest left to sue for mercy. These heroes, now no longer slaves, bore away immediately for Malta; but were soon pursued by the two frigates and a Ragusian ship, whom, by crowding sail, they escaped; and the 8th, this ship, mounting 68 fine brass guns, but boarded for 74, was brought safe into the harbour of Valatte, amidst the acclamations of the people.

The order of Malta, as an encouragement to such brave fellows, has made them the sole proprietors of the ship and slaves, as well as of all the contribution money, which latter is said to amount to a million and a half of florins, and other effects on board. Deeds equal to this in heroism, though not in value, have been atchieved by our own countrymen, several times during the course of this war; which at once proves what presence of mind and resolution may surmount, and what an almost incredible effect it has where it is not expected.

The grand signior was, on this occasion, so highly offended with the conduct of his admiral, that he dismissed him from his service.

1761 Ofnaburg taken and pillaged by the French.

The tide ebbed and flowed four times in an hour, at Whitby, July 17.

Potatoes sold this year at 29s. the barrel.

His late majesty's statue erected in Cork.

The duke de Broglio obliged prince Ferdinand to abandon all his conquests, to raise the blockade of Zingenhayn, and the siege of Cassel, and retire behind the Dymel. Broglio was afterwards repulsed with the loss of 5000 men.

Belleisle taken by commodore Keppel and general Hodgson.

Pondicherry in the East-Indies taken from the French. General Lally and the garrison, made prisoners by colonel Coote.

Foundation of Poolbeg light-house laid. Finished in 1768.

Mareschal

1761 Mareshal Broglio and the prince de Soubife, defeated at Kirch Denckern, by prince Ferdinand of Brunfwick, and the British forces under the marquis of Granby; 2000 men were killed and wounded, and 3000 prisoners.

Prince Henry gained a signal victory over the Auftrians and Imperialifts in Saxony, took 4000 prifoners, and 365 waggons.

The garrifon of Dorften taken by prince Ferdinand.

Prince Xavier of Saxony, took Wolfenbuttle.

Coals firft difcovered in Scotland, Nov. 1ft.

Colberg taken by the Ruffians under general Butterlin.

Dominico taken from the French, by lord Rollo and fir James Douglas.

A violent shock of an earthquake at Cork and Kinfale, March 31ft.

April 22d, The election for members of parliament began in this city, and ended the 28th; for John Hely Hutchinfon, efq; 567 votes; fir John Freke, bart. 370 votes, and Thomas Newenham, efq; 295 votes; whereupon the two former were returned duly elected.

June 18th and 19th, We had the moft conftant thunder and lightning, attended with the heavieft rain ever known. In the fouth liberties, a bull and two cows were ftruck dead by lightning. At Donybrook, the feat of the rev. Boyle Davies, a large beam which fupported a floor over the cellar, was fplit fo wide that a 24 pound ball may be put into the chafm. There was not the leaft thunder or rain at Bandon or Kinfale.

September 15th, Illuminations in Cork for queen Charlotte's arrival in England.

Illuminations for the king and queen's coronation.

October 4th, The wooden-bridge adjoining the north wier, fell down; a woman and a boy were unfortunately drowned by this accident.

A fox went into the houfe of Mr. M'Carthy, brewer, in Hanover-ftreet, and killed eleven fowl. He attempted

attempted it again, but was seized by the brewers, and killed in the presence of several sporting gentlemen. He made great havock among the poultry in St. Finbarry's, and was supposed to have run into town.

Died at Koningsberg in Prussia, captain Bromfish, aged 112; 93 years of which he had been in the service of Prussia.

Died at Philadelphia, Mr. Charles Cottrel, aged 120 years; and in three days after his wife died, aged 115. They lived together in matrimony ninety-eight years.

A farmer's wife at Glencairn, was delivered of four sons, three of which survived. The father was 74 years old, and the mother 44.

In an engagement between the Tuscany of Bristol, captain Power, and the duc de Biron privateer of Dunkirk, the Tuscany blew up, and sunk in a few minutes, and out of 211 persons, only the captain and four or five were saved; among whom was a young infant that was blown into the privateer, and found on her deck after the explosion, without having received the least injury.

A cause was tried in the court of king's-bench, Westminster, wherein Mr. Butler was plaintiff, and one Bell defendant, on an action for the defendant's dog being loose and biting the plaintiff's hand, so that he lost the use of three of his fingers. The jury brought in a verdict of two hundred pounds damages.

The wife of Mr. Bandon, page to the late king, delivered of a son, at the age of 58, and her husband 70.

Died at Mitchelstown, John Newell, esq; aged 127, and grandson to old Parr, who died at the age of 152.

Worksop Manor, the seat of his grace the duke of Norfolk, burnt to the ground; the loss was computed at 100,000l.

At

1762 At Gratz in Voigtlan, a man lived to the age of 135 years, without any illness; he had seen seven emperors of Germany.

Died, a peasant in Poland, in the 157 year of his age; till within 12 days of his death, he worked as day labourer.

A poor labouring family, near Biddestown in Norfolk, had been lately afflicted with a terrible disorder; the limbs of several of them having rotted off, though without any injury to their health, or the other parts of the body.

A centinel on duty at Chatham, was struck with lightning; the upper leather of his shoe on his left foot was shattered; a hole was made through the blade of his sword, and about two inches of the edge melted; the hilt was melted and soldered to his bayonet, as was one of the locks of his musket to the iron ramrod; his face was scorched, and he lay an hour speechless, but afterwards recovered.

A prosecution commenced against Mr. Foote, for introducing the character of Mr. George Falkner, upon the public stage; after a long hearing, a verdict was given in favour of Mr. Falkner, and Mr. Foote was severely fined.

Cornelius Nepos, published at Moskow, being the first classical book printed in Russia.

Queen Charlotte's annuity settled at 100,000l. after the king's death.

Martinico taken from the French, together with St. Lucia, St. Vincent's, and Grenada islands, by a detachment of admiral Rodney's fleet, under the command of commodore Swanton, with brigadier Walsh and lieutenant-colonel Scott.

The Havannah taken from the Spaniards by the British forces, under the command of general lord Albemarle, admiral sir George Pocock, and commodore Keppel. The treasure found here may be said to equal a national subsidy. The Neptune of

EVENTS.

1762 of 70 guns, Afia 64, and Europa 64, Spanifh line of battle fhips, were funk at the entrance of the harbour; the Tyger of 70 guns, Reyna 70, Soverano 70, Infanta 70, Aquilon 70, America 60, Conqueftado 60, San Genaro 60, San Antonio 60, Vinganaza 24, Thetis 24, and Marte 18 guns, furrendered to the Britifh commanders in the harbour of the Havannah, befides two fhips of war that were on the ftocks, and feveral merchant fhips in the harbour.

The firft payment of the Havannah prize-money, amounted to 516,185l. 3s.

Preparatory to the taking of the Havannah, the Englifh troops found great difficulty in taking Moro; at laft a breach was made, and they were ordered to ftorm it, which they did with fo much fpirit and order, that the garrifon was quite difconcerted: 400 were cut to pieces, the reft threw down their arms, and received quarter. Don Lewis de Velafco, the governor, having collected a fmall body of determined men, in an intrenchment around the flag ftaff, glorioufly fell in defending the enfign of Spain, which no intreaties could induce him to ftrike. The generous and civilized victors watered his body with their tears, inftead of exulting over it like barbarians, or tearing it in pieces like favages, in vengeance of their fufferings.

Elizabeth, emprefs of Ruffia died, and was fucceeded by her nephew the duke of Holftein, under the name of Peter III. who, on coming to the throne, ordered a ceffation of arms, and foon after entered into an alliance with the king of Pruffia, and joined part of his forces to drive the Auftrians out of Silefia.

Prince Henry of Brunfwick killed in a fkirmifh with Broglio, near Munfter.

The king of Pruffia obliged marefhal Daun to abandon his ftrong pofts, and leave Schweidnitz uncovered.

The

1762 The Czar depofed, and Catherine invefted with the Imperial enfigns; he was thrown into prifon, and died in three days.

The Emprefs withdrew her troops out of Silefia, Pruffia, and Pomerania.

The king of Pruffia defeated marefhal Daun, and obliged Schweidnitz to furrender.

American philofophical fociety eftablifhed in Philadelphia.

The Englifh forces arrived at Lifbon,

Miranda in Portugal, taken by the Spaniards.

Braganza in the fame kingdom taken by the Spaniards.

The city of Chaves alfo furrendered to the Spaniards under count O'Reily.

War declared by Portugal againft Spain.

The Danes invefted Hamburgh.

France declared war againft Portugal.

St. John's in Newfoundland taken by the French, but retaken September the 18th.

A dreadful cannonade at Bucker Muhl. This poft was no more than a Bridge over the Ohme, defended by a flight redoubt on one fide, and by a mill on the other. The allies had no cover except the redoubt, nor the French except the mill. A dreadful fire and cannonade with grape fhot was fupported between thefe two refolute bodies, without a moment's intermiffion, or the leaft flackening on one fide or the other, for near fifteen hours, from the dawn of day to dark night: Neither fide gave way, and this moft bloody conteft for a very trifling object in the end, left the allies in the poffeffion of their redoubt, and the French of their mill; the whole compafs of military hiftory furnifhes no inftance of fo obftinate a difpute. The allies loft 600 men in killed and wounded; towards the clofe of the day the dead bodies ferved to raife a parapet for the redoubt, in the place of that which had been beat to pieces by the cannonade.

The

1762 The Manilla and Philippine Islands taken from the Spaniards by the English, under the command of admiral Cornish and brigadier general Draper.
National debt in 1762: Principal 110,613,836l. 8s.
Annual intereft - - - 3,792,594l. 3s. 4d.

114,406,430l. 11s. 4d.
June 4th, Bow Bells rung for the firft time; the weight of them are as follows: Firft bell 8 Ct. 3 qrs. and 7 lb. Second bell, 9 Ct. 2 lb. Third bell, 10 Ct. 1 qr. 4 lb. Fourth bell, 12 Ct. 7 lb. Fifth bell, 13 Ct. 24 lb. Sixth bell, 17 Ct. 11 lb. Seventh bell, 20 Ct. 2 qrs. 26 lb. Eighth bell, 24 Ct. 2 qrs. 5 lb, Ninth bell, 34 Ct. 2 qrs. 6 lb. Tenth bell, 53 Ct. 22 lb.

At the fale at St. Paul's coffee-houfe, of Mr. Gills collection of coins, &c. the following fold as under: One penny of Henry I. for 2l. 2s. one ditto of Edward I. 1l. 9s.—one groat of Henry VIII. 1l. 2s.—one crown, half-crown, fhilling, and fixpence of queen Elizabeth, 3l. 18s.—one halfcrown and three-pence of Charles I. 2l. 15s.— a gold ring with an ancient Runic infcription, 15l.

June 6th, A dreadful fire in Cat-lane, Cork, which confumed 150 houfes.

Doctor Brambel, lord primate of Ireland, died.

Sale of Dunkirk to the French, by king Charles II.

Andrew Franklin, efq; mayor of Cork, obliged a ferjeant and twelve men to mount guard regularly every day at his houfe, during the laft 3 months he remained in office; he was oppofed by colonel Molefworth, lieutenant-governor of the city; but the mayor, who was an upright fpirited magiftrate, foon humbled the military jurifdiction; he fhewed his prerogative as chief magiftrate of the fecond city in the kingdom, and left an example to his fuccefsors not unworthy of imitation.

1763 The definitive treaty of peace between Great-Britain, France, Spain, and Portugal, concluded at Paris, February 10th; which confirmed to Great Britain

Britain the extensive provinces of Canada, East and West Florida, and part of Louisiana, in North America; also the islands of Grenada, St. Vincent, Dominica, and Tobago, in the West Indies.

The Jesuits expelled from France.

The pensions on the Irish establishment this year, amounted to 66,477l. 5s.

The definitive treaty of peace between the empress Queen and the king of Prussia, signed the 15th of February.

John Wilkes, esq; member of parliament for Aylesbury, arrested on a general warrant signed by lord Hallifax, one of the secretaries of state, and committed to the tower, under a warrant signed by him and the other secretary, lord Egremont, April 30th.

The new excise on cyder took place, when the right honourable George Grenville was first lord of the treasury.

The political paper, called the North-Briton, No. 45, was publickly burnt, by order of both houses of parliament.

May 9th, The workmen began to clear the channel of the harbour of Cork, in order to build the New Wall; and on Monday the 30th, several hundred labourers paraded the city with spades and shovels on their shoulders, quitted their work at the New Wall, and turned out for eight-pence per day, being then allowed but 6d.h.

One side of the North main-street flagged.

The Red-house Walk began to be improved.

1764 The parliament granted 10,000l. to Mr. Harrison for his discovery of the longitude by his time-piece.

Famine and pestilence in Italy,

An earthquake at Lisbon.

Lady Molesworth and her three children, burnt in her house.

On the 13th of June, the mayor and corporation of Limerick,

Limerick, proceeded by water to Scattery-Island, where he called a court of admiralty, and then he sailed to the mouth of the river Shannon, where ends the boundary of the city liberties. Here the mayor, as admiral of the Shannon, ordered a gun to be fired, to bring to one of his majesty's sloops of war then in the river, which she not regarding, only by hoisting out a flag, another gun was fired, and soon after the mayor boarded the sloop; the crew of which, on hearing his errand, were immediately ordered to compliment his worship with three cheers.

Regulations with respect to franking letters, took place.

Prince Frederick, his majesty's second son, elected bishop of Osnaburg in Germany, by a conge d'elire from his father, as elector of Hanover.

December 28th, Henry, earl of Shannon, one of the lords justices of Ireland, died.

1765 His majesty's royal charter passed for incorporating the society of artists.

An act passed for annexing the sovereignty of the Isle of Man to the crown of Great Britain.

Grand Canal begun for making a navigation from Dublin on the south side to the Shannon; incorporated in 1772. Passage-boats plied to Sallins in 1783; to Monastereven 1786.

Otaheite, or George the Third's Island, discovered June 18th.

Oak saw-dust first discovered useful in tanning.

There was a scarcity, caused by the failure of potatoes in general throughout the kingdom, which distressed the common people; the spring corn had also failed, and grain so high, that it was thought necessary to appoint a committee to enquire what might be the best method to reduce it; and to prevent a great dearth, two acts were passed early in this session, to stop the distillery, and to prevent the exportation of corn for a limited time. In the spring of 1766, those fears seem to have been

1765 well founded; several towns were in great distress for corn, and by the humanity of the lord-lieutenant (lord Hertford) money was issued out of the treasury to buy corn for such places as applied to his lordship for that purpose.

The years 1770 and 1771, were seasons of great distress in Ireland; and in the month of February in the latter year, the high price of corn was mentioned from the throne, as an object of the first importance, which demanded the utmost attention.

In the years 1778 and 1779, there was great plenty of corn, but the manufacturers were not able to buy, and many thousands of them supported by charity; the consequence was, that corn fell to so low a price, that the farmers in many places were not able to pay their rents.

The bed of the river Ayre was quite dry for more than half a mile, which continued so till the tide returned; the same was never known to happen before or since.

The river at Bourdeaux ebbed an hour and half, then flowed fifteen minutes, and then ebbed again for an hour and half more; which last unusual ebbing was followed by an ordinary flood, that continued the usual time.

M. Peter Kretzchmar set one grain of barley in a rich spot, from which he reaped in 18 months, 15,000 ears, by transplantation sixteen times.

The peruke-makers petitioned the king to cut off his hair and wear a wig; to which his majesty answered, "That he held nothing dearer to his heart " than the happiness of his people; and they " may be assured, he should at all times use his " endeavours to promote their welfare." Several of the peruke-makers, who attended on this occasion, gave such offence by their inconsistency in wearing their own hair, that they had it cut off by the mob.

A negro

1765 A negro at Lisbon, named Firmein de Costa, gave the following most surprising instance of fidelity and affection: "Hearing that his master Emanuel Cabral, was taken up for killing a soldier, he quitted the woods to which he had fled for refuge, and voluntary surrendered himself into the hands of justice, declaring that he alone was guilty of the assassination, and that his master was innocent; accordingly the master, after a long examination, appearing innocent, he was set at liberty, and the negro hanged."

Died, Mr. Farrol, in Maygard-street, St. Giles's, who, by letting two-penny lodgings, amassed upwards of 6000l.

Died at Carowby, Mr. Dominick Joyce, aged 120.

At an ordination at the chapel royal, a black was ordained, whose devout behaviour attracted the notice of the whole congregation; he was shortly after priested.

At a stable in Piccadilly, two coach geldings were sold by weight at one shilling per lb. and produced 57l.

At Surry assizes, Samuel Berry was tried for actually committing a rape on his wife's grandmother, aged 91.

A life-guard-man of Poland, celebrated for his great voraciousness, was presented to the court of Saxony, and in the presence of it devoured near twenty pounds of beef and half a calf roasted, besides other things.

Nicholas Wolley, esq; of Bletchington, Cumberland, who died lately, left the best part of his estate to his footman, who saved his life about two years before.

Died in Hog-lane, St. Giles's, a man of the name of Duncan, who in a few years amassed 1200l. by letting out barrows at sixpence per week.

A captain in the 95th regiment of foot, obtained a verdict with 400l. damages, against a tradesman, for a malicious prosecution on the charge of murder,

1765 der, for which he stood his trial in the city of Cork, and no profecutor appearing, he was acquitted.

June 1ſt, The Engliſh colours were hoiſted on the caſtle of Caſtletown, the capital of the Iſle of Man, the ſovereignty of that iſland being now annexed to the crown of Great Britain; in a few days after, his majeſty was proclaimed throughout the iſland, for which his majeſty paid the duke of Athol 70,000l. By an abſtract of the clear revenue of this iſland, from 1754 to 1763, the medium was 7293l. per ann. of which the land revenue for the laſt year was 1409l. 17s. 6d. and the income of the lands in the hands of the lord of the Iſle, 107l.

The following articles, part of the curious collection of Egyptian, Roman, and other antiquities, made by Ebenezer Muſſel, eſq; lately deceaſed, ſold by auction, viz.

King Charles II's hat-button, for 2l. 13s. The curtana of James II. of England, and the ſword of James IV. of Scotland, taken at Floddenfield, 1l. 12s. A ſcymeter taken from the baſhaw of Damaſcus at the ſiege of Vienna, 5l. 5s. King of Madagaſcar's ſhirt, the queen's ſhift, their ſaſhes, belts, &c. 1l. 3s. Queen Elizabeth's gloves, knife and fork, work-bag, pincuſhion, and a toothpick; Mary queen of Scots hair-cap, Oliver Cromwell's night-cap, camp-pillow, ſilk ſaſh, tobacco-ſtopper, and king Charles II's. night-cap, 2l. 12s. Queen Elizabeth's ſtriking-watch, given by her to one of the warders of the tower when ſhe quitted her impriſonment there, 2l. King Charles I's. watch, given by him to biſhop Juxon the morning of his martyrdom, 2l. 17s. An earthen cann of St. Thomas a Becket, finely wrought, 16s. Sir Edmundbury Godfrey's dagger; a large parcel of curious ancient gloves; the ſtar and garter worn by the duke of Marlborough at Blenheim battle; ditto of James II. William III. and queen Anne; and a piece of fringe work made by Mary queen of

1765 of William III. 2l. By this the curious may form some judgment of the price of virtu in England.

Two mowers near Wells, in Somersetshire, cut down four acres of grass in an hour and seventeen minutes for a wager of 20l. which they won by performing it only one minute within the time: two to one were laid against them.

Nine whiteboys were killed and twenty made prisoners, in a skirmish with a party of dragoons near Dungannon.

The wife of a collier at Sitzeroda, near Torgau in Saxony, was lately delivered of five daughters, who were all baptised, but died soon after. In the year 1732, a woman of the same village, was twice delivered in the space of eleven months, of three children at a birth.

In Lapland 120 head of rein-deer, in one herd, were struck dead by lightning.

A young woman walked 72 miles in one day, viz. from Blencogo to within two miles of Newcastle.

A red cow, the property of Mr. Thomas Stubbing, of Hempsted in Essex, brought forth three milk-white-cow calves, with red ears.

The emperor of Germany died.

A boat with three men, a boy, and a large dog, overset in crossing the river near Aberdeen; the dog brought ashore one of the men, and then went into the water and brought out the boy; the other two men got ashore of themselves.

As lord William Campbell was fishing near Henley upon Thames, he heard the cry of a man from a distance, calling out boat! boat! several of which, however, passed not far off without taking the least notice. At last a man from the point of an island, called out that there was a man drowning: upon which lord William Campbell immediately set out, and came to the place, where he was shewn something like a man lying at the bottom of the water. His lordship stirred the body
with

with the pole of his boat, which was twenty feet long; but as the pole had no hook to it, and his lordship finding it was losing too much time, he instantly pulled off his coat only (his lady and sister being in the boat) and jumped into the water, which was sixteen feet deep, and although the man was under the trunk of an old tree, he brought him up, and swam to shore with him. His lordship then ordered him to be blooded, and by his great care, in a short time brought him to breathe; when, being carried home, he soon after perfectly recovered. He was a servant to lord Palmerston, who was then on a visit to a gentleman near that place.

The late Mrs. Wolfe, mother of the brave general, left 1000l. to the incorporated society in Dublin, for promoting English Protestant working-schools in Ireland, and the residue, after a few legacies were paid, to be disposed of among the widows and families of the officers who were employed in the military land service under her son.

Thomas Scott, of York, rode his own horse from that city to London, in thirty-two successive hours and forty minutes, being 192 miles.

His royal highness the duke of Cumberland, died suddenly, and on opening him a coagulation of blood about the size of a pigeon's egg, was found in the right ventricle of the brain. As he died intestate, the earl of Albemarle administered to him, by virtue of his majesty's sign manuel. John Mezo, one of his hussars, having been given a suit of his cloaths, with all the visible pockets turned out, he found in a private one bank notes to the amount of 1751l. which he was so honest as to return to the gentleman in waiting.

At Avranches, in France, a woman, who had been long afflicted with vapours and convulsions, which at last degenerated into a palsy, having been lately blooded by order of her physician, and in his presence, the blood ran freely a little while, and then stopped;

1765 stopped; when, upon examing the orifice, there appeared in it a small white body, which, on being drawn out with the point of a pin, proved to be a live worm with two eyes, which were very visible, and a muzzle with long hairs upon it, like a cat's whiskers. This curiosity is still preserved in spirits of wine.

Two bricklayers were fined, one in a hundred pounds the other fifty, for suffering rubbish to remain a long time before some buildings carrying on by them near red-lion square.

A child at Portisham, near Weymouth, not two years old, discharged a worm out of one of her eyes, about an inch and half long.

A diamond of considerable value was found in the stomach of a woodcock, lately shot at Seaton in Northumberland.

The Pope's bull was suppressed by the parliament of France, when it was declared that no bull or brief for the future should be received, unless attended with the king's letters patent.

1766 April 21st, A spot or macula of the sun, more than thrice the bigness of our earth, passed the sun's centre.

The American stamp-act repealed, March 18th.

A great earthquake at Constantinople.

The Jesuits expelled from Bohemia and Denmark.

The chevalier de St. George, died at Rome, Jan. 2d.

The army commissions regulated in their prices, by a board of general officers.

Gibraltar nearly destroyed by a storm, Feb. 3d.

Died, the reverend Mr. Mattinson, curate of Patterdale in Westmoreland, 60 years. The first infant he christened after he got holy orders, when she was 19 years old agreed to marry him, and he asked her and himself in the church. By this wife he had one son and three daughters, and married them all in his own church himself. His stipend, till within these 20 years, was only 12l. per annum, and never reached to 20l. yet out of this,

by

1766 by the help of a good wife, he brought up his children very well, died at the age of 83, grandfather to 17 children, and worth 1000l. sterling.

Peter McKinley, Andres Zeckerman, George Gidley, and Richard St. Quintin, four pirates, who inhumanly murdered captains Cochran and Glass, on board the Sandwich, were executed near St. Stephen's green, Dublin.

Count Lally, commander in chief of the French forces the laft war in the East Indies, beheaded at Paris.

Her royal highness the princefs Matilda, was espoused by proxy, to Christian VII. king of Denmark.

James Marquis of Kildare, created Duke of Leinster, Nov. 14th.

Wines imported on an avarage of three years, ending 1766 — — — 4425 tons
1776 — — — 3331 ditto
1787 — — — 2061 ditto

In 1754 The return of houses in Dublin were 12,857.

Ellen Ellis, at Beaumaris in Derbyshire, aged 72, was brought to bed May 10th; she had been married 46 years, and her eldest son was 45 years old. She had not had a child for 25 years.

The number of houses this year in Dublin, were 13,194.

Patrick Redmond, taylor, was executed at gallows-green, the 10th of September, for robbing the dwelling-house of John Griffin. Glover the player (who was then in Cork) took an active part in this man's restoration; after he hung nine minutes and was cut down, he was perfectly restored to life by constant friction and fumigation. He afterwards made his escape, got drunk, went to the play-house door (the night of his execution) to return Mr. Glover thanks, and put the whole audience in terror and consternation. He was the third taylor that made his escape from the gallows since the year 1755.

1767 The Jesuits expelled from Spain, Venice, and Genoa, April 2d.

Martinico almost destroyed by an earthquake.

The Protestants tolerated in Poland, Nov. 2d.

The avarage export of pork, for the last five years, was about 40,000 barrels; the like, ending 1774, was 46,924 barrels; the like, ending 1782, was 87,085 barrels; and in the year 1787, it rose to 101,859 barrels.

The avarage export of cattle, for the last five years,
ending 1767 about — 500 head
in 1774 — — 1,088 ditto
in 1782 — — 2,993 ditto
in 1787 — — 12,993 ditto

Phelix M'Carthy, baker, fined fifty pounds, and to suffer three months imprisonment, for offering a bribe to Samuel Maylor, esq; mayor of Cork; he was convicted on Saturday, 19th of September, before prime-serjeant Hely Hutchinson, in the city court.

Hugh Carleton, esq; was elected Recorder of the city of Cork, August 24th.

The mayoralty-house finished. James Chatterton, esq; was the first mayor who inhabited it.

October 8th, A prodigious flood and spring-tide. A boat plied for some time in the North Main-street.

1768 Academy of painting established in London.

The Turks imprisoned the Russian ambassador, and declared war against that empire.

The Jesuits expelled from Naples, Malta, and Parma.

Duration of Irish parliaments limited to eight years.

A bill passed to impose a tax on tea, paper, painters colours, and glass imported into America.

A vessel was seized at Boston, in consequence of her having neglected some new regulations; on which the mob attacked the houses of the commissioners, destroyed the collector's boats, and obliged the custom-house officers to take refuge in Castle-William.

July

July 21st, The election in the county court-house, Cork, for knights of the shire; the numbers stood as follows, viz. For Richard Townsend, esq; 673 votes; Arthur Hyde, esq; 671; Sampson Stawell esq; 402; and sir Robert Deane, bart. 394 votes; Richard Townsend and Arthur Hyde, esqrs. were returned duly elected.

The right hon. John Hely Hutchinson, and Brabazon Ponsonby, esq; were elected members for the city.

Tonson's bank opened in Paul-street, August 1st.

Septem. 8th, Hennessy's salt-house, at Cold-harbour, was accidentally blown up with powder. His son and maid-servant unfortunately lost their lives.

1769 Paoli fled from Corsica June 13th. The island then reduced by the French.

Foundation of the Hibernian Hospital, for the reception of soldiers children, Phœnix-park, laid. Opened in 1770.

The sums remitted from Ireland to absentees, amounted this year to 1,208,982l. 14s. 6d.

The foundation stone of the royal exchange, laid by lord viscount Townsend, lord-lieutenant of Ireland. It was designed by Mr. Cooley, and opened for transacting business in 1779. The expence amounted to 40,000l. was defrayed by lottery-schemes conducted by the merchants of Dublin.

A flash of lightning penetrated the theatre at Venice, during the representation; 600 people were in the house, several of whom were killed; it put out the candles, melted a lady's gold watch-case; the jewels in the ears of others, which were compositions, and split several diamonds.

George lord viscount Townsend, lord-lieutenant of Ireland, arrived in the city of Cork, June 3d, dined with the corporation at the mayoralty-house on Monday the 4th, and went to Christ church on Sunday the 10th of September.

Buttons first numbered on officers coats. Buff waistcoats and breeches for soldiers.

Foundation

1770 Foundation laid of the Hibernian Marine Nurſery, Rogerſon's-quay. Opened 1773.

An earthquake at St. Domingo.

Government repealed all the duties laid on articles imported into America, except that on tea, which was oppoſed as much as all the others.

1771 Dr. Solander and Mr. Banks, in his majeſty's ſhip the Endeavour, captain Cook, returned from a voyage round the world, having made ſeveral important diſcoveries in the South-ſeas.

An emigration of 500,000 Tourgouths from the coaſts of the Caſpian Sea to the frontiers of China.

Solway Moſs, bordering on Scotland, ten miles from Carliſle, began to ſwell, owing to heavy rains, and upwards of 400 acres of it roſe to ſuch a height above the level of the ground, that at laſt it rolled forward like a torrent, and continued its courſe above a mile, ſcooping along with it houſes, trees, and every thing in its way; it then divided into iſlands of different extent, from one to ten feet deep, upon which were found hares, wild fowl, &c. It has covered near 600 acres at Netherby, to which it removed, and deſtroyed about thirty ſmall villages; it continued in motion from Saturday to Wedneſday, Dec. 31.

Commodore Knight in the Ramillies of 90 guns, with the Defence of 74, Centaur 74, Ajax 74, Rippon 64, and the Solebay of 28 guns, arrived in Cork harbour, Jan. 31.

1772 The king of Sweden changed the conſtitution from ariſtocracy to a limited monarchy.

The Pretender married a princeſs of Germany, grand-daughter of Thomas, late earl of Ayleſbury.

The emperor of Germany, empreſs of Ruſſia, and the king of Pruſſia, ſtripped the king of Poland of a great part of his dominions, which they divided among themſelves, in violation of the moſt ſolemn treaties.

Negroes adjudged to be free whilſt in this country.

T   Exploſion

Explosion of gunpowder at Chester, which destroyed many of the spectators of a puppet-show, and greatly damaged several houses, Nov. 5.

1773 Captain Phipps was sent to explore the North Pole; but having made 81 degrees, was in danger of being locked up by the ice, and his attempt to discover a passage in that quarter, proved fruitless.

The English East India company having, by conquest, or treaty, acquired the extensive provinces of Bengal, Orixa, and Bahar, containing fifteen millions of inhabitants, great irregularities were committed by their servants abroad; upon which, government interfered, and sent out judges, &c. for the better administration of justice.

The war between the Russians and the Turks proved disgraceful to the latter, who lost the islands in the Archipelago, and on the sea were every where unsuccessful.

The Americans destroyed 342 chests of tea.

General Gage arrived in America, and removed the assembly to Salem.

Powel, a lawyer, walked from London to York and back again in six days, being about 402 miles.

Protections by noblemen and foreign ambassadors, restrained by parliament.

Several thousand hands are now employed in the cotton manufacture in this kingdom; and there is every reason to believe, that the manufacture has taken root amongst us. It progress will be seen by inspecting the importations of the wool and yarn at different periods; on an avarage of three years, ending

	Cotton Wool.			Cotton Yarn.		
	Ct.	qr.	lb.	Ct.	qr.	lb.
1773	2550	3	2	2226	0	0
1783	3236	1	18	5405	0	0
1787	7153	2	0	21615	- 0	0

The glass manufacture has arisen to considerable consequence within a few years; and the degree of excellence to which it is at present arrived, has

has eſtabliſhed it in our own, and forced it into foreign markets. Our avarage imports of one article alone, may convey an idea of its general increaſe, viz. That of drinking glaſſes, for three years, ending

 1773 was in number 399,222 glaſſes
 1783 ditto 22,240 ditto
 1767 ditto 4,648 ditto

The firſt ſtone of the blue-coat hoſpital in Dublin, laid by the lord-lieutenant.

1774 Peace was proclaimed between the Ruſſians and the Turks.

The American colonies ſent deputies to Philadelphia, who aſſumed the title of "The Congreſs of the "Thirteen United Provinces," and all the powers of government.

A bill paſſed for blocking up the port of Boſton; in conſequence of which, the inhabitants entered into a ſolemn league, by which they bound themſelves to break off all communication with Britain, 'till the obnoxious acts were repealed.

The Congreſs met at Philadelphia, petitioned the king, addreſſed the Britiſh nation, and the Colonies, and wrote a letter to general Gage, ſtating their grievances, and entered into ſeveral new and ſpirited reſolutions, &c. &c.

General Gage fortified the Neck which joins the town of Boſton to the Continent, ſeized the Provincial powder, ammunition, and military ſtores at Cambridge and Charleſtown, and deprived John Handcock of his commiſſion as colonel of the Cadets; all which was remonſtrated againſt by the Americans. The governor, to reſtore tranquility, if poſſible, called a general aſſembly, but ſo many of the council had reſigned their ſeats, that he was induced to countermand its ſitting by proclamation. This meaſure was deemed illegal; the aſſembly met at Salem, and after waiting a day for the governor, voted themſelves into a provincial Congreſs, of which Mr. Handcock was chosen

1774 chosen president. A committee was appointed, and waited on the governor with a remonstrance, concerning the fortifications at Boston Neck.— Winter was approaching; every one saw that the Spring was to be the season for commencing hostilities; a list of all the fensible men was made out, magazines of arms, &c. collected, and money provided for the payment of troops.

The Americans began to seize on the military stores belonging to government, which commenced at New-Port in Rhode Island, where the inhabitants carried off 40 pieces of cannon. New Hampshire followed the example, and seized a small fort, and the ammunition it contained.

In Pennsylvania, a convention was held, which expressed a desire of reconciliation with the Mother-Country, though at the same time declaring, They were resolved to defend their just rights, and defend to the last, their opposition to the late acts of parliament.

Stamp Act commenced in Ireland, March 25th.

February 12th, Early in the morning, Mr. Daniel M'Carthy, sub-sheriff of the county of Cork, and a party of the 28th regiment, commanded by Mr. King, attacked the fortifications and intrenchments of Pratt and his forces at Kilrush, who were lodged in the county gaol, Feb. 13.

The Cork Society for the relief and discharge of Persons confined for small debts, instituted June 17th.

1775 General Gage sent a detachment under colonel Smyth and major Pitcairn, to destroy the stores at Concord, which they effected with the loss of 250 men killed; the Americans lost 60 men.

The spirit of the Americans was so raised, that an army of 20,000 men formed a line of encampment from Boxbury to Myftle, and afterwards joined a a large body of Connecticut troops, under general Putnam; by this force Boston was blocked up, until generals Howe, Burgoyne, and Clinton, with a considerable reinforcement, arrived.

On

1775 On the 17th of June, the English attacked the Americans at Bunker's Hill, where the British lost 1000 men, the Americans only 500; in this engagement Charlestown was burnt by the English.

Colonels Easter and Allen, without receiving any orders from Congress, or communicating their design to any body, with only 250 men, surprized the forts of Crown-Point, Ticonderago, and the rest that form a communication between the Colonies and Canada; 200 cannon, mortars and military stores, and two armed vessels, with materials for the construction of others, fell into their hands.

The Americans shut up the troops in Boston, who were reduced to such distress, that they were obliged to send out armed vessels to make prizes indiscriminately, of all that came in their way.

The congress in the mean time continued to act with all the vigour which its constituents had expected. Articles of confederation and perpetual union were drawn up and solemnly agreed upon, by which they bound themselves and their posterity for ever. These were in substance as follows:

1. Each colony was to be independent within itself, and to retain an absolute sovereignty in all domestic affairs.
2. Delegates to be annually elected to meet in congress, at such time and place as should be enacted in the preceding congress.
3. This assembly should have the power of determining war or peace, making alliances; and in short, all that power which sovereigns of states usually claim as their own.
4. The expences of war to be paid out of the common treasury, and raised by a poll-tax on males between 16 and 60; the proportions to be determined by the laws of the colony.
5. An executive council to be appointed to act in place of the congress during its recess.
6. No colony to make war with the Indians, without consent of congress.

7. The

7. The boundaries of all the Indian lands to be secured and ascertained to them; and no purchases of lands were to be made by individuals, or even by a colony, without consent of congress.

8. Agents appointed by congress should reside among the Indians, to prevent frauds in trading with them, and to relieve, at the public expence, their wants and distresses.

9. This confederation to last until there should be a reconciliation with Britain; or, if that event should not take place, it was to be perpetual.

General Washington appointed commander in chief, by the congress.

Generals Montgomery and Arnold attacked Quebec, but were repulsed, the former was killed.

Mr. Spooner at Tamworth, in Warwickshire, died in the 75th year of his age; he weighed 40 stone 9lb. and measured four feet three inches across the shoulders.

Laurence Kennedy was executed at gallows-green, Cork, April 29th, for the murder of his father; he was prosecuted by his mother.

April 6, 7 & 8, The 35th, 49th, & 63d regiments of foot, embarked at Cork for Boston.

May 12th, The 22d, 40th, 44th, & 45th regiments of foot embarked for New-York.

September 27th, The 17th & 55th regiments embarked for Boston.

Dec. 22d, About 7 o'clock at night, the Marquis of Rockingham, transport from Portsmouth, with three companies of the 32d regiment and their baggage on board, besides women and children, was, in a hard gale of wind, drove into Roberts's Cove, and at three in the morning was dashed to pieces on the rocks, and every soul on board (except three officers and about thirty private men) perished.

1776 General Howe permitted the inhabitants to evacuate Boston, but was soon after obliged to abandon it himself, and leave several articles of value behind

1776 behind him; the Americans took poffeffion, and fortified it, and declared themfelves independent of Great Britain.

Several of the nobility, under Mr. Beanjeu, fallied forth from Canada to relieve the capital, but were defeated by the Provincials.

The Britifh reinforcements joined general Carleton, and obliged the Americans to fly.

The Americans were drove out of Canada with the lofs of 1000 men, of whom 500 were made prifoners.

Lord Dunmore driven out of Virginia.

The Britifh fleet attacked Charleftown, but was repulfed.

The Americans fitted out a fleet under commodore Hopkins of 5 fhips, who failed to the Bahama iflands, and made himfelf mafter of the military ftores.

General Howe landed on Staten Ifland, where he was joined by a number of the inhabitants. Lord Howe foon after joined him, who was armed with a commiffion to make peace, which was rejected.

General Putnam repulfed at Long Ifland, with the lofs of 3000 men; on which lord Howe fent general Sullivan, who was taken prifoner, to congrefs, to requeft a conference with any of them as individuals. They appointed a committee, confifting of doctor Franklin, Mr. Adams, and Mr. Rutledge, to wait on him, who were politely received, but which proved fruitlefs, as their final anfwer was, That they were willing to enter into any treaty with Great Britain that might conduce to the good of both nations; but that they would not treat in any other character but Independent States. On this lord Howe determined to profecute the war with the utmoft vigour, and fet about the moft proper methods for reducing New-York, and advanced fo far, that the Americans abandoned it; and in a few days, fome that ftaid behind, fet fire to it; and, though all poffible means were

1776 were used by the British to extinguish the flames, one quarter of it was consumed.

The two armies met at White Plains; the Americans were worsted, and were obliged to abandon Fort-Washington and Fort-Lee.

General Clinton took Rhode-Island.

General Lee taken prisoner by colonel Harcourt.

General Washington defeated the Hessians at Trenton, took 1000 prisoners, and seized their artillery.

Norfolk and Portsmouth in Virginia, destroyed by the British forces, Jan. 1.

Duchess of Kingston tried for Bigamy, convicted, and degraded, April 22.

Captain Cook first circumnavigated the globe.

Sir Peter Parker, in the Bristol of 50 guns, arrived at the Cove of Cork, Jan. 6th.

The Solebay arrived at Cove, with colonel Ethan Allen, and other American prisoners on board, Jan. 21st.

Sir Peter Parker, in the Bristol, with the Acteon, Solebay, Active, Lively and Phinx frigates, sailed for America from our harbour, with the 15th, 28th, 33d, 37th, 46th, 54th, and 57th regiments on board.

Montreal taken by the Americans, Nov. 13th.

May 21st, The election began in the city of Cork, and ended on the 29th, when the numbers stood as follows, viz. Richard Longfield, esq; 602; the right honourable the Provost 457; John Bagwell, esq; 372; and Arthur Gethin Creagh, esq; 24 votes. Richard Longfield, esq; and the Provost were returned duly elected.

Sheriff Lawton died in office; he was succeeded by Charles Denroche, esq; on the 12th, and sworn into office the 26th of August.

Guineas of 5 pwts. 8 grs. took place in the city of Cork, August 26th.

Jan. 16th, John Hayes and William Downey were tried in Clonmell by special commission, before

Baron

EVENTS.

Baron Scott and Juſtice Henn, and convicted of the murder of Ambroſe Power, eſq; of Barret's-town; they were immediately taken from the dock, and executed by torch light in the main-ſtreet, near the court-houſe.

Jan. 18th, William Mackey and Philip Berregrath, were tried, convicted, and executed the ſame day, oppoſite the gaol in Clonmell, being found guilty on the white-boy act, for breaking into the houſe of John Watſon, eſq; at Cartigan's-town.

April 5th, The rev. Mr. Grainger died ſuddenly in England, as he was adminiſtering the ſacrament.

1777 General Preſcot taken by the Americans.

The Britiſh army landed at the head of the Elk, and came to a general engagement with the Americans, who were defeated with the loſs of 1000 killed and wounded, and 400 taken priſoners.

General Howe took poſſeſſion of Philadelphia, Oct. 3.

The Americans attacked the royal army at Germain Town, but were defeated.

Ticonderago taken by general Burgoyne.

The Americans retired to Saratoga.

General Burgoyne, diſtreſſed for want of proviſions, made an attempt on the Provincial magazines at Bennington; a detachment under colonel Baum, advanced for this purpoſe, but were utterly defeated, and the colonel taken priſoner.

The Americans under general Gates, attacked the royal army at Stillwater, and were with great difficulty repulſed.

The Americans made a dreadful attack on the royal army, in which general Frazer was killed, and the Germans were defeated with great ſlaughter.

The royal army, in danger of being ſurrounded, attempted to retreat without ſucceſs, and having only proviſions ſufficient for three days, were obliged to ſurrender by capitulation, at Saratoga.

Print-ſellers properly ſecured.

The penſions this year amounted to 89,095l. 17s. 6d.

Charitable Muſical Society, Dublin, incorporated.

Jack

- Jack the painter, executed March the 10th, for setting fire to Portsmouth dock-yard.

The rev. doctor Dodd executed at Tyburn for forgery, June 27th.

The earl of Harcourt drowned in a well in Oxfordshire, Sept. 17th.

The first stone of the new guard-house, in Tuckey's-street, was laid by Hugh Lawton, mayor of Cork, September 11th.

The Boyne society first reviewed by colonel Bagwell, in White's bowling-green, Nov. 4th.

1778 Treaty between France and America.

Lord North's bill, received with indignation by the royal army, and despised by the colonists.

Philadelphia evacuated.

French fleet arrived in America.

Lord Howe attempted, with a very inferior force, to engage D'Estaing off Rhode Island, but the fleets were parted by a violent storm.

The British army took possession of Georgia.

General Prevost defeated the American's at Briar's-Creek.

D'Estaing defeated at Savannah, by general Prevost.

A treaty of alliance, amity, and commerce, signed between the French and Americans, Feb. 6th.

The earl of Chatham interred in Westminster-abbey, June 9th.

June 18th, The Licorne French frigate of 32 guns, struck to the America, one of admiral Keppel's fleet, after first discharging her broadside into the America, being the first French ship of war captured since the commencement of the present hostilities.

July 10th, The French fleet appeared off the Edystone, near Plymouth, and took the Folkstone cutter, commanded by lieutenant William Smith.

The court of France issued a declaration for making reprisals against Great Britain.

July 27th, Admiral Keppel, with 30 ships of the line, engaged the French admiral D'Orvilliers,

with

1778 with an equal number of ships. This was the first general engagement at sea, since the commencement of the present hostilities; admiral Keppel had 133 men killed, and 373 wounded: there was no ship taken or destroyed on either side.

July 29th, Great Britain issued orders for making reprisals against the court of France.

August 8th, The French fleet repulsed at Rhode-Island.

The American magazines destroyed in Bedford harbour, September 5th.

The island of Dominica, under the command of lieutenant-governor Stewart, surrendered to the French troops, under the marquis d'Bouille.

The islands of St. Pierre's and Miquelon in the West-Indies, taken from the French, by commodore Evans.

Pondicherry, in the East Indies, under the command of general de Bellecombe, taken from the French by major-general Munro.

The island of St. Lucia taken by the French.

The French repulsed at St. Lucia, and the island retaken by the British troops.

Parliament, that always raises money in Ireland on easy terms, when there is any to be borrowed in the country, this year gave 7 and a half per cent. in annuities, which in 1773 and 1775, were earnestly fought after at 6l. then thought to be a very high rate.

The sums remitted by Ireland, from 1751 to this year, to pay the troops serving abroad, amounted to 1,401,925l. 19s. 4d.

The sums raised by Great Britain, in time of peace, are about ten millions; in Ireland about one million. The circulating cash of the former is estimated at twenty-three millions, of the latter at two millions.

In 1698, The export of our wool to England amounted to 377,520 stone three-fourths; at a
medium

medium of eight years to Lady-Day 1728, it was only 227,049 stone, which is 148,000 less than in 1698, and was a loss of more than half a million yearly to England. In the last ten years, the quantity exported has been so greatly reduced, that in those years it only amounted to 1007 stone 11 lb. and in the last year, did not exceed 1665 stone, 12 lb.

September 7th, The first general field-day of all the armed societies belonging to the city of Cork.

Roman Catholics first permitted to take long leases; several of them attended at the city court-house, and testified their allegiance, Sept. 29th.

Parliament Beer took place; and at this time all the signs were taken down, pursuant to the act which commenced August 1st.

A boat going from Cork to Cove, with twenty men and women on board, was lost near Passage, and all perished except one man.

1779 A most extraordinary eruption of Vesuvius, August 8th.

The siege of Gibraltar begun by the Spaniards, July 8th.

Irish parliament addressed the king for a free trade, October 12th.

Armed Associations (to the number of 80,000) formed in every part of Ireland, under the denomination of *Volunteers;* which were cloathed, armed, and disciplined at their own private expence, for the purpose of repelling any hostile attempt from a foreign enemy, and of preserving tranquility and a due observance of the laws within the kingdom. By the spirited applications of these Associations, *Poyning*'s law, and all the obnoxious acts declaring the supremacy of England over this Kingdom, were repealed, and the Crown of Ireland rendered *independent of that of Great Britain.*

Spain joined the confederacy against Britain.

Fort Omoa taken by the British, but afterwards evacuated.

The

1779 The combined fleets of France and Spain joined at Cadiz, amounting to between 60 and 70 sail of the line, and paraded up the English channel; sir Charles Hardy, with 35 sail of the line, was cruising in the Bay of Biscay, and was passed by this great armament, without their having any knowledge of each other. Sir Charles, afterwards, the wind being in his favour, gained the entrance into the channel, without their being able to prevent him. The combined fleets retired to their own Ports early in the month of September, without effecting any thing.

The island of St. Martin taken from the French by the British troops, under the command of the honourable Thomas Hodge, esq; Jan. 5th.

Island of St. Bartholomew taken from the French, Feb. 11th.

Mahie and all its dependencies on the Malabar coast in the East-Indies, taken from the French by the British troops, under the command of colonel Braithwait.

The reverend Mr. Hackman executed at Tyburn, for the murder of miss Ray, April 19th.

The island of St. Vincent's taken by the French.

The British court issued a manifesto, for making reprisals against the court of Spain.

The American army, under the command of general Lincoln, repulsed at Stono-Ferry, South-Carolina, by the troops under the command of major-general Prevost.

The island of Granada, commanded by lord Macartney, taken by the French troops under the command of count d'Estaing.

Major-General Tryon, on an expedition in the Sound, at Newhaven, Fairfield and Norwalk, had different skirmishes with the Americans, where he had 20 men killed, 96 wounded, and 32 missing.

The king's troops under the command of lieutenant-colonel Johnson, defeated by the Americans at Stoney-Point.

1779 The British troops under the command of colonel M'Lane, on an expedition to Penobscot, had 23 men killed, 33 wounded, and 11 missing. At this time sir George Collier destroyed the large American fleet.

Goree taken by sir Edward Hughes.

Fort-Baton Rouge, on the Mississipi, in West-Florida, commanded by lieutenant-colonel Dixon, of the 16th regiment, surrendered to the Spanish troops under the command of Don Ferdinando de Galvez.

Post-horses first taxed.

Pitch and tar made from pit coal, discovered at Bristol.

The bridge at Puerta de St. Maria, near Cadiz, fell down soon as finished, while receiving the benediction, and killed several hundred persons that were over and under it, Feb. 22.

Jersey attempted by the French, and their shipping destroyed in Concale-Bay, May 1.

Lord chancellor Thurlow, pressed by a lieutenant and his gang, in Long-Acre, London, July 15.

The first fancy ball introduced in the city of Cork by lady Fitzgerald, Jan. 1st.

The Tartar privateer sailed from Cove, March 4th.

Edward Newton, surgeon, killed in a duel with lieutenant Dixon, April 16th.

June 4th, The city of Cork was alarmed with the news of a French fleet having appeared off Bantry Bay; drums instantly began to beat to arms, through every quarter of the city; the volunteers assembled on the Mall; the True-Blue society took charge of the main-guard, the Highlanders quitted it and joined the remaining part of the regiment in the old barrack. Palms Westropp, esq; mayor of Cork, summoned a council to consider what was necessary to be done on such an alarming occasion. Several Roman Catholics took up arms, offered their assistance to the volunteers, and distinguished themselves loyal subjects in the defence

1779 of their country. About ten at night, the Highland regiment marched from the old barrack towards Bandon, they were met exprefs on the road, countermanded, and returned next morning; upon the whole, it appeared to be an Englifh fleet hovering off Cape Clear, who, on firing feveral guns in honour of his majefty's birth-day, gave rife to the alarm and expected invafion.

Auguft 2d, Six regiments of infantry and two of cavalry, with a train of artillery, encamped at Ballinrea near Carrigaline, and did not break up till Wednefday the 24th of November following.

Auguft 23d, Six hundred and forty French prifoners arrived here from Kinfale, and on the 25th were efcorted moft part of the way to Kilkenny, by the different armed focieties of the city of Cork.

September 24th, Another alarm took place; the army in camp at Ballinrea ftruck their tents, croffed the country near Kinfale, and returned the fame evening; it proved to be the homeward-bound Jamaica fleet which appeared on the coaft, that occafioned this alarm.

October 19th, The ftatue of Hugh Lawton, efq; late mayor, was erected in the exchange.

1780 Sir George Rodney, appointed commander in chief in the Weft Indies, proceeded in his way to relieve Gibraltar, and met with 15 fail of Spanifh merchantmen richly laden, under convoy of a 64 gun fhip and 4 frigates, all of which he captured.

About a week afterwards, fir George fell in with a Spanifh fquadron of 11 fail of the line, took the admiral's fhip and four others, blew up the San-Domingo of 80 guns, another of 70 guns was loft on the rocks, and only 4 efcaped, much damaged into Cadiz.

After relieving Gibraltar, admiral Rodney proceeded to the Weft-Indies, leaving the bulk of the fleet, together with the Spanifh prizes under the conduct of admiral Digby, who, in his way to England, took

1780 the Prothe, a French 64, with part of a convoy laden with military stores. Thus, six ships of the enemy's line were added to the royal navy of England.

Jan. 14th, 6 h. A. M. the thermometer suspended in the open air at Glasgow, stood 46° below 0.

Declaration of the armed neutrality at Petersburgh.

Captain Cornwallis, on the Jamaica station, acquired great honour by the gallant defence he made with a very inferior force, against M. de la Mothe Picquet, who was himself wounded in the action.

Three naval actions between sir George Rodney and admiral Guichen, productive of no decisive consequences.

A large and valuable convoy, under the conduct of commodore Moutray, bound for the East and West Indies, were taken by the combined fleets; the men of war escaped.

Colonels Baillie and Fletcher defeated by Hyder Ally, at Perenbancum in the East Indies, after a desperate engagement, in which colonel Fletcher was killed, and colonel Baillie wounded and taken.

Arcot besieged and taken by Hyder.

General Clinton went on an expedition to Charles-Town, which surrendered on capitulation.

The Provincials attacked Staten-Island, but made a precipitate retreat.

A large body of French troops landed at Rhode-Island.

General Knyphausen attempted to surprise the advanced posts of general Washington's army, but retreated without effecting any thing material.

Earl Cornwallis obtained a very signal victory over general Gates, in South-Carolina.

Colonel Tarleton, with 350 men, surprised general Sumpter, and totally destroyed or dispersed his detachment, which consisted of 700 men, killed 150, and made 300 prisoners.

General Arnold deserted the service of Congress.

Major André taken in disguise within the American lines, and hanged as a spy. Major

1780 Major Ferguſon, with 1,400 men, totally defeated by the Americans at King's-Mountain.
General Sumpter with 1000 men, defeated at Black-Storks, by colonel Tarleton, with only 150 men.
Dec. 20th, Hoſtilities commenced againſt Holland.
Firſt ſtate lottery drawn at Dublin.
A dreadful inſurrection in London, and riots in many other places in the kingdom.
Lord Cornwallis defeated the Americans at Camden.
A dreadful hurricane in the Leeward Iſlands, Oct. 9.
An extraordinary ſtorm of wind in England.
Woollen goods firſt exported from Ireland to a foreign market.
The caſtle of St. John's, in Look-out-Iſlands, taken from the Spaniards by the Britiſh troops under the command of captain Polſon.
Fourt-Moultrie, on Sullivan's Iſland, taken by the Britiſh troops.
Five Eaſt-Indiamen, and 50 merchant ſhips, bound for the Eaſt and Weſt Indies, were captured by the combined fleets of France and Spain.
Forts Ann and George, ſurrendered to the Britiſh forces, under the command of major Carleton.
Baſſan, on the coaſt of Mallabar, ſurrendered to general Goddard.
Illuminations in Cork, for the defeat of count d'Eſtaing at Savannah, and for the firſt part of a free trade granted to Ireland.
An act of parliament took place, that no perſon ſhould be impriſoned for any debt under five pounds.
1781 Penſacola taken by the Spaniards, after a very gallent defence.
Iſland of St. Euſtatius, taken by admiral Rodney and general Vaughan.
A valuable Dutch fleet of 30 ſail, with a 60 gun ſhip, commanded by admiral Were, taken by the Monarch and Panther, and Sybil frigate, after a ſhort engagement; the Dutch admiral was killed.

1781 The Settlements of Demerary, Issequibo, and the Berbices, surrendered to the British.
Island of Tobago taken by the French.
Sir Eyre Coote defeated an immense force commanded by Hyder Ally.
Dutch Settlements on the Island of Sumatra, taken.
Negapatam taken by sir Edward Hughes, and sir Hector Munro.
Trincomale taken from the Dutch.
A second attempt was made on the Island of Jersey, by a French army, under the command of M. de Buttecourt, who landed in the night and surprised St. Helier the capital of the Island, and compelled major Corbert the deputy-governor, to sign a capitulation, and summoned Elizabeth castle to surrender, but was gallantly attacked in the town by major Pierson of the 95th regiment, at the head of some regulars and the militia of the island. The French commander was killed, and his remaining troops surrendered prisoners of war. The brave major Pierson was unfortunately slain in the instant of victory.
Dreadful cannonade and bombardment of the town and garrison of Gibraltar, from the Spanish camp, in which the town was destroyed, and many of the inhabitants perished.
Fifteen merchantmen from St. Eustatius, taken by M. de la Mothe Piquet.
Commodore Johnstone was attacked by M. Suffrein, in Port-Prayer-Bay.
Commodore Johnstone took a fleet of Dutch Indiamen, in Saldanha Bay.
General Elliot made a grand sally from Gibraltar, by which he destroyed the enemy's batteries and works.
Desperate engagement on the Dogger-Bank, between admiral Parker and the Dutch fleet commanded by admiral Zoutman.
Admiral Kempenfelt took part of a convoy of French East and West Indiamen.

Colonel

EVENTS. 235

1781 Colonel Tarleton totally defeated by general Morgan at Ninety-Six.
Lord Cornwallis defeated the Americans at Guilford.
Lord Rawdon attacked general Greene in his camp, and defeated him.
General Greene attempted to storm the garrison at Ninety-Six, but was repulsed and obliged to retire.
A partial action between the British and French fleets, off the Capes of Virginia.
General Greene defeated by colonel Stuart in South-Carolina.
Fort Grifwold taken by storm.
Action between the British and French fleets, off the Chefapeak.
Lord Cornwallis blocked up in York town, by general Washington.
General Clinton embarked at New-York with 7000 men, to relieve lord Cornwallis, but arrived too late.
Lord Cornwallis with his army, consisting of 6000, surrendered to general Washington.
Officers of the Board of Works, Great Wardrobe, Treasurer of the Chamber, and Jewel Office, with the Board of Green Cloth, and Cofferer of the Houshold, abolished by parliament.
The foundation of the custom-house of Dublin laid, and built from the designs of James Grandon, esq; who conducted the execution. The estimate was 163,363l. but as numerous unforeseen incidents must be added, with finishing the offices, &c. the total expence will probably amount to, or exceed 200,000l. it is 209 feet deep, by 375 long, with four fronts; the long-room is 65 feet by 70, and 30 feet high.
Prince William Henry, third son of his present majesty, was the first prince of the Blood Royal that ever landed in North America.
Captain Donnelan executed at Warwick, for poisoning sir Theodosius Boughton, April 9th.

The

1781 The garrison of Gibraltar relieved by admiral Darby, April 13th.
  General Arnold destroyed several American ships, and a vast quantity of Tobacco, at Petersburgh.
  Sir Samuel Hood, with 18 ships of the line, engaged Count de Grasse with 24.
  Thomas Lonergan, executed in Dublin, for poisoning Thomas O'Flaherty, esq; in Kilkenny.
  Henry Laurens, esq; late President of the American congress, admitted to bail, by lord chief justice Mansfield; he was taken prisoner in an American packet near Newfoundland, the 3d. of September, and committed to the Tower of London on a charge of high-treason, the 4th of October.
  The Spitfire sailed from the Cove of Cork the 3d, and returned with a Dutch prize the 9th Feb.
  Shrove-Tuesday, Feb. 27th, There was a violent hurricane in the city of Cork.
  March 18th, The 3d, 19th, and 30th regiments of foot, embarked at Monkstown for America.
  June 12th, Carlisle Fort was this day named by general Mocher.
  Sept. 16th, Admiral Rodney arrived at Cove in the Gibraltar man of war.
  Sept. 22d. The inhabitants of Cork were greatly alarmed by the report of an invasion; the army was under arms most part of the day; in the evening when the alarm subsided, the 66th & 67th regiments of foot, the Athol Highlanders, with the 13th and 18th regiments of light dragoons, were drawn up on the Mall. General Irwin, commander in chief, general Mocher, general Gabbet, lord Ross, colonel Lyons, colonel Crosbie, and several other field-officers, were present.
  George Brereton, esq; one of the Duhallow Rangers, was killed by an officer in the army; he was interred with military honours in Christ church-yard, attended by several parties of horse volunteers.
  The Volunteers of Ireland received the thanks of both houses of parliament.

St. Chris-

1782 St. Christopher's taken by the marquis de Bouille, after a most gallant defence;—Nevis and Montferrat taken.

Memorable engagement of the 12th of April, between admiral Rodney and M. de Graffe, in the West-Indies, which lasted from sun-rise till sun-set, in which the French fleet were entirely routed; the count de Graffe was taken in the Ville de Paris, four other ships of the line were taken, and one sunk.

Minorca taken by the Spaniards.

Admiral Barrington fell in with a French convoy, and took the most of them, with the Pegase and l'Actionaire, two French ships of the line.

Grand attack by the Spaniards on Gibraltar, which was returned by a dreadful cannonade and bombardment from the lines, the battering ships, and the garrison; the Spanish admiral's ship and another were set on fire, and blew up in the night; the admiral and many officers and men were saved by the extraordinary exertions of captain Curtis and his seamen, in the gun-boats, but the Spanish battering ships were entirely destroyed.

Lord Howe relieved Gibraltar with troops, ammunition and provisions, and repassed the Straits without interruption from the combined fleets.

Several indecisive engagements between sir Edward Hughes and M. Suffrein, in the East-Indies.

Trincomale in Ceylon, taken by the English.

Onore taken by storm, by general Matthews.

Cundapore taken by general Matthews.

General Matthews defeated by Tippoo Sultan, and afterwards besieged in Bedmore, which he surrendered by capitulation. The capitulation was violated by Tippoo; the general and principal officers were seized and imprisoned, the army plundered and inhumanly treated, and the general officers are said to have been barbarously murdered.

Ramillies, Centaur, Ville de Paris, le Glorieux, and le Hector,

1782 le Hector, with many other merchant ships, lost in a violent storm.
Georgia and South-Carolina, evacuted by the king's troops.
Callicut on the coast of Mallabar, taken by major Abingdon.
Colonel Braithwaite, with a detachment of British troops, were taken prisoners by Hyder Ally.
Vermont in North America, allowed by Congress to be a free state.
The States of Holland refused to treat of a peace with Great Britain.
The Bahama Islands taken by the Spaniards.
Twenty thousand seamen for the British navy, unanimously voted by the Commons of Ireland.
Seven thousand houses destroyed by fire at Constantinople.
The marquis of Rockingham died, June 12th.
Geneva taken possession of by the troops of France and Sardinia.
Earl Shelburne appointed first Lord of the Treasury, July 5th.
Count de Graffe (prisoner to admiral Rodney) arrived in London, August 3d.
Contractors with government disqualified for sitting in parliament.
Influence of the Crown abridged by parliament: revenue officers deprived of their votes.
Six thousand charity children met at St. Paul's, May 2.
Holland allowed the American indepedency.
Cape River Fort, on the coast of Hunduras, taken from the Spaniards by storm.
David Tyre, a French spy, executed at Portsmouth.
The Royal George of 100 guns, overset at Portsmouth; admiral Kempenfelt with 400 seamen and officers, and 200 women were drowned.
Numerous meeting of the Ulster Volunteer Delagates held at Dungannon, who published a Declaration of Irish Rights, Feb. 15th.
Parliament of Ireland voted its independence, and

1782 made a declaration of constitutional rights, August 16th.

British house of commons addressed the king against further prosecution of the American war, March 4.

British parliament repealed the 6th George I. whereby it renounced legiflating for Ireland, June 20.

Irish parliament passed an act for the restoration of the constitution of Ireland, July 28th.

Henry Grattan, esq; made a speech in the Irish house of commons, relative to the rights and independence of Ireland; for which he was voted 50,000l. by parliament.

Earl Temple sworn lord lieutenant of Ireland.

The combined fleets damaged by a storm in Algeciras Bay, and the St. Michael, a Spanish 74, drove on shore under the guns of Gibraltar, and taken by the garrison.

Captain Asgill set at liberty from his severe confinement in America, by order of Congress, and arrived at New York.

An embargo laid on all corn in Ireland, Nov. 16th.

Three men were smothered in a brew-house in Cork, by the steam of the beer.

In June and July, a disorder called the influenza, raged in Cork, very few escaped the malady; it began with a sneezing and running at the nose, a severe cough, attended with a fever, heaviness, and pain in the head, or with a weariness and a pain in all the bones; it commonly went off in three or four days.

Shocking inclement weather during the whole harvest; in October there was a great scarcity of bread which continued to the year's end, and perhaps the worst that ever was made, owing to the continual rains which totally ruined the corn.

Admiral Graves arrived at Cove in the Bella merchantman; the Ramillies to which he belonged, having foundered at sea.

Peter's Church thrown down in order to be rebuilt.

The Ocean of 98 guns, admiral Milbank, Foudroyant

ant 80, Afia 64, Panther 64, Fortitude 74, and Dublin 74, part of lord Howe's fleet, arrived at Cove.

A criminal confined in the bridewell, made a hole through the roof, out of which he leaped, and fell on a number of barrels on the head of a barrel-carrier, who was paffing along, by which means he fortunately faved his life, and made his efcape.

Four criminals broke out of North gaol, three of whom made their efcape.

1783. Preliminary articles of peace figned at Paris, between Great Britain and America; on behalf of Great Britain, by Mr. Fitzherbert and Mr. Ofwald; and by Meffrs. Franklin, Jay, Adams and Jefferfon, on behalf of America. By thefe preliminaries the king of Great Britain formally acknowledges the Thirteen United Colonies to be *The free, fovereign, and independent States of America.*

A dreadful earthquake, attended with many extraordinary circumftances in Italy and Scicily.

The fun obfcured by a kind of fog, during the whole fummer.

A volcanic eruption in Iceland, furpaffing any thing recorded in hiftory. The lava fpouted up in three places to the height of two miles perpendicular, and continued thus for two months; during which time it covered a tract of 3600 fquare miles of ground, in fome places more than one hundred feet deep.

A large meteor appeared to the northward of Shetland, and took its direction fouthward, with a velocity little inferior to that of the earth in its annual courfe round the fun. Its trak obferved for more than one thoufand miles.

The emperor obtained by treaty from Holland, the navigation of the Schelde, from Antwerp to Seftingen, with the ceffion of fome forts and territories.

Order of the knights of St. Patrick inftituted Feb. 15.

Treaty

1783 Treaty of alliance between France and the States-General.

Independence of the Irish Courts of Justice established by act of parliament.

Irish National Bank established June 25th.

Christnings taxed in England.

Air-Balloons invented in France by monsieur Montgolfier; introduced into England, and Mr. Lunardi ascended from Moorfields, Sept. 15th.

National debt of England this year was 272 millions, which were it to be laid down in guineas in a line, would extend 4,300 miles in length; if laid down in shillings, would extend three and a half times round the globe; if in solid silver, would require 60,400 horses to draw it, at 15 cwt. for each horse.

The Count Belgioso East-Indiaman, lost off Dublin Bay, and all on board perished; she had 130,000 dollars, besides a very valuable cargo.

The ingenious Mr. Spalding, perished in his diving-bell, in attempting to recover some of the materials of the above ship.

Charles Byrne, the famous Irish giant, died in London; his corpse measured eight feet four inches.

Died at Norwich, the Widow Keepas, who had been tapped for the dropsy eighty times, and 6,553 pints of water taken from her.

The Bank of Paris, commonly called Caisse de Escompte, stopped payment, Oct. 2d.

A violent shock of an earthquake in the Island of Sicily, in the Two Calabrias, and at Messina, which continued to be felt for some months.

The ports of Dover and Calais, were opened for passengers to and from Great-Britain and France.

Another earthquake in Italy, which destroyed the remainder of Messina.

A violent hurricane at Venice, which caused the sea to rise so high as to overflow the whole city, April the 11th.

1783 A terrible fire at Attendam, in the Dutchy of Westphalia, which consumed 300 houses, July 13th.

The Irish parliament dissolved, July 25th.

A terrible fire in the town of Berolzheim, in the Margravate of Anspach, which consumed 200 houses, Aug. 2d.

The bishop of Osnaburg took possession of his bishoprick, October 15th.

More than half of Busdorf, a large town of Prussia, was consumed by fire, Nov. 4th.

The Prince of Wales first took his seat in the House of Peers as Duke of Cornwall, Nov. 11th.

Sir Eyre Coote arrived at Madrafs, and brought with him two lacks of rupees; he died in two days after, April 24th.

Christopher Atkinson was expelled the British House of Commons for perjury, Dec. 4th.

The Duke of Kingston East-Indiaman, burned by accident at sea, and 79 souls lost, Aug. 23d.

On the fee-lands of the bishop of Dromore, were found a pair of moose-deer horns, which measured fourteen feet four inches from tip to tip, as also most of the entire skeleton (in the most perfect preservation) of the enormous animal that wore them; who, from the length of the bones of his fore leg, is judged to have been about twenty hands high.

Patrick Lynch, for firing a pistol at and wounding Mr. Dowling, was executed out of one of the windows at the new prison in Green-street, Dublin.

Accounts were received at the admiralty of the loss of the Centaur, and of the dreadful hardships suffered by capt. Inglefield, 16 days in an open boat.

The new coalition took place; lord North and the honourable Charles Fox, were sworn secretaries of state.

Colonel Brathwaite defeated by Hyder Ally's son on the 18th of February; the surrender of Cuddamore on the 4th, and of Trincomali on the 17th

of

1783 of April following, to the arms of the French king.

January 6th, About 10 o'clock this morning, John Dwyer, Calvin Booth, John Fisher, alias Dogherty, of the 4th, and James Ward of the 49th regiment of foot, four soldiers who were sentenced by a general court-martial, to be shot for desertion, were taken from the guard-house in Tuckey's-street to the Lough of Cork, the place of execution, where Dwyer suffered; the remaining three were then called forward and pardoned conditionally, on receiving five hundred lashes, and to be sent to Africa.

The corporation admitted John Marsh, esq; his majesty's commissary at Cork, to the freedom at large of that city, and ordered it to be presented to him in a silver box, as a testimony of their approbation of his upright conduct and uniform integrity, in the faithful discharge and execution of his office.

The Two Friends of Cork, sailed from our harbour for Philadelphia, and carried the first cargo legally shipped from Ireland, since the commencement of the American war.

Porter reduced to three-pence half-penny per quart; it was first argued and determined before the commissioners of his majesty's revenue in Dublin; and secondly, on a solemn hearing before the commissioners of appeal, it was finally determined to be sold at the above price all over the kingdom.

The Enterprize, an American ship, from Rhode-Island, arrived at Cove; she had the Thirteen Stripes flying at her top-mast head.

The first dawn of Irish liberty broke out in 1779; Ireland obtained her legislative independence, with the consent of the British Senate, the 16th day of April, 1783.

The election for Knights of the Shire of the county of Cork, began the 23d of August, 1783; William Chetwynd, esq; high-sheriff. Sir James L. Cotter, bart. proposed Richard Townsend and

James Bernard, esqrs.—Richard Longfield, esq; proposed Robert King, commonly called Lord Kingsborough; and, Lord Kingsborough proposed Sir John Conway Colthurst, bart.—State of the poll for each:

B. 1665.— T. 978.— K. 1198.— C. 209.

Number of freeholders polled, 1627. Election ended October 3d.

Election for the City commenced Aug. 13th, when the votes were, for the right hon. J. Hely Hutchinson, 650; Richard Longfield, esq; 615; John Bagwell, esq; 564; and Augus. Warren esq; 475.

Ratification of the treaty for the independence of the United States of America.

Definitive treaty between England and Holland.

The following new ministers were appointed: Mr. Pitt first lord of the treasury and chancellor; Marquis of Carmarthen, secretary of state; Lord Sydney, secretary for the home department; Earl Gower, lord president.

1784 Slave-Trade abolished in Pennsylvania.

Lord Strangford, of Ireland, suspended from voting in the Irish house of lords, for soliciting a bribe in the cause of Rochfort and Ely.

Mail-coaches first established to Bristol.

Postage of letters advanced.

The first bishop in America was doctor Seabury, consecrated Nov. 14.

Great Seal stolen from the lord chancellor, and destroyed, March 24th.

Printing-house commenced in Constantinople.

Clodagh-castle, now in ruins, said to have been built by the Mac-Swineys' who were anciently famous for Irish hospitality. On the west side of the road near Dunusky, there was a stone set up (which now lies in a ditch, signifying to all persons, to repair to the house of Edmond Mac-Swiney for entertainment.

A charitable Infirmary and Dispensary instituted at Youghall.

Mr. Bag-

EVENTS.

1784 Thurſday, July 29th, was obſerved throughout the kingdom, as a general day of thankſgiving, in conſequence of the late peace.

Mr. Bagwell having petitioned the Houſe of Commons againſt the late return of members to repreſent this city in parliament, which being tried before a committee of the Houſe, the election of Richard Longfield, eſq; was ſet aſide, and on January 8th, came on the election to fill up the vacancy, when Auguſtus Warren, eſq; was unanimouſly elected, Mr. Bagwell having declined the poll.

Between the hours of 10 and 11 o'clock at night, a rick of furze took fire, near the back of the North-Chapel, by means of which ten cabbins were burnt to the ground, Aug. 26th.

Engliſh parliament diſſolved, March 25th.

Sept. 3d, Some reapers in a field near Ballincollig, diſcovered the body of a man exceedingly putrified; it was ſuppoſed that the unfortunate wretch got drunk at the races, and throwing himſelf in that ſituation, where he could not poſſibly be ſeen, was ſtifled for want of aſſiſtance.

Prince Frederic, biſhop of Oſnaburgh, created Duke of York and Albany in the kingdom of Great-Britain, and Earl of Ulſter in the kingdom of Ireland; theſe titles are to deſcend to his Highneſs's heirs male lawfully begotten.

The right hon. William Pitt narrowly eſcaped being ſhot, by a gardiner near Windſor, Aug. 17th.

The remains of Dr. Samuel Johnſon, were interred in Weſtminſter-Abbey, Dec. 20th.

December 18th, At Hciro (one of the Canary Iſles ſubject to Spain) thirty-ſeven convicts from Ireland were landed out of the ſhip Dublin, for mutiny; they were all immediately put to the ſword, by order of the governor, on an idea that the plague raged among them.

REMARKABLE

August 5th, Died at Matlock in Derbyshire, Ann Clowes, aged 103; she measured three feet nine inches in height, and weighed only 48lb. The house she resided in was as diminutive, in proportion as herself, containing only one room, eight feet square.

Ten thousand houses destroyed by fire in Constantinople, most of which had been built after the fire of 1782.

1785 East-India Company revived in France.

First air-balloon in Ireland ascended from Ranelagh Gardens, Dublin, Jan. 19th.

A congress of representatives from the different counties of Ireland held in Dublin, for promoting a parliamentary reform, Jan. 20.

System of commercial intercourse between Great-Britain and Ireland, proposed in the Irish house of commons; but being strongly opposed, was withdrawn, August 13.

At Winster in Derbyshire, near sixty people met at a puppet-show, when the upper floor of the house was blown up with gun-powder, and no hurt done to the people below, Jan. 25.

Attorney's tax commenced.

Female servant tax commenced.

Party Walls regulated by parliament.

Patent medicines taxed.

Canal, which joins the Baltic and North Sea, opened to all nations.

Mr. Christopher Atkinson, an expelled member of parliament, stood in the pillory for perjury.

On Callan mountain, there is a large stone or monument, with an inscription in *Ogham* characters, denoting it to be the burial place of the famous *Conan*, one of the Connaught knights who fell in battle; the stone is eleven feet six inches long, three feet broad, and one foot thick; it lies on an eminence above a small lake facing the south, on a soft flat quarry, about eight miles from Ennis; it was discovered this year by the right honourable W. B. Co-

W. B. Conyngham in company with Mr. O'Flanagan; the latter gentleman being sent from Dublin for that purpose, by the Royal Irish academy.

The floor of the Sessions House in New-Molton in York-shire, gave way, when 300 persons fell 12 feet deep, but no lives were lost, Dec. 9.

The merchants of the city of Cork, fitted out a vessel well supplied with bread, water, beef, &c. to cruise off Cape Clear, for the purpose of relieving any vessels which the long continuance of easterly winds might keep at sea, April 30th.

June 15th, M. Pilatre de Rozier, and M. Romain, ascended in M. Montgolfeir's fire balloon, from Bologna, with an intent to cross the Channel; in about twenty minutes after their ascent, the balloon took fire, by which means these unfortunate gentlemen lost their lives.

August 27th, A violent hurricane at Jamaica, which did considerable damage; the like happened at Carthagena in South America.

The Danube overflowed its Banks, in consequence of which the adjacent country suffered great injury.

January 7th, Mr. Blanchard, accompanied by Dr. Jefferies, took their departure from the Castle of Dovor, in his balloon for the Continent; they ascended at one o'clock, and descended on the coast of France at three.

Died at Broadway-Farm, near Great Berkhampsted in Hertfordshire, the person distinguished by the appellation of Peter the Wild Boy, who was picked up in a wood in Germany, in the latter end of the reign of George the First, while he was hunting, and by that monarch brought to England, who placed him under proper masters to have him instructed in the English language, but their endeavours proved fruitless, as he could not be brought to articulate a single word.

October 26th, Their Graces, the Duke and Dutchess of Rutland, arrived in the city of Cork, from the seat of the right hon. Lord Doneraile. Next day his

1785 his Grace was waited on by the Corporation, and addreſſed in a moſt dutiful and loyal manner by the Recorder. His Grace received them graciouſly, and returned a very polite anſwer to their addreſs, and conferred the honour of knighthood on the mayor. He was alſo attended by the lord biſhop of Cork and the clergy of the dioceſes, with an addreſs, which his Grace received in the moſt favourable manner, and gave them the ſtrongeſt aſſurances of his countenance and protection.— They afterwards viſited Kinſale, where his Excellency was preſented with his freedom, dined with the corporation, and conferred the honour of knighthood on James Carty, ſovereign thereof; and on the 12th of Nov. a deputation from the town of Youghall waited on his Excellency to invite him to that town, which he graciouſly accepted; viſited it on the Monday following, received his freedom in a gold box, dined with the corporation, and offered to confer the honour of knighthood on the mayor, which he declined; after which there was a very brilliant aſſembly at which their Graces made their appearance, where they were much pleaſed.

Dec. 7th, A large part of the rock back of Mr. Newenham's houſe, North-Abbey, fell down, which entirely deſtroyed his ſtables and buried three horſes in its ruins.

March 23d, Count Zembecari and ſir Edward Vernon, accompanied by miſs Grice, attempted to make an aerial excurſion from London, but the balloon not being intended for ſo great a weight, the young lady was (much againſt her inclination) obliged to come out of the car, on which the balloon aſcended with great velocity, took a weſtern direction, and in a few minutes was out of ſight; in about an hour the aeronouts deſcended ſafe, near Horſham in Suſſex, about 37 miles diſtant from the place they aſcended from. In the following month Mr. Decker aſcended at Briſtol, and

and in an hour and seven minutes, descended on the other side Chippenham, about thirty miles distant.

His Excellency, John Adams, accompanied by colonel Smith as secretary (who was aid-de-camp to general Washington during the American war) arrived in London, as an ambassador from the United States of America.

A Marine Society established in Bristol; many poor lads were cloathed and admitted into that seminary for maritime knowledge; a charity worthy of imitation in this rising country.

The Montague East-Indiaman, burnt by accident at Calcutta, Dec. 6th.

Died, in Berry-street, London, in the 29th year of her age, Mrs. Kelly, the noted Irish Fairy, who was only 34 inches high; she was that morning delivered of a child twenty-two inches long, with much difficulty; the child did not live longer than about two hours after its birth. Mrs. Kelly had been shewn in Norwich some time previous to her death; the smallness of her figure, and the circumstance of her being pregnant, caused a vast number of people to see her, and she was reckoned the greatest curiosity ever seen.

1786 Foundation of the New Four Courts and Public Offices, Dublin, laid.

Royal Irish Academy at Dublin, incorporated January 28th.

A Police established at Dublin, and other parts of Ireland.

June 6th, The Halsewell East-Indiaman was unfortunately wrecked at Seacombe in the Isle of Purbeck, on the coast of Dorsetshire; 166 persons lost their lives, amongst whom were captain Pierce, his two daughters, and a number of young ladies, besides other passengers.

In the church-yard of Aghabolloge, there is a stone called St. Olan's Cap, by which the vulgar people swear on all common occasions; and they pretend

1786 if this stone was carried off, it would return to its own place of residence.

At Montpellier in France, a Booth wherein a play was performing, fell down and killed 500 persons, July 31.

The Cork Society (one of the most useful Charities in the City of Cork) commenced, lending three guineas instead of two, *interest free*, once a fortnight, to fifteen poor tradesmen.

August 11th, A shock of an earthquake at Whitehaven in England, which continued for a few minutes.

Jan. 31st, Died at Paris, Count de Grasse, who commanded the French fleet on the 12th of April 1782.

October 31st, Princess Amelia died at London, aged 76 years.

Aug. 2d, His majesty George III. attempted to be stabbed by Margaret Nicholson, at St. James's, for which she was confined to a mad-house. This book records two similar attempts on different monarchs—how different the punishment!

May 25th, Died at Lisbon, Don Pedro Clement, king of Portugal, and F. R. S. aged 69 years.

The San Pedro D'Alcantara, a Spanish galloon from Lima to Cadiz, with eight millions of dollars on board, was stranded at Paniche, and 186 persons perished.

Articles of impeachment presented by Mr. Burke, against Warren Hastings, esq;

George Robert Fitzgerald, esq; executed for the murder of Patrick Randal Mac-Donald, esq; &c.

Edward Aylette, an attorney, stood in the pillory in Westminster, for wilful and corrupt perjury.

Frederick II. King of Prussia, died.

1787 Turkish manifesto and declaration of war against Russia, preceded on the 16th, by committing the Russian ambassador to the castle of the Seven-Towers.

. The

1787 Died at London, Mr. Frederick Pilion of Cork, who wrote the following dramatic pieces: The Invasion; Liverpool Prize; He Wou'd be a Soldier; Illumination, or Glazier's Conspiracy; Deaf Lover; Siege of Gibraltar, &c. &c.

Disturbances in Holland, which produced armaments on the part of France, England, and Prussia, and terminated in the suppression of the fomenting party in Holland by an army of Prussians.

Treaty of alliance between England and Holland.

Remarkable Aurora Borealis, Oct. 6.

Duke of Rutland, lord lieutenant of Ireland, died October 24th. Grand funeral procession, Nov. 17.

Prince of Wales's debts paid by parliament.

Botany Bay settlers first sailed from England.

Bishop of Nova Scotia first appointed, August 11.

Cotton wool used in English manufactures this year, was valued at 7,500,007l. and weighed about 22,600,000 lbs.

Quantity of rum imported into England this year was, 2,253,657 gallons, besides what was smuggled. Its duty was 46,943l. 10s.

Scarcity Root, a kind of parsnip introduced and propagated in England, first by doctor Letsom.

The play-house in Bury, in Lancashire, containing upwards of 300 persons, fell down during the performance, and buried the audience under its ruins; five were killed on the spot, and many had their limbs broke.

Dec. 3d, Arrived at the Cove of Cork, his majesty's ship Pegasus, Prince William Henry commander; who honoured the City with his presence for several days, dined with the corporation at the Mansion-house, and with the merchants at the King's-Arms; went frequently to the assembly, and danced with several ladies; passed some days with the earls of Shannon and Grandison; dined with the corporation of Youghal, and received his freedom of both places.

Dec.

1787 Dec. 27th, Prince William Henry, in the Pegafus frigate, arrived at Plymouth from Cork; on his paſſage, a thunder ſtorm broke over the ſhip ſo violently, as to tear ſome of the ſails and ſhiver the main maſt.

Sept. 2d, A violent hurricane at the Bay of Hunduras, which did conſiderable damage.

April 2d, One of the market boats from Cork to Cove, was overſet, and eight people unfortunately drowned.

The Parliament of Paris entered on their journals, the letters patent which aboliſhed the droits de aubaine, and by which all Engliſh ſubjects dying in France, are to be conſidered as natural born ſubjects.

May 9th, Mr. Haſtings was taken into the cuſtody of the Black Rod, and brought to the bar of the Houſe of Lords, to anſwer the charges of high crimes and miſdemeanors brought againſt him by the Commons of Great Britain.

An extraordinary eruption of Mount Ætna, July 18.

Sept. 3d, Thomas Stone, a lunatic, taken up for writing an extraordinary letter to the queen, in which he avowed a paſſion for the Princeſs Royal.

Some villains found means to conceal themſelves in the Palace of the Arch-Biſhop of Dublin, where they murdered the porter and houſe-maid, and afterwards ſet fire to the Palace in ſeveral places; the flames were extinguiſhed in a ſhort time.

Auguſt 3d, Violent ſtorms at the Iſland of Dominica, which nearly deſtroyed it.

Lord George Gordon excommunicated from the pariſh church of St. Mary le Bonne.

July 10th, A Public Diſpenſary, for the purpoſe of ſupplying the ſick poor of the city of Cork with medical advice and medicines gratis, was eſtabliſhed, by benefactions and voluntary ſubſcriptions. To this charity, all poor patients confined to their beds by fevers, or any other acute diſeaſes, are admitted on the recommendation of a benefactor

factor or subscriber. The number of patients who have received the benefits of this truly valuable institution, from its commencement unto the last annual meeting, April 13th, 1791, are 12,462.— To this laudable charity, a Humane Society is annexed, for the purpose of recovering persons apparently drowned; a proper apparatus is always kept in readiness, and handsome gratuities given to the persons most active in taking up such unfortunate objects, and giving the first information to any of the physicians of the medical committee, or any other physician resident in the city, or to the apothecary of the dispensary, that the proper means may be immediately used for their recovery.

1788 Jan. 31st, Prince Charles Stuart died at Rome.

Feb. 13th, The trial of the impeachment of Warren Hastings, esq; commenced in the House of Lords.

March 27th, A large bog, of 1500 acres, lying between Dundrum and Cashel, in the county of Tipperary, began to be agitated in an extraordinary manner. The rumbling noise from the bog gave the alarm; and on the 30th it burst, and a kind of lava issued from it, which took its direction towards Ballygriffin and Golden, overspreading and laying waste a tract of fine fertile land, belonging to John Hyde, esq; every thing that opposed its course was buried in ruins.

April 7th, Died at Constantinople, Abdub Hamied, the Ottoman Emperor; he was born on the 20th of March 1725, and ascended the throne on the 21st of January 1774, by the name of Achmet the Fourth.

April 11th, A violent gale of wind at the Mauritius, by which the French suffered to the amount of 14,400,000 livres.

May 25th, The Protestant bishops of Scotland unanimously resolved, that his majesty king George and all the royal family, should be prayed for in all their chappels for the future.

before

1788 June 1ſt, The famous St. Euſtatius cauſe was heard before the Houſe of Lords, when Lord Rodney was caſt with full coſts.

June 3d, The earl of Mansfield reſigned the office of Lord Chief Juſtice of the King's-Bench.

June 4th, His Royal Highneſs the Dauphin, died at Verſailles, in the eight year of his age.

June 10th, Three ambaſſadors from Tippoo Saib, arrived in France.

June 18th, The Ruſſians gained a deciſive victory at Sea over the Turks.

June 31ſt, Robert Keon, eſq; received ſentence of death for the murder of George Nugent Reynolds, eſq; and was executed February 16th.

July 3d, In London a violent ſtorm of thunder, lightning, and rain, by which part of the wall on Tower-Hill was torn away, and the river Thames moſt violently agitated.

July 13th, A dreadful ſtorm happened at Paris; the devaſtation was dreadful beyond deſcription: the country for many ſquare leagues was totally laid waſte; during the ſtorm, enormous pieces of ice fell, of ſeveral pounds weight, which deſtroyed a vaſt number of cattle; the damage done exceeded one hundred millions of livres.

July 25th, The foundation ſtone of St. Patrick's-Bridge laid. Mr. Michael Shanahan, architect and contractor.

Definitive treaty between England and Pruſſia.

Sept. 30th, A violent ſhock of an earthquake was felt in the town of Borgo de San Sepulcro, in Italy, which laſted two minutes; it threw down ſeveral churches, the palace, and a number of houſes.

A Committee for the regulation of Pilotage and other purpoſes, tending to promote trade and commerce, eſtabliſhed in the Port of Youghall.

Inſurrection in the Auſtrian Belgic provinces.

The new Meat, Fiſh, Poultry, and vegetable Markets, the moſt convenient in their kind in Europe, opened in the city of Cork, Auguſt 1ſt, 1788.

War

EVENTS.

1788 War between Sweden and Ruffia. This war had nearly annihilated the naval power of Sweden.

The duty on coal this year amounted to 306,718l. when the quantity confumed in London, amounted to 765,880 chaldrons.

Doctor Kaye, dean of Lincoln, finding in his parifh three poor families, having from ten to twelve children each, claimed the tenth child from each family, and the parents joyfully complying with his demand, the Doctor has taken them under his protection, and humanely feeds, cloathes, and educates them.

The Quakers in America have given freedom to their flaves; erected and liberally endowed a very capital fchool at Philadelphia for their inftruction; and fuch of thefe poor Africans as chofe to continue in fervice, are paid wages, and put upon the fame footing with the Whites.

The town of New Orleans deftroyed by fire.

The king of England attacked by a fevere illnefs, attended by a derangement of intellect, for four months.

1789 Died, the right. honourable Wolfran Cornwall, fpeaker of the Englifh houfe of commons.

The right honourable William Wyndham Grenville, elected fpeaker.

During his majefty's illnefs, the Prince of Wales paid the annual donation of 1000l. to the poor of the city of London, out of his own pocket.

The city of London refufed to vote an addrefs of thanks to Mr. Pitt, for his conduct during the regency.

Regency bill for the term of the king's illnefs, introduced in the Britifh parliament.

During the king's illnefs, a motion was made in the Englifh houfe of commons and agreed to, that an addrefs be prefented to the Prince of Wales, praying him to take upon himfelf the regency of the kingdom; and alfo an addrefs to her majefty, praying

1789 praying her to take upon herself the controul of the houshold.

The resolutions of the house of commons to address the Prince and the Queen, were agreed to in the house of lords.

Feb. 21, The House of Lords and Commons of Ireland, waited upon his Excellency the Marquis of Buckingham, with their address to his Royal Highness the Prince of Wales, requesting him to accept of the unlimited Regency of this kingdom, during the continuance of his majesty's unhappy indisposition; which address his Excellency refused to transmit; whereupon the Lords appointed his Grace the duke of Leinster, and the right hon. the earl of Charlemont; and the Commons named the right hon. J. O'Neil, right honourable Thomas Conolly, right hon. William Brabazon Ponsonby, and James Sturat of Killymoon, esq; as commissioners to present the address of both houses, to his Royal Highness.

The parliament passed a vote of censure on the lord-lieutenant, for expressions contained in his answer to their application for conveying the said address, February 20th.

The king declared perfectly recovered, 26th Feb.

The king resumed the royal authority, signified by commission to parliament.

Jan. 24, The king of France resolved to convoke the States-General.

Pole Renier, Doge of Venice, died March 4th.

The body of Edward IV. discovered by some workmen employed in repairing St. George's Chapel, Windsor—the body was in good preservation.

The Sirius and Supply, with transports, under the command of commodore Philips, made good their voyage to Botany Bay. These were the first convicts sent to the above settlement, of which 40 died upon the voyage, and 42 infants were born.

Captain Rodney, son of the gallant lord Rodney, was formally acquainted, that his claims to the appointment

1789 appointment of a guardianship, according to promise, were forfeited by his father's voting for the Prince of Wales.

Lodovico Marinei, procurator of St. Mark, elected Doge of Venice, April 16th.

Sept. 23d, The king, queen, and all the royal family, attended by both houses of parliament and the whole court, attended Divine Service at St. Paul's, to return public thanks for his majesty's recovery; this was the most splendid procession ever seen in England.

Prince William Henry arrived at Portsmouth in the Andromada frigate from Hallifax, April 29th.

The right honourable Lord Lifford, Lord Chancellor of Ireland, died April 29th.

May 4th, States-General of France met at Versailles.

Great disturbances in France, in consequence of which many families of distinction came over to England.

The abolition of the Slave Trade first agitated in the house of commons, May 12th.

The honourable W. Townsend put a period to his existence, May 13th.

Prince William Henry created Duke of Clarence, May 18th.

June 4th, General Washington, president of the United States of America, gave a grand entertainment on account of the recovery of his Britanic majesty from his late dangerous illness. The envoys of England, France, Holland, and Portugal, and persons of the first distinction, were present.

June 9th, His majesty went to the House of Peers for the first time since his happy recovery.

June 17th, The opera house in the Haymarket, consumed by fire.

June 17th, The Tiers Etat, declared themselves duly constituted the National Assembly of France, and proceeded to business; a few days previous thereto, his Royal Highness the duke of Orleans, and several

1789 veral others of the nobility and clergy, joined them.

Mr. Grenville, speaker of the house of commons, appointed Secretary of State, vice Lord Sydney.

Mr. Addington elected speaker of the house of commons, vice Mr. Grenville.

The king's theatre in the Hay-market, totally destroyed by fire, June 17.

June 20th, Mr. Shine a cooper, was found suffocated in a hole near Wandesford's-bridge, Cork.

June 20th, The right honourable John Fitzgibbon, was sworn into the office of Lord High Chancellor, and the seals delivered into his custody; the first Irishman that ever filled this important office.

June 22d, Every member of the National Assembly took a solemn oath never to separate, but to assemble together whenever circumstances shall require, until the Constitution shall be established.

The French and Swiss guards refused to serve against the nation.

June 29th, The nobles and clergy, at the request of the king, joined the Tiers Etat.

July 8th, His majesty's royal mail-coach, established by Messrs. Anderson, Fortescue, and O'Donnoghue (from Dublin to Cork) arrived this day for the first time, with his majesty's mail.

The duke of Orleans put himself at the head of forty of the nobility and two hundred of the clergy.

A duel was fought between col. Lenox and Mr. Swift, on account of some expressions used by the latter in a pamphlet; the colonel wounded his adversary in the body.

The duke of Orleans was elected president of the National Assembly.

Mr. Whaley arrived in Dublin from his journey to Jerusalem. By which he gained a wager of 20,000l.

July 8th, Great tumults in the French provinces; a great mob arose at Metz, on account of the dearth of flour: the governor ordered out two French regiments, who refused to act against the mob:

two

1789) two German regiments were then brought out, which raised the indignation of the National troops, who burst from their quarters, and joined the populace; a dreadful havock was the consequence; upwards of 1000 men were killed on each side; and at length the German troops were overpowered;—the governor made his escape.

An army of 35,000 men, encamped between Paris and Versailles, under the command of M. Broglio.

The National Assembly addressed the king to dismiss the Swifs troops, which he refused.

The king dismissed M. Neckar.

In consequence of the dismission of M. Neckar, the populace began to arm themselves, and were immediately joined by the French guards.

The populace forced the convent of St. Lazare, in which was found a considerable quantity of corn, arms, and ammunition. The following day, the Hospital of Invalids was taken possession of; all the cannon, small arms and ammunition, were immediately seized upon, and every one who chose to arm himself, was supplied with what was necessary. The cannon was distributed in different parts of the town.

A detachment with two pieces of cannon, went to the Bastile to demand the ammution deposited there: a flag of truce had been sent before them, which was answered by the governor (the marquis de Launay) who nevertheless ordered the guard to fire on them, and several were killed. The populace enraged, rushed forward to the assault, when the governor agreed to admit a certain number, on condition that they should commit no violence. A detachment of forty accordingly passed the drawbridge, which was instantly drawn up, and the whole party massacred.

The populace, enraged at this breach of faith, aggravated by such glaring inhumanity, soon made a breach in the gate, and the fortress surrendered. The marquis de Launay was carried before the

Council

1789 Council at the Hotel de Ville, and ordered to be beheaded, which was immediately put in execution at the Place de Greve; several other suspected persons underwent the same fate, and their heads were fixed on poles and carried round the city:—
the same evening, the whole of the French guards joined the people.

The king ordered the troops to retire from Paris and Versailles, and recalled M. Neckar.

July 26th, An engagement between the fleets of Russia and Sweden.

August 1st, The Prince de Cobourgh defeated an army of 30,000 Turks, in Wallachia.

An insurrection took place in the Austrian Netherlands, August 10th.

The Swedes gained a complete victory over a body Russians, August 22d.

Fermentations increased at Brussels, August 24th.

August 30th, A Doge of Genoa elected.

Sept. 7th, A deputation of Ladies from Paris, presented their jewels to the National Assembly, for the use of their cavalry, to the amount of 600,000 livres.

Sept. 17th, The National Assembly declared itself permanent, and resolved upon its unity.

A complete victory gained by the Imperialists and Russians over the Turks in Moldavia; and another victory gained by them in Transylvania, Aug. 31.

The Prince Bishop of Liege left that city abruptly.

The celebrated Vandernoot, the patriot, attempted to be assinated at Brabant.

The emperor published a proclamation against the patriots of the Austrian Netherlands, and exiled Vandernoot.

Liege, by the flight of its bishop, obtained its freedom, Sept. 12th.

The Manilla trade opened to ships of all nations for three years.

The Prince of Wales was presented with the freedom of Drogheda, by the mayor and recorder, Sep. 17.

A riot

EVENTS.

1789 A riot at Troyes, in which the populace tore the mayor to pieces, on account of some regulations he had made respecting bread.

The Ruſſians gained a complete victory over the Swedes, Sept. 25.

The aſſembly granted to the king the ſuſpending Veto.

The Iſland of Corſica declared a part of the French empire, and its inhabitants to be governed by the French conſtitution. All the fugitive Corſicans allowed to return, and exerciſe the rights of French citizens.

Sept. 22d, The allied armies, under the command of the Prince de Cobourgh, obtained a complete victory over the Turks, on the Banks of the Rimnick.

September 29th, The Quay-Stone of the laſt arch of the New Bridge, was laid by Lord Donoughmore, Grand Maſter of Ireland, attended by the ſeveral Lodges of ancient and honourable Free-Maſons in the city of Cork, at which time it got the name of St. Patrick's-Bridge.

Two boys arrived from Otaheite, Oct. 6th.

Dreadful exceſſes committed at Paris by the women.

October 14th, Lord Weſtmoreland appointed lord-lieutenant of Ireland, in the room of the Marquis of Buckingham.

A victory gained by the Imperial army over the Turks, Oct. 19.

An earthquake near Florence, which overthrew a cathedral, and Palace of the Prætor.

A tumult at Liege between the ſoldiers and patriots.

The king of Spain made a public entry into Madrid, October 21ſt.

Oct. 6th, The king and queen of France were conducted by the Poiſſardes from Verſailles to the Palace of the Thuilleries.

October 9th, The States of Brabant revolted from the Emperor.

Martial

1789 October 20, Martial law decreed by the National Assembly.

October 22d, The remuneration of the king's physicians, was settled as follows: to doctor Willis, the father, 1500l. per ann. for twenty-one years; to doctor Willis, the son, 650l. per ann. for life; to the other physicians, thirty guineas for each visit to Windsor, and ten guineas for each visit to Kew.

The National Assembly agreed to affix to the king the title of *restorer of the liberty of France.*

The National Assembly began to debate on the rights of men and citizens.

Commotions at Bruffels, on account of the refugees who took shelter there. Every part also of Imperial Flanders shewed a disposition to follow the example of the French.

An insurrection at Boulogne sur Mer.

Spain and Sardinia refused to supply the court of of France with troops.

An artificial scarcity of corn was made at Paris.

Mr. Gorden executed at Northampton, for shooting a sheriff's officer, who come to arrest his father.

The Duke of Fitzjames experienced violent insult from the populace at Dunkirk.

An approaching revolution in the constitution of Austrian Flanders.

The new Sultan Selim, caused the grand vizier and all his relations, to be strangled, and their effects to be confiscated.

The plague broke out at Constantinople and Smyrna.

The Roman Catholics presented addresses to their majesties, on the king's happy recovery.

A fine pillar of oriental granite discovered at Rome, twelve palms in height, and one and a half in diameter; a statue of a consul, and two marble urns, in the excavations going on in the ground belonging to the sepulture of Nero.

The earl of Caithness put a period to his existence.

Illuminations,

1789 Illuminations, the moſt general ever known in London, on the reſtoration of the health of George III. March 10th.

Parliament of Ireland paſſed a two months money-bill, 23d March.

A diſpute happened between the duke of York and colonel Lenox (nephew and heir to the duke of Richmond) which terminated in a duel.

Count Montſera was the firſt who fell a victim to popular fury in Paris.

Nov. 3d, Eccleſiaſtical poſſeſſions aboliſhed in France.

Nov. 5th, The National Aſſembly decreed, that in future there ſhould be no diſtinction of orders in France; by this decree, all titles of nobility are aboliſhed.

Dec. 14th, The National Aſſembly decreed, that all the Proteſtant refugees, their heirs (of whatſoever degree) and ſucceſſors, ſhould be recalled, naturalized, and put in full poſſeſſion of their anceſtor's landed property.

The following is the ſtate of the Carron manufactory in Scotland, the greateſt perhaps of the kind ever known in the world: the weekly conſumption of coals amounts to 11,000 tons, at 4s. per ton; and the conſumption of each day is equal to that of the city of Edinburgh during the whole week. As many coals, therefore, are conſumed in the Carron founderies as would ſuffice to ſupply a city of 700,000 inhabitants. A thouſand workmen are daily employed in this manufactory, whoſe wages amount to 700l. per week, and 36,400l. per annum. The demands from abroad, and particularly from Spain, continue yearly to encreaſe.

Royal Canal Company for making a navigation from Dublin on the north ſide to the Shannon, incorporated 1ſt October.

Belfaſt contains 30,000 inhabitants; Kilkenny 20,000; Galway 15,000.

Limerick contains 40,000 inhabitants, and is three miles in circumference.

Charity,

1789 The duke of Orleans arrived in London from Paris, October 21st.

A dangerous conspiracy discovered at Brussels.

An edict was published at Brussels, to inform every one to surrender their arms within twenty-four hours, October 27th.

Nov. 3d, A victory gained by the Swedes over the Russians.

An engagement between the Imperial troops and the patriots of Brabant, in which the patriots were victorious, Nov. 7th.

A spirited manifesto to the emperor, published by the patriots of Brabant, Nov. 14th.

The city of Ghent surrendered to the patriots of Brabant, Nov. 23.

Lord-Aukland appointed ambassador to the States-General of the United Provinces, Nov. 28th.

Nov. 30th, The national assembly voted an address of thanks to lord Stanhope, and the members of the Revolution Club.

Dec. The court of Chatelet, at Paris, proceeded to the trial of Monf. de Bezenval.

The patriots of Brabant meet with great success.

A massacre at Marli, in which many lives were lost.

Dec. 12th, The capture of Brussels by the patriots.

Ghent restored to tranquility, Dec. 24.

The Ottoman emperor caused to be proclaimed by the sound of trumpet, his intention of putting himself at the head of his army; also, of the surrender of Bender to the Russians.

The assembly of the States of Brabant, were received at Brussels with great rejoicings.

Charity, Working, and Sunday Schools, established in Youghall.

In Youghall, the Mall formed, and an elegant large square building erected thereon, consisting of an assembly, card, coffee, and billiard-rooms, at the corporation expence.

Great rejoicings in the city of Cork, on account of his majesty's happy recovery.

On

Jan. 17th, The City of Cork exhibited a melancholy spectacle. A great fall of snow for some days, dissolved by a heavy fall of rain which cont'nued twenty-four hours, swelled the river beyond any thing hitherto known; it rushed through every avenue leading into the city, and by four o'clock in the evening, all the flat part thereof was covered: it continued to rise until nine o'clock; in many parts it was five feet, and in some seven feet high. The inhabitants were terrified at the unusual sight; many of them were obliged to ascend to the second floor of their houses, without meat or drink for their families; several boats plied through many parts of the city, and afforded relief to those who had not a mouthful of bread to give their frightened children. Considerable damage was sustained by many; happily but one life was lost, (a man of the name of NOAH.) A cellar on the North Mall, an house at Baldwin's corner, and two in Globe-lane, and a considerable part of some of the quays, were swept away; several other houses narrowly escaped the same fate. St. Patrick's Bridge, which at that time was erecting, suffered considerable damage; two of its arches that were nearly finished, were thrown down; a vessel which broke from her moorings at the Sand-quay, beat with such violence against the above bridge for several hours, as to accelerate its fall, on which the waters above the bridge rapidly diminished; and at three o'clock in the morning, retired within their usual bounds. The other bridges received no very material injury.

Though many falls of snow and rain, much heavier than the above, have repeatedly happened in this city and its neighbourhood, yet no flood equal to the above, is supposed to have ever happened in Cork. Providentially it happened in the day time, had it been otherwise, many lives must have been lost; the loss of property must have been immense; beds, tables, chairs, implements of husbandry, hay, straw, and timber, were brought down the river in great abundance; a boat well manned at Leitrim kept a look out for such prizes, and put off when they saw them approach; fortunately for Mr. Montjoy, who was swept off Batchelor's-quay, and miraculously escaped the piers of the north bridge, they perceived him also, and with some difficulty brought him to shore, where the mode adopted by the Humane Society, for the recovery of persons apparently drowned, was practised on him with success.

The wretched poor, whose lowly habitations particularly exposed them to this furious element, were relieved by their fellow-citizens, who have ever been highly distinguished for benevolence, humanity, and every other virtue which expands the feeling heart to relieve a fellow-creature.

1790 Jan. 5th, His Excellency the Earl of Westmoreland, arrived in Dublin.

Jan. 26th, The national assembly decreed, that none of its members can accept from government any place, employment, gift, pension, or gratification of any kind whatever, even though he should relinquish his seat in the assembly.

Feb. 4th, The king of France went to the national assembly, and declared his assent to the new constitution.

The emperor Joseph II. died Feb. 20th.

Feb. 24th, The national assembly abolished all honorary distinctions, superiority, and power, resulting from the feudal system.

March 14th, Captain Bligh arrived in London, and brought intelligence of a mutiny on board the Bounty armed ship in the South Sea, on the 28th of April, 1789, when the captain and seventeen others were put into an open boat, and after traversing the ocean for 48 days, the extent of 4000 miles, arrived at Timor on the 12th of June.

March 19th, An experiment in aerology was made at Portsmouth, which drew together the greatest concourse of people ever seen in that place. Mr. Murray,

1790 Murray, an eminent optician and man of science, descended from the church tower in a parachute, and came to the ground without receiving the smallest injury. Mr. Murray went through the whole process without the least embarrassment or fear, and when elevated to the vast height of the tower, waved his hat, saluted the multitude, and seemed totally undismayed, though the place on which he stood was scarcely nine inches in diameter.

March 20th, A very curious discovery in natural history, took place at Blackwall. Mr. Perry, the ship-builder, planned and made one of the most extensive wet docks in the kingdom; for which great undertaking, he appropriated seven acres of land. In digging the ground, regular strata of sand, clay, &c. were found, which afforded materials for bricks; and at the depth of 12 or 14 feet from the surface, under the above strata, numbers of very large trees were discovered; and what is most remarkable, a hazel nut hedge, with considerable quantities of nuts as they grew on the trees.

March 22d, A person convicted at the assizes of Hertford, for the robbery of a farmer, was discovered by the sagacity of a dog in the following manner: the offender, some time after the fact was committed, being at St. Alban's market, though at first unknown to the farmer, was singled out among the crowd by the dog, which by barking, snarling, and other offensive dispositions, so much irritated the former, that not knowing the owner of the animal, he told him that he ought to be prosecuted for keeping such a dog unmuzzled. This exciting the farmer's attention, he so far recollected the person of the other, his dress, &c. that he was apprehended, and was convicted of the robbery.

The celebrated Mr. Howard, died at Cherson.

April 8th, Irish parliament dissolved.

1790 April 17th, Doctor Benjamin Franklin died at Philadelphia, aged 84. He requested that the following epitaph (which he compofed for himfelf fome years ago) might be infcribed on his tombftone:

" The body of
BENJAMIN FRANKLIN, Printer,
(like the cover of an old book,
its contents torn out,
and ftript of its lettering and gilding)
lies here food for worms:
yet the work itfelf fhall not be loft,
but will (as he believed) appear once more,
in a new
and more beautiful edition,
corrected and amended
by
THE AUTHOR."

The parliament of Thouloufe, having pronounced an Arreté againft the national affembly, the national troops in the neighbourhood affembled, feized all the members, and upwards of fifty others of high rank, marched them to the Great Square, where gibbets were inftantly erected, and they were all executed, to the number of 182.

His majefty's fhip, the Guardian man of war, arrived fafe at the Cape of Good Hope, after a moft miraculous efcape from an ifland of ice.

May 1ft, The election for members to reprefent the city of Cork in parliament ended, when the numbers ftood as follows: for the right hon. Richard Longfield, 696; hon. John Hely Hutchinfon 605; Benjamin Bousfield, efq; 450; whereupon the two former were declared duly elected.

The Swedifh army repulfed the Ruffians at Karnankofky, May 4th.

Notification to parliament of the Spanifh hoftilities at Nootka-Sound, and confequent armaments.

Liberty of the prefs decreed in the national affembly.

1790 May 22d, The national affembly referved to themfelves the exclufive privilege of making war or peace.

June, At the final clofe of the poll for the election of members to reprefent this county in parliament, it appeared that the majority was in favour of James Bernard, efq; and the right honourable Lord Kingfborough; whereupon the high-fheriff declared them duly elected. Mr. Morris petitioned; and being tried by a committee of the houfe, lord Kingfborough was declared not duly elected ;¡ Mr. Bernard died in the interim. Writs were iffued for two other members, whereupon lord Kingfborough and Mr. Morris, were elected without oppofition.

June 7th, Grand proceffion of the Nabob from Chitpore to Calcutta, in order to pay his compliments to earl Cornwallis, on his arrival in India.

Rhynwick Williams (commonly called the monfter) found guilty.

July 4th, A defperate engagement between the Ruffian and Swedifh fleets, in which the duke of Sudermania was wounded, and the Ruffians gained a complete victory.

July 9th, The king of Sweden having reinforced his fleet, attacked the Ruffians, and after a very obftinate engagement, totally defeated them.

Treaty of Riechenbach between Auftria and Pruffia, whereby Auftria relinquifhed to the Turks, all her conquefts, July 27th.

July 28th, The important event of opening the Forth and Clyde navigation from fea to fea, took place by the failing of a track-barge belonging to the company of proprietors, from the bafon of the canal near the city of Glafgow, to the river Clyde at Bowling-Bay.

The voyage, which is upwards of twelve miles, was performed in lefs than four hours, during which period the veffel paffed through nineteen locks, defcending thereby 150 feet from the fummit of the canal into the Clyde. It required only four minutes

1790 nutes to pafs each of the locks, in which fpace the veffel defcended eight feet into the reach of the navigation immediately below.

In the courfe of the voyage from Glafgow to Bowling-Bay, the track-boat paffed along that ftupendous bridge, the great aqueduct over the river Kelvin, 400 feet in length exhibiting to the fpectators below, the fingular and new object of a veffel navigating feventy feet over their heads.

The extreme length of the navigation from the Forth to the Clyde, is exactly 35 miles, 16 of which is upon the fummit of the country, 160 feet above the level of the fea.

To this fummit the voyager is raifed by means of twenty locks from the eaftern fea, and nineteen from the weft. Each lock is exactly twenty feet wide, and feventy-four long within the gates. The depth of the canal is precifely eight feet from the furface of the water, and its breadth twenty-eight feet.

The toll-dues payable upon the navigation, are 2d. per ton for each mile, or 5s. 10d. per ton for the extreme length of the canal.

Auguft 1ft, A fhallop belonging to the fhip Ulyffes, captain Campbell of Glafgow, by a fudden fquall fhipped a fea in Montego-Bay, by which fhe was inftantly funk, and only one failor befides the captain faved. Captain Campbell fortunately got hold of an oar, and the failor of a gun-cafk, which he held by the bung-hole. In this perilous fituation, the captain touched fomething with his foot, which proved to be a fhark: this new terror, inftead of difheartening, animated him; and, till five o'clock in the morning, when he was taken up by fome negroes who heard his cries, he was found defending himfelf againft the fhark. The method he took was fometimes by preffing with his hands and the whole weight of his body with the oar upon the fhark, which made him fheer off; at other times getting to the extremity of the oar,

and

1790 and striking him; and by these, and other stratagems that the moment suggested, he wonderfully preserved himself from being destroyed by the voracious animal. The shark was about 11 feet long.

August 6th, Austria renounced her alliance with Russia, and concluded a separate peace with the Porte.

Preliminaries of peace between Sweden and Russia, August 14th.

August 17th, The grand fleet, under the command of lord Howe, sailed from Portsmouth.

August 18th, It was decreed by the national assembly, that Protestants of every denomination should be equally eligible as Catholics, to places of public trust.

In August 18th, 1788, the lightning was so great as to split part of the rock of the Giant's Causeway 20 yards, and a cow had one half of her skull entirely separated from the other.

Aug. 26th, The national assembly ordered the navy of France to be augmented to 45 sail of the line, for the purpose of supporting the family compact.

Leopold II. king of Hungary, chosen king of the Romans, August 30th.

The celebrated Barrington, the pickpocket, sentenced to seven years transportation.

Belgic Provinces submitted to the emperor.

Hostilities in the East Indies, between Tippoo Saib and English India Company.

House of Commons voted the prosecution of the impeachment of Warren Hastings, esq; governor-general of Bengal, notwithstanding the dissolution of parliament, which necessarily discontinued it.

Sept. 13th, A detachment from general Meadows's army, under the command of lieutenant-colonel Floyd, consisting of 4000 men, were attacked by Tippoo Saib at the head of 14,000 cavalry, and 20,000 infantry, and a formidable train of artillery; when, after an obstinate engagement, the enemy were defeated; a number of British officers were

1790 were killed and wounded:—two days afterwards the colonel was joined by general Meadows.

Sept. 18th, His royal highnefs the duke of Cumberland died.

The Turkifh fleet defeated by the Ruffians on the Black fea.

October 10th, A great victory obtained by the Ruffians near the Cuban.

October 25th, His Excellency the earl of Weftmoreland, lord lieutenant of Ireland, arrived in Cork; he conferred the honour of knighthood on Henry Brown Hayes, efq; one of the high fheriffs.

Convention between Great Britain and Spain, the 27th of October.

Nov. 6th, The widow of Kaddoo Ghofe, who died at Sinlay, near Calcutta, afcended the funeral pile of her hufband with the ufual ceremonies. Her refolution was fo determined, that, previoufly to the cuftomary preparations for this fatal event, fhe diftributed her fortune, confifting of feveral thoufand rupees, among her family; and the Bramin priefts were not forgot in the appropriation. She was alfo poffeffed of feveral houfes, and a talook, or farm, which were conveyed to her relations, together with her jewels and furniture; fo that the apprehenfion of poverty could have no influence in this facrifice of her life.

Foundation Stone of firft lock of the Royal Canal, on Glafsmanogue road, laid by lord Weftmoreland, and named Weftmoreland Lock, Nov. 12th.

Coronation of the emperor at Prefburg, Nov. 15.

A ftandard of weights and meafures eftablifhed in France.

Dec. 1ft. M. Blanchard made his 37th aerial excurfion from Prague.

Dec. 2d, The States of Brabant returned to their allegiance.

Dec. 31ft, There was fo thick a fog at Amfterdam, that upwards of 230 perfons were drowned in the Canals,

1790 Canals, before any affiftance could be given them, though their cries could be diftinctly heard.

The Charlemont Packet loft, and 114 fouls perifhed, only 16 efcaped.

The Auftrians, with an army of 2440, defeated the Turks with 6000 picked men.

The chief magiftrate of the city of Cork, Richard Harris, efq; iffued near two hundred cards, inviting company to dine with him on Chriftmas Day, the guefts till then entertained at the mayoralty-houfe, were of the firft fafhion; but his was of a different defcription—the diftreffed houfe and room-keepers. The invitation cards were given to the different clergymen of all perfuafions in the city, to diftribute among the indigent of their feveral parifhes.

Macleod, a Scotchman, aged 102, walked ten miles on the Hammerfmith Road for one hundred guineas; two hours and a half were allowed him, but he performed the tafk in two hours and twenty-three minutes.

A large Sunfifh caught near Cable-Ifland, and brought into the harbour of Youghall.

At Leicefter affizes, a clergyman aged 63 years, was convicted of felonioufly folemnizing a marriage, without publication of banns, or licence firft obtained, and was ordered to be tranfported for fourteen years.

1791 Jan. 17th, A Sunday and Daily School was opened on Hammond's-Marfh in the city of Cork, where about 400 children of both fexes, and all perfuafions, are inftructed in reading, writing, and accompts gratis; proper books, &c. are procured for the fcholars, at the expence of the charity, which is fupported by fubfcriptions and donations.

March 2d, The Albion mills in London, burnt to the ground; the lofs was immenfe; 41,000l. of which was infured; the buildings and machinery coft 55,000l. befides a vaft ftock of grain, flour, &c. Out of 4,000 facks of corn, only 30 were faved.

March

1791 March 21st, Bangalore taken by storm by earl Cornwallis.

April 9th, The king attempted to go to St. Cloud, but was stopped by the populace; the national guard refused to disperse the multitude, and M. de la Fayette seeing his orders disobeyed, resigned his command, but was afterwards prevailed on to resume it.

The reverend John Wesley died, aged 88.

June 21st, The king, queen, and royal family of France, escaped from Paris, but were stopped near the borders of the kingdom, and brought back on the 25th.

July 14th, In consequence of a meeting of gentlemen at the hotel, Birmingham, to celebrate the French Revolution, a large mob assembled, and broke the windows of the hotel; they afterwards destroyed the Presbyterian meeting-houses, doctor Priestly's house and valuable library, and many other houses belonging to the principal Dissenters in the town and neighbourhood.

Sept. 29th, His royal highness the Duke of York, married to to the princess royal of Prussia.

Dreadful insurrection of the Negroes in St. Domingo, where a great number of Whites were killed, and plantations destroyed to an immense value.

Nov. James Haslar, an attorney, stood in the pillory in Dublin for perjury; he was afterwards struck off the list of attornies.

Nov. 21st, Their royal highnesses the Duke and Dutchess of York, arrived in London.

Lord Cornwallis attacked and defeated Tippoo Saib's army, and made them retreat under the walls of Serengapatam; but on account of the monsoons, was obliged to relinquish the object of his enterprize, and return to Bangalore. The monsoons likewise obliged general Abercrombie to descend the Gauts, leaving behind him four 18 pounders, and a quantity of provisions, stores, and camp equipage.

Armaments

1791 Armaments of England, Holland, and Pruffia, obliged Ruffia to make peace with the Turks.

Parliament granted 45,000l. for making wet and dry docks on thofe parts on the north and fouth fides which communicate with the ports of Dublin.

An Apothecaries' Hall eftablifhed at Dublin.

A Mining Company eftablifhed.

Declaration of the Court of Ruffia of her being willing to yield up to the Turks, all her conquefts during the war, excepting Oczakow and its immediate dependencies, as a barrier.

This year the Church at Youghall, a large antient Gothic ftructure, underwent a greater improvement than it did thefe hundred years paft.

The church now building at Peterfburgh is the largeft in Europe; 2000 men have been working at it thefe twenty years, and are not yet at the top of the walls. It is of polifhed marble, both infide and out; the pillars are of one piece, 50 feet high; the bafe and capitals of folid filver; but the greateft curiofity of all, is the wooden box which covers the whole from the weather, conftructed in a particular manner. All the Emprefs's buildings are on the fame immenfe fcale.

Fort-Weftmoreland Battery, on Spike-Ifland, at the entrance of the harbour of Cork (intended to mount one hundred guns) began to be built by Mr. Michael Shanahan, architect, under the direction of that able engineer, colonel Vallancy.

The infulating wall and guard-houfe for the intended gaol for the county of Cork, began Dec. 6th, by Mr. Michael Shanahan, architect.

Caftle-Street widened, and the merchants Coffee-Room built.

A houfe for the reception of lunatics, began to be built in Cork, for which purpofe near 200l. was collected by a charity play, owing to the very active exertions of Richard Harris, efq; mayor.

French

REMARKABLE

French ships of war taken by the English, since the commencement of hostilities with that kingdom, which took place the 17th day of June, 1778.

	Guns.		Guns.
La Ville de Paris	110	De Clinton	32
Le Glorieux	74	Minerva	32
Le Pegafe	74	L' Ellis	28
Le Ardent	64	Le Neckar	28
Le Actionaire	64	Unicorn	28
Le Caton	64	La Duguesseau	28
Le Jason	64	Le Hercule	24
La Prothee	64	L'Audacieux	24
Solitaire	64	Rouen Soubife	24
Le Compte d'Artois	64	Duc de Cogny	24
Le Fayet	40	Sphynx	24
La Fortune	40	L'Adventure	24
Le Artois	44	Le Chevireul	24
La Blanche	40	Sophie	22
Le Bellipotent	40	La Princefs de Robecque	20
La Hebe	40	La Dunquerquoife	20
L'Aigle	40	Pearl	18
L'Imperieux	36	Senegal	18
La Prudente	36	Duc d'Eftifac	16
La Nymphe	36	Guay Trouin	14
Le Monfieur	36	L'Abondance	18
La Belle Poule	36	Ceres	18
Menagere	40	M. d'Seignaly	16
Le Sartine	36	Albicore	16
La Pallas	32	Pelican	16
La Licorne	32	Pigmy	14
La Danae	32	Duc d'Chartres	14
La Oifeau	32	Le Goree	14
L'Alcmene	32	Mutine	14
L'Americaine	32	Pilote	14
La Magicienne	32	L'Caereur	14
L'Eperance	32	Maurepas	12
La Colagne	32	Le Jeune Lion	12
L'Aimable	32	Le Renard	12
La Convert	32	La Gloire	8

Befides

EVENTS. 277

Besides the Le Cæsar, of 74 guns, blown up, and La Diademe of 74, sunk by admiral Rodney on the 12th of April 1782; Valeur 26, and Recluse 24 guns, burnt by sir James Wallace's squadron, in Concale Bay; La Capricieuse, 32 guns, taken by the Prudent, and burnt; La Legere, 36 guns, destroyed by the Nonsuch; and several others of lesser force.

Spanish ships of war taken by the English, since the commencement of hostilities with that kingdom, which took place the 18th of June, 1779.

	Guns.		Guns.
Phœnix (now Gibraltar)	80	Santa Catilina	34
Princessa	70	San Carlos	32
Diligente	70	San Raphael	30
Monarca	70	Santa Teresa	28
Guipuscano (now the Prince William)	64	San Bruno	26
		Santa Leocadia	36
St. Joseph Del Carlos	52	Grana	28
St. Michael	74	Santa Pedrosa	28
Santa Monica	36	San Fermin	16
Santa Margarita	36	San Vincent	16

Besides the San Domingo of 70 guns, blown up; the San Eugenio of 70, and the San Julian of 70, driven on shore by admiral Rodney, and destroyed.

Dutch ships of war taken by the English, since the commencement of hostilities with the State of Holland, which took place the 20th day of December, 1780.

	Guns.		Guns.
Mars (now Prince Edward)	60	Germantine	32
		Accra	32
Princess Carolina	54	Hercules	24
Rotterdam	50	Mars	24
Mars	32	Fort Mouree	20
St. Eustatia	28	Apam	22
Castor	36	Berricoe	18

	Guns.		Guns.
Dogger Bank	20	Pylades	18
Orestes	18	Zeuse	18

Besides a 74 gun ship, sunk by admiral Hyde Parker, off the Dogger Bank; and a Dutch Dogger of 18 guns, blown up by the Cameleon.

Congress ships of war taken by the English, since the commencement of hostilities with America, which took place the 14th day of June, 1774.

	Guns.		Guns.
Confederacy	36	Cumberland	20
Providence	32	Sullivan	20
Raleigh	32	Jason	20
Trumbull	32	Morning Star	14
Delaware	28	Tobago	14
Virginia	28	Hetty	20
Charles-Town	28	Mifflin	20
Hussar	28	Alfred	20
Boston	32	Columbus	20
Hancock	32	Independence	26
Washington	24	Ranger	20
Alexander	24	Dalton	20
Lexington	32	Montgomery	18
Effingham	28	Sturdy Beggar	18
Protector	26	Mentor	18
Portsmouth	26	Rattlesnake	16
Bellisarius	24	Surprise	16
Oliver Cromwell	24	Cabot	14
Bunker's-Hill	20	Rover	14
Tartar	20		

Together with the Bon Homme Richard, of 40 guns, commanded by Paul Jones, sunk in an engagement with the Serapis of 44 guns, which she took before she went down. The Randolph of 36 guns, blown up near Barbadoes, by the Yarmouth of 64 guns, and only five of the crew saved. The Warren of 64 guns burnt, with sixteen others of inferior force, at Penobscot, by sir George Collier's

EVENTS. 279

lier's fleet: forty-four fail of armed floops, privateers, and fchooners, with the Wafhington and Effingham frigates, of 32 guns each, burnt on the Delaware by captain Henry, of lord Howe's fleet. The number of privateers, armed veſſels, brigs, fchooners, cutters, and floops of private property, that have been taken and deſtroyed, belonging to the Americans, ſince the commencement of hoſtilities, are almoſt innumerable.

Engliſh ſhips of war taken by the French, ſince the commencement of the preſent hoſtilities, in 1778.

	Guns.		Guns.
Ardent	64	Ariel	20
Experiment	50	Germaine	20
Hannibal	50	Gronoque	20
Romulus	44	Ceres	18
Iris	32	Weaſel	16
Richmond	32	Senegal	16
Montreal	32	Alert	14
Minerva	32	Alligator	14
Fox	28	York	12
Active	28	Thunder Bomb	8
Creſcent	28	Zephyr	14
Lively	24		

Beſides the Charon of 44, Guadaloupe 28, Fowey 24, Bonetta 24, and Vulcan fire-ſhip, taken and deſtroyed at York in Virginia; the Quebec of 32 guns, blown up in an engagement with the Surveillant of 40 guns; captain Farmer, of the Quebec, finding his ſhip totally on fire, ſuffered himſelf to be blown up, ſooner than ſurrender.

Captured by Spain: The Penelope Engliſh frigate of 28 guns, who had taken the Margate Spaniſh ſhip of war, and was conducting her to port, when the priſoners fell upon the crew of the Penelope, killed her captain, and carried both ſhips ſafe into the iſland of Cuba. One ſhip ſince June 1779.

English ships of war captured by the Americans, since the commencement of hostilities in 1774: Serapis 44 guns; Scarborough 20; Sandwich 24; Drake 16; Atalanta 16; Thorn 16; and the General Monk of 14 guns.

English ships of war, lost by accident, since the commencement of the American war.

	Guns.	
Ville de Paris	110	
Royal George	100	Lost in Portsmouth Harbour.
Glorieux	74	
Ramillies	74	} Lost on their passage from Jamaica; most of the crews perished.
Hector	74	
Centaur	74	Lost near the Azores.
Culloden	74	Lost at Gardiner's Island.
Thunderer	74	} Lost in a hurricane in the West-Indies, and all on board perished.
Sterling-Castle	64	
Somerset	70	Lost near Boston.
Augusta	64	Burnt near Philadelphia.
Terrible	74	Lost near the Chesapeak.
Repulse	32	Lost on her passage from New-York.
Flora	32	
Juno	32	
Lark	32	
Orpheus	32	} Burnt at Rhode-Island to prevent their being taken by the French fleet; the crews were saved.
Cerberus	28	
Falcon	18	
King's Fisher	16	
Arethusa	32	Lost near Brest.
Actæon	28	Burnt near Charles-Town.
Syren	28	Lost near Rhode-Island.
Mermaid	28	Lost near Philadelphia.
Liverpool	28	Lost near New-York.
Vestal	20	} Lost on the Newfoundland station.
Pegasus	16	
Mercury	20	Lost near New-York.
Ferret	14	Lost on the Jamaica station.
Pomona	14	Lost on the Antigua station.
Merlin	16	Burnt near Philadelphia.
Cruiser	8	Burnt on the coast of Carolina.
Savage	8	Lost near Louisbourg.

EVENTS.

	Guns.	
Otter	16	Loft near St. Auguftine.
Supply	26 }	Burnt in the Weft Indies.
Glafgow	20	
Swan	18	Loft near the Saltees (Ireland)
Spy	20	Loft near Newfoundland.
Phœnix	44 }	
Andromeda	28	
Laurel	28	Loft in the Weft Indies, at the time of the terrible hurricane, which happened there the 10th day of October, 1780; moft of the crews perifhed.
Beaver's Prize	18	
Scarborough	24	
Deal-Caftle	24	
San Vincente	16	
Victor	16	
Barbadoes Brig	16	
Cameleon	14	
Blonde	32	Loft near New York.

                                                                         Years.

The Revolution War lafted from 1688 to 1696, both included — — — } 9

The Succeffion War, from 1702 to 1713 — 11

Spanifh and French, from 1739 to 1748 — 10

The late War, from 1755 to 1762 — — 8

The American War, from 1775 to 1782. — 8

Total of years from the firft period to the prefent — — — } 92

                Total of war — 46

                Total of peace — 46

REMARKABLE
ROMAN CATHOLIC MAYORS OF CORK.

PROVOSTS.
Years. KING JOHN's Reign.
1199 John Difpenfer,
HENRY III.
1236 Walter Eynoff,
1249 Eliah Stackpole,
1251 John Wenchedon,
1252 Walter Wright.
MAYORS.
EDWARD I.
1272 Richard Morren,
1273 Richard Wine,
1274 Richard Lee,
1279 Walter Tardiff,
1281 Walter Rute,
1285 Peter Ruffel,
1287 William Pollard,
1290 Walter Tardiff,
1291 Walter O'Heyn.
EDWARD II.
1293 John Lavallan,
1310 John Walters,
1311 William Bond,
1312 Nicholas de la Weily,
1313 William Hadvivre,
1314 Walter de Kerdiff,
1315 Nicholas O'Heyn,
1316 John de Ligré,
1317 Nicholas de la Weily,
1318 Adam Milkfbury,
1319 Stephen Coppinger,
1320 Richard Delahoide,
1321 Abraham de Stacpole
1322 Walter Reifch,
1323 Gilbert Monk,
1324 John le Difpenfer,
1325 Richard Morraine.

Years. EDWARD III.
1326 Edward de Tailour,
1327 Roger Tryal,
1328 Roger le Blon,
1329 William Albus,
1330 Nicholas Murraine,
1331 Richard Poftwind,
1332 Richard Leleigh,
1333 Richard Leleigh,
1334 Robert Lebolout,
1335 Bernard de Montibus,
1336 John Wedlock,
1337 John de Efpencer,
1338 John de Briftol,
1339 John Fitz-Abraham,
1340 David de Montibus,
1341 Peter Rafhall,
1342 Elias de Stacpole,
1343 Walter Reifch,
1344 William Pollard,
1345 William Pollard,
1346 Walter de Kerdiff,
1347 Walter O'Heyn,
1348 John Wallen,
1349 Wm. de Wandefpar,
1350 Walter de Kerdiff,
1351 Nicholas O'Heyn,
1352 Nicholas Delahoide,
1353 Walter de Kerdiff,
1354 Percival Hunt,
1355 John Gallengar,
1356 Walter de Kerdiff,
1357 John Gallengar,
1358 Adam Ruth,
1359 Walter de Kerdiff,
1360 Percival Vincent,
1361 Percival Vincent,
1362 William

EVENTS.

Years.		Years.	HENRY IV.
1362	William Drooper,	9	John Mainen,
3	Adam Ruth,	1400	John Kapp,
4	William Skiddy	1	Richard Lavallan,
5	William Skiddy,	2	William Sughin,
6	Percival Vincent,	3	John Benefiat,
7	William Skiddy,	4	John Skiddy,
8	Jordan Kerdiff,	5	John Lignee
9	William Drooper,	6	William Sughin,
1370	John Leblown,	7	John Wright,
1	John Leblown,	8	William Sughin,
2	Thomas Thiſh,	9	Thomas Morton,
3	William Drooper,	1410	John Warner,
4	William Downane,	1	Thomas Murray,
5	Thomas Thiſh,		HENRY V.
6	William Drooper,	2	Thomas Mordonton,
	RICHARD II.	3	Patrick Rice,
7	William Downane,	4	Thomas Mollenton,
8	Thomas Thiſh,	5	Robert Gardiner,
9	David Miagh,	6	Robert Gardiner,
1380	John Lombard,	7	Robert Gardiner,
1	David Miagh,	8	Robert Gardiner,
2	Robert Drooper,	9	Thomas Mollenton,
3	John Mynne,	1420	Thomas Mollenton,
4	John Mynne,	1	Robert Bordernor,
5	John Mynne,		HENRY VI.
6	Robert Drooper,	2	Thomas Mollenton,
7	John Malby,	3	Pierce Drooper,
8	John Malby,	4	Robert Gardiner,
9	John Lombard,	5	David Landebrook,
1390	William Polent,	6	Geoffry White,
1	Redmond Kerrick,	7	David Landebrook,
2	Andrew Stacpole,	8	Edward Dantz,
3	Redmond Kerrick,	9	Geoffry Waile,
4	Robert Flemming,	1430	Geoffry Gallaway,
5	John Warriner,	1	William Anaſey,
6	Thomas Honeybeard,	2	William Anaſey,
7	Thomas Burdeys,	3	John Menia,
8	John Warriner.	4	Geoffry White,

John

Years.

5 John Murrogh,
6 Godfrey Gallaway,
7 John Murrogh,
8 John Skiddy,
9 John Skiddy,
1440 John Meagh,
1 John Murrogh,
2 William Gold,
3 William Gold,
4 John Murrogh,
5 John Gold,
6 Richard Skiddy,
7 John Gold,
8 Patrick Gallaway,
9 John Gallaway,
1450 Richard Skiddy,
1 John Gold,
2 Richard Skiddy,
3 William Gallaway,
4 William Skiddy,
5 Richard Lavallan,
6 William Gallaway,
7 Richard Skiddy,
8 William Skiddy,
9 Patrick Gallaway.

EDWARD IV.

1460 Thomas Murrogh,
1 Richard Skiddy,
2 John Gallaway,
3 William Gold,
4 John Gold,
5 John Skiddy,
6 Richard Skiddy,
7 John Meagh,
8 Godfrey Naiole,
9 John Mezca,
1470 Richard Skiddy,
1 John Gallaway,
2 William Gallaway,

Years.

3 Thomas Murrogh,
4 William Skiddy,
5 Richard Lavallan,
6 John Gallaway,
7 William Gallaway,
8 Richard Skiddy,
9 William Skiddy,
1480 William Skiddy,
1 William Gallaway,
2 Richard Gallaway,
3 William Gallaway,
4 William Skiddy.

HENRY VII.

5 Patrick Gallaway,
6 William Gallaway,
7 William Skiddy,
8 Maurice Roche,
9 William Gallaway,
1490 John Walters,
1 Maurice Roche,
2 John Lavallan,
3 William Gold,
4 John Walters,
5 Thomas Coppinger,
6 John Lavallan,
7 Maurice Roche,
8 John Lavallan,
9 John Walters,
1500 Maurice Roche,
1 William Gold,
2 William Gallaway,
3 Edmond Gold,
4 John Gallaway,
5 William Terry,
6 William Skiddy,
7 John Skiddy,
8 Richard Gallaway.

HENRY VIII.

9 Edmond Gallaway,

Edmond

EVENTS.

Years.
- 1510 Edmond Gold,
- 1 Edmond Terry,
- 2 John Gallaway,
- 3 John Roche,
- 4 Edmond Terry,
- 5 Richard Skiddy,
- 6 Walter Gallaway,
- 7 John Skiddy,
- 8 Nicholas Skiddy,
- 9 Patrick Terry,
- 1520 Edmond Roche,
- 1 David Terry,
- 2 Richard Gold,
- 3 Maurice Roche,
- 4 Edmond Gold,
- 5 William Terry,
- 6 John Skiddy,
- 7 Walter Gallaway,
- 8 John Skiddy,
- 9 Patrick Terry,
- 1530 Edmond Roche,
- 1 Richard Gold,
- 2 Patrick Gallaway,
- 3 David Roche,
- 4 James Gold,
- 5 William Coppinger,
- 6 Robert Meagh,
- 7 Thomas Ronayne,
- 8 William Terry,
- 9 James Roche,
- 1540 Richard Terry,
- 1 Christopher Creagh,
- 2 William Sarsfield,
- 3 William Skiddy,
- 4 James Gold,
- 5 Richard Gold,
  EDWARD VI.
- 6 William Gold,

Years.
- 7 William Gold,
- 8 Patrick Meagh,
- 9 Thomas Ronayne,
- 1550 Dominick Roche,
- 1 William Terry,
- 2 James Roche,
  MARY I.
- 3 Patrick Gallaway,
- 4 Richard Terry,
- 5 Christopher Meagh,
- 6 William Sarsfield,
- 7 William Skiddy,
  ELIZABETH.
- 8 Dominick Roche,
- 9 Edmond Gold,
- 1560 Edward Gallaway,
- 1 John Gallaway,
- 2 Andrew Gallaway,
- 3 Maurice Roche,
- 4 Stephen Coppinger,
- 5 Rich. Roche,
- 6 William Gallaway,
- 7 Edmond Gold
- 8 John Gallaway,
- 9 Andrew Gallaway,
- 1570 John Meagh,
- 1 Maurice Roche,
- 2 Stephen Coppinger,
- 3 John Walters,
- 4 Walter Terry,
- 5 James Ronayne,
- 6 William Roche,
- 7 John Gold,
- 8 Walter Gallaway,
- 9 Maurice Roche,
- 1580 Thomas Sarsfield,
- 1 Christopher Walters,
- 2 Patrick Gallaway,

James

REMARKABLE

Years.
- 3 James Roche,
- 4 George Gold,
- 5 Stephen Walters,
- 6 Stephen Terry,
- 7 Robert Coppinger,
- 8 Edmond Terry,
- 9 John Skiddy,
- 1590 Dominick Roche,
- 1 David Terry,
- 2 Henry Walſh,
- 3 Patrick Gallaway,
- 4 Francis Martel,
- 5 James Meagh,
- 6 Patrick Gallaway,
- 7 George Gold,
- 8 John Skiddy,
- 9 James Sarsfield,
- 1600 William Mead,
- 1 John Mead,

JAMES I.
- 2 John Coppinger,
- 3 Thomas Sarsfield,
- 4 Edmond Terry,
- 5 Robert Coppinger,
- 6 William Sarsfield,
- 7 Philip Martel,
- 8 David Terry,
- 9 Dominick Roche,
- 1610 Edmond Gallaway,
- 1 George Gold,
- 2 Dominick Terry,
- 3 William Skiddy,
- 4 David Terry,
- 5 William Gold,

Years.
- 6 John Coppinger,
- 7 Patrick Terry,
- 8 William Gold,
- 9 John Coppinger,
- 1620 William Terry
- 1 Andrew Skiddy,
- 2 John Coppinger,
- 3 John Roche,
- 4 John Roche,

CHARLES I.
- 5 Henry Gold,
- 6 Edmond Martel,
- 7 William Hoare,
- 8 David Terry,
- 9 James Murrogh,
- 1630 Thomas Ronayne,
- 1 Maurice Roche,
- 2 Jefferey Gallaway,
- 3 William Roche,
- 4 Richard Roche,
- 5 Thomas Martel,
- 6 Robert Meagh,
- 7 David Meagh,
- 8 Patrick Lavallen,
- 9 Thomas Sarsfield,
- 1640 Thomas Gold,
- 1 Melcher Lavallen,
- 2 Maurice Roche,
- 3 John Roche,
- 4 Robert Coppinger,
- 5 James Lombard,
- 6 ☞ For ten years, no Civil Magiſtrate during Cromwell's uſurpation.

PROTESTANT

EVENTS.

PROTESTANT MAYORS & SHERIFFS of CORK.

KING CHARLES II's. REIGN.

Year.	Mayors.	Sheriffs.
1656	John Hodder, firſt Proteſtant mayor.	William Hodder, Philip Matthews firſt Proteſtant Sheriffs.
7	William Hodder,	Richard Covet, Timothy Tuckey,
8	Philip Matthews,	Richard Baſſet, John Bailey,
9	Jonas Morris,	R. Lane, Noblet Dunſcomb,
1660	Chriſtopher Oliver	Thomas Farren, John Flynn,
1	Walter Cooper,	Chriſtopher Rye, Nicholas King,
2	Richard Covet,	Robert Williams, Thos. Crook,
3	James Vandeluen,	Wm. French, Richard Purdon,
4	Richard Baſſet,	James Finch, Matthew Deane,
5	Noblet Dunſcomb,	Jn. Newenham, Pat. Ronayne,
6	Thomas Farren,	Jn. Hawkins, Timothy Tuckey,
7	Chriſtopher Rye,	Thomas Mills, George Wright,
8	Chriſtopher Rye,	T. Kitcherman, R. Fletcher,
9	Matthew Deane,	Wm. Field, Richard Harvey,
1670	James Finch,	Wm. Wren, Thomas Walker,
1	John Newenham,	Jonathan Perry, John Bailey,
2	John Hawkins,	Thomas Franklin, John Terry,
3	Thomas Mills,	James Mills, Thomas Wills,
4	John Bailey,	Robert Rogers, William Hull,
5	George Wright,	John Wright, Edward Webber,
6	William Field,	Edward Youd, John Sealy,
7	Timothy Tuckey,	William Allen, Chriſt. Crofts,
8	Thos. Hickerman,	Wm. Malebom, Richard Terry,
9	John Baily,	William Ballard, Wm. Howel,
1680	Robert Rogers,	Randall Hull, H. Fitzgerald,
1	William Allwin,	Thomas Cronepn, Stephen Cook,
2	Richard Covet,	W. Charters, Eleazer Lavers,
3	John Wright,	Zachary Cook, Samuel Bailey.

JAMES II.

4	Edward Webber,	Edward Hoare, John Bailey,
5	Chriſtopher Crofts,	Daniel Crone, J. Champion,
6	Edward Hoare,	Thomas Brown, Edw. Tucker,
7	W. Ballard & Ignatius Gold,	Wm. Coppinger, W. White.

WILLIAM

WILLIAM and MARY's REIGN.

Year.	Mayors.	Sheriffs.
8	Patrick Roche,	Bate French, Thos. Murrogh,
9	Dominick Sarsfield	Patrick Meade, Patrick Nagle,
1690	William Ballard,	Wm. Roberts, Wm. Green,
1	Daniel Crone,	Peter Renew, Samuel Love,
2	William Charters,	John Whiting, Richard Slocond,
3	William Howel,	James French, Simon Dring,
4	Peter Renew,	John Rains, William Goddard,
5	Samuel Love,	Edm. Knapp, Jona. Trifillian,
6	James French,	Theo. Morris, F. Pennington.
7	William Roberts,	Rich. Crabb, Thos. Kinfmell,
8	William Goddard,	W. Andrews, Edw. Yeamans,
9	Theophilus Morris,	Barth. Taylor, John Allen,
1700	John Sealy.	Jos. Reddeck, Fran. Cottrel.

QUEEN ANN's REIGN.

1	Simon Dring,	Jos. Franklin, Bernard Poye,
2	John Whiting,	W. Mafters, Abraham Watkins,
3	Edmond Knapp,	Mathias Smith, Edw. Brown,
4	William Andrews,	D. Perdriau, Row. Delahoide,
5	Francis Cottrel,	Wm. Cockeril, Daniel Pierce,
6	Bernard Poye,	Noblet Rogers, P. Hamilton,
7	Jofeph Franklin,	Edward Hoare, John Hawkins,
8	Rowland Delahoide	W. Lambly, James Morriffon,
9	Noblet Rogers,	Richard Phillips, Sam. Wilfon,
1710	Edward Hoare,	Thomas Barry, Samuel Allen,
1	Richard Philips,	John Terry, Richard Addis,
2	Daniel Perdriau,	Phil. French, Anthony Gofs,
3	John Allen.	Abraham French, Jofeph Lavit,

GEORGE I.

4	Edward Brown,	Jn. Morriffon, Hugh Millerd,
5	Philip French,	John Morley, Francis Power,
6	William Lambly,	Thomas Sheares, Thos. Brown,
7	Abraham French,	W. Hawkins, Charles Cottrel,
8	John Morley,	Edw. Brocklefby, Jos. Auftin,

John

Year.	MAYORS.	SHERIFFS.
9	John Terry,	John Maunsel, George Fuller,
1720	Joseph Lavit,	Samuel Croker, James Foucalt,
1	William Hawkins,	W. Owgan, Augustus Carey,
2	Daniel Pierce,	Robert Atkins, G. Bennett,
3	Edw. Brockelsby,	Ambrose Cramer, James Hulet,
4	George Bennett,	Fran. Rowland, T. Pembroke,
5	Ambrose Cramer,	W. Busteed, Joseph Franklin,
6	Robert Atkins.	Js. Crook, Ambrose Jackson.

GEORGE II.

7	Thomas Brown,	John Atkins, William Lane,
8	Hugh Millerd,	Daniel Eagan, Thomas Austen,
9	John Atkins,	Francis Healy, Harding Parker,
1730	Joseph Austen,	Whitwell Hignet, J. Baldwin,
1	James Hulet,	James Piersy, Robert Travers,
2	Samuel Croker,	W. Newenham, A. Newman,
3	Thomas Pembroke	Robert Dring, Walter Lavit,
4	George Fuller,	Thomas Farren, W. Delahoide,
5	Ambrose Jackson,	Wm. Fuller, Thomas Brown,
6	Thomas Farren,	Daniel Crone, Richard Bradshaw
7	John Baldwin,	C. Carleton, H. Townsend,
8	Adam Newman,	Randall Westropp, Na. Barry,
9	William Fuller,	John Terry, Noblet Phillips,
1740	Harding Parker,	George Fuller, William Clark,
1	Richard Bradshaw,	William Taylor, W. Winthrop,
2	William Owgan,	Mathias Smith, H. Millerd,
3	Randall Westropp,	Robert Wrixon, W. Harding,
4	William Winthrop	Sir R. Cox, bt. Usher Philpott,
5	Walter Lavit,	Nicholas Ford, David Bruce,
6	William Taylor,	Phineas Bury, W. Holmes,
7	Hugh Millerd,	W. Busteed, George Hodder,
8	Daniel Crone,	James Chatterton, John Reily,
9	William Holmes,	John Webb, John Swete,
1750	Robert Wrixon,	Sir J. Freke, bt. R. Newenham,
1	William Busteed,	Francis Carleton, Hugh Swayne,
2	Mathias Smith,	John Wrixon, Stephen Denroche
3	Sir John Freke, bt.	John Cossart, Kevan Izod,
4	George Hodder,	John Smith, Joseph Witheral,

Year.	Mayors.	Sheriffs.
5	John Reily,	Samuel Maylor, Godfrey Baker,
6	William Harding,	Thomas Newenham, John Roe,
7	Usher Philpott,	Boyle Travers, P. Westropp,
8	John Swete,	W. Parks, Christopher Collis,
9	Phineas Bury,	And. Franklin, Dan. Connor.

GEORGE III.

1760	Joseph Witheral,	H. Harding, Thomas Owgan,
1	Andrew Franklin,	W. Fitton, James Morrisson,
2	John Wrixon,	Walter Travers, Robert Lane,
3	John Smith,	Francis Rowland, Wm. Coles,
4	Boyle Travers,	Henry Wrixon, Wm. Butler,
5	William Parks,	Samuel Rowland, W. Wilcocks,
6	Samuel Maylor,	John Travers, John Harding,
7	James Chatterton,	S. Twogood French, H. Lawton,
8	Noblet Phillips,	Sober Kent, Richard Lloyd,
9	Godfrey Baker,	Benj. Bousfield, Rich. Kellet,
1770	Christopher Collis,	Peter Coffart, Jasper Lucas,
1	John Webb,	John Wrixon, Henry Puxley,
2	John Roe,	Richard Harris, John Franklin,
3	Francis Rowland,	Kingf. Berry, Fr. Carleton, junr,
4	John Travers,	Thomas Fuller, Philip Bennett,
5	William Butler,	W. Lawton, M. R. Westropp, Charles Denroche,
6	Hugh Lawton,	John Day, William Leycester,
7	Thomas Owgan,	Thos. Harding, Richard Lane,
8	Palms Westropp,	Chrif. Lawton, Richard Purcell,
9	John Harding,	Michael Busteed, Vesian Pick,
1780	Francis Carleton,	James Kingston, Aylmer Allen,
1	Walter Travers,	K. Hutchinson, Peter Dumas,
2	Sober Kent,	John Thompson, J. Lindsay,
3	Richard Kellet,	John Shaw, Thomas Waggett,
4	James Morrison,	Philip Allen, Hum. Crowley,
5	Sir John Franklin,	William Lumley, Hen. Sadlier,
6	Sir Sam. Rowland,	Christ. Allen, Christ. Waggett,
7	James Kingston,	Rowland Morrisson, Jef. Piercy,
8	Richard Purcell,	J. Herbert Orpen, Paul Maylor,

Henry

EVENTS. 291

Year.	Mayors.	Sheriffs.
9	Henry Harding, who died, and was succeeded by Hum. Crowly,	Thos. Harding, jun. N. Johnson,
1790	Richard Harris,	C. Fergufon, Sir H. B. Hayes,
1	Henry Puxley,	James Sadleir, Thomas Dorman.

GOVERNORS of the CITY of CORK, since the Revolution.

Lord Clare and Mon. Boileau, for King James,	1689
The Earl of Tyrone, and Colonel Roger McElligot, governors;—lord-lieutenant of the County for King James, Lord Mount-Cafhel;—deputy-lieutenants, Pierce Nagle, Daniel McCarthy Reagh, O'Sullivan Bear, and Charles M'Carthy, alias Donough,—in the year.	1690
Colonel Hales and Colonel Haftings, for King William, upon the furrender of the city	1691
Sir Richard Cox, knt.	1691
Sir Toby Purcell, knt.	1692
Sir James Jeffereys, knt.	1701
James Jeffereys, efq;	1722
General Gervais Parker,	1746
Lieutenant-General James St. Clare,	1752
Lord Robert Bertie,	1764
Colonel John Wynne,	1769
Nicholas Lyfaght, efq;	1778
Thomas Pigott, efq;	1782
Mountifort Longfield, efq;	1789

SHERIFFS of the COUNTY of CORK.

Year.	High-Sheriffs.	Sub-Sheriffs.
1753	Richard Townfend,	Charles M'Carthy,
4	John Lyfaght,	Thomas Allen,
5	Philip Oliver,	Edward Daunt,
6	Robert Rogers,	William Heard,

REMARKABLE

Year.	High-Sheriffs.	Sub-Sheriffs.
7	John Lyfaght,	Rider Doe,
8	Richard Longfield,	Thomas Farren,
1760	Abraham Morris,	Edward Irwin,
1	Wallis Colthurst,	Daniel M'Carthy,
2	Abraham Devonshire,	Robert Reeves,
3	Walter Baldwin,	John Warren,
4	Emanuel Moore,	Jonas Lander,
5	Nicholas Dunfcomb,	Daniel M'Carthy,
6	Walter Aikin,	James Wherland,
7	Roger Bernard,	Francis Kiernan,
8	Nicholas Lyfaght,	Benjamin Hayes,
9	Jonas Morris,	Daniel M'Carthy,
1770	Hon. John S. Barry,	Thomas Chatterton,
1	Benjamin Bousfield,	John Warren,
2	John Wallis,	James Gregg,
3	Sir Robert Deane,	Daniel M'Carthy,
4	Maffey Hutchefon,	Peter Deane,
5	Matthew Freeman,*	Noblet Rogers,
6	James Uniacke,	George Jack,
7	Henry Baldwin,	Daniel M'Carthy,
8	William Wrixon,	William Philips,
9	William Wrixon,	Noblet Rogers,
1780	Hon. Hayes St. Leger,	George Jack,
1	Sir James Cotter,	Daniel M'Carthy,
2	Abraham Morris,	Abraham Abbott,
3	William Chetwynd,	Thomas Warner,
4	Thomas Hungerford,	John Minton,
5	R. Boyle Townfend,	John Pyne,
6	Broderick Chinnery,	George Jack,
7	Wm. W. Newenham,	John Barry,
8	Sir N. Con. Colthurst,	John Franklin,
9	George Dunfcombe,	John Pyne,
1790	Joseph Capel,	William Allen,
1	Arthur O'Connor.	William Lane.

* *Mr. Freeman died in office, and was fucceeded by John Longfield.*

JUDGES

JUDGES in CORK, from 1753, to 1791.

Year.	Spring Assizes.	Summer Assizes.
1753	Baron Mountney, Juftice Blenerhaffet,	Lord chief jus. Caulfield, Juftice French,
4	Lord chief juf. Caulfield, Juftice French,	Lord chief Baron Bowes, Boylen Whitney, efq;
5	Lord chief juftice York, Juftice Marfhall,	Lord chief jus. Caulfield, Juftice Marfhall,
6	Lord chief jus. Caulfield, Juftice French,	Baron Mountney, John Smyth, efq;
7	Lord chief jus. Caulfield, Juftice French,	Lord chief jus. Caulfield, Juftice French.
8	Juftice Marfhall, Juftice Robinfon,	Lord chief jus. Caulfield, Juftice Robinfon,
9	Lord chief jus. Caulfield, Baron Dawfon,	Lord chief jus. Willes, Prime Serjeant Scott,
1760	Baron Dawfon, Juftice Marfhall,	Lord chief jus. Caulfield, Serjeant Malone,
1	Lord chief jus. Flood, Juftice Scott,	Baron Dawfon, Prime Serjeant Tennifon,
2	Lord chief jus. Afton, Serjeant Malone,	Juftice Tennifon, Pr. Ser. H. Hutchinfon,
3	Lord chief jus. Flood, Juftice Scott,	Lord chief juftice Afton, Baron Mountney,
4	Lord chief Baron Willes, Serjeant Patterfon,	Lord chief juftice Afton, Baron Mountney,
5	Lord chief Baron Willes, Juftice Tennifon,	Lord chief Baron Willes, Solicitor-gen. Patterfon,
6	Lord chief jus. Clayton, Serjeant Malone,	Baron Mountney, Serjeant Dennis,
7	Baron Mountney, Juftice Malone,	Juftice Malone, Pr. Ser. H. Hutchinfon,
8	Lord chief jus. Clayton, Serjeant Dennis,	Lord chief Baron Forfter Serjeant Dennis,
9	Lord chief jus. Clayton, Baron Scott,	Lord chief Baron Forfter Serjeant Malone,
1770	Lord chief jus. Clayton, Juftice Henn,	Lord chief Baron Forfter Juftice Malone,

Year.	Spring Assizes.	Summer Assizes.
1771	Justice Henn, Counsellor Fitzgibbon,	Lord chief jus. Forster, Justice Malone,
2	Justice Henn, Solicitor-General Lill,	Lord chief jus. Patterson, Justice Robinson,
3	Justice Henn, Baron Power,	Justice Robinson, Justice Henn,
4	Baron Power, Thomas Maunsell, esq;	Justice Henn, Baron Hamilton,
5	Lord chief jus. Patterson, Justice Henn,	Justice Robinson, Justice Tennison,
6	Baron Power, Justice Lill,	Justice Henn, Justice Lill,
7	Serjeant Carleton, Justice Lill,	Lord chief jus. Patterson, Justice Henn,
8	Lord chief Baron Dennis, Baron Power,	Lord chief Baron Dennis Justice Henn,
9	Justice Henn, Solicitor-Gen. Carleton,	Baron Power, Justice Lill,
1780	Lord chief jus. Patterson, Justice Henn,	Lord chief Baron Dennis Justice Henn,
1	Lord Tracton, Justice Lill,	Justice Henn, Baron Power,
2	Lord Tracton, Justice Lill,	Lord chief jus. Patterson, Justice Henn,
3	Lord chief Baron Burgh, Baron Power,	Justice Henn, Baron Hamilton,
4	Baron Power, Justice Kelly,	Lord Baron Earlsfort, Chief Justice Patterson,
5	Lord chief B. Yelverton, Baron Hamilton,	Lord Earlsfort, Justice Henn,
6	Justice Kelly, Sir Samuel Bradstreet,	Chief Baron Yelverton, Justice Henn,
7	Baron Hamilton, Sir Samuel Bradstreet,	Lord Baron Earlsfort, Justice Henn,
8	Baron Hamilton, Justice Kelly,	Chief Baron Yelverton, Justice Henn,
9	Lord chief jus. Carleton, Hon. Geo. Hamilton,	Chief Baron Yelverton, Justice Henn,

EVENTS.

Year.	Spring Assizes.	Summer Assizes.
1790	Juſtice Kelly, Baron Metge, Baron Hamilton, Juſtice Kelly,	Juſtice Henn, Sir Samuel Bradſtreet, Chief Baron Yelverton, Juſtice Hellen.

ROMAN CATHOLIC MAYORS of YOUGHALL.

****

Year. Henry VIII.
1542 M. Portingall,
   3 J. Forreſt,
   4 W. Walſh,
   5 R. Bluet.
      Edward VI.
   6 D. Portingall,
   7 R. Gough,
   8 W. Walſh,
   9 C. Walſh,
1550 J. Bluet,
   1 R. Gough,
   2 F. Tobin,
      Mary I.
   3 W. Anyas,
   4 W. Shears,
   5 R. Gough,
   6 T. Uniacke,
   7 T. Bluet.
      Elizabeth.
   8 P. Ronayne,
   9 T. Bluet,
1560 T. Uniack,
   1 J. Portingall,
   2 F. Gallevan,
   3 R. Gough,
   4 T. Coppinger,
   5 J. Walſh,
   6 T. Bluet,

Year.
   7 P. Bluet,
   8 P. Forreſt,
   9 F. Anyas,
1570 J. Portingall,
   1 M. Bluet,
   2 J. Portingall,
   3 T. Coppinger,
   4 T. Bluet,
   5 J. Collins,
   6 F. Anyas,
   7 P. Bluet,
   8 P. Forreſter,
   9 P. Coppinger,
1580 J. Gallevan,
   1 F. Anyas,
   2 T. Coppinger,
   3 P. Brennet,
   4 P. Brennet,
   5 J. Kerring,
   6 T. Coppinger,
   7 H. Portingall,
   8 Sir W. Raleigh,
   9 W. Magner,
1590 J. Ronayne,
   1 J. Bluet,
   3 J. Forreſt,
   4 J. Kerny,
   5 H. Portingal,
      J. Bluet,

Year.		Year.	
6	J. Bluet,	6	J. Gough,
7	P. Walsh,	7	J. Every,
8	J. Forrest,	8	C. Hartford,
9	J. Ronayne,	9	W. Blunt,
1600	C. Collegue,	1620	W. Lewellan,
1	J. Kerny,	1	T. Holdship,
2	J. Gallevan.	2	E. Gough,
	JAMES I.	3	W. Lewellin,
3	J. Gallevan,	4	W. Bluet.
4	E. Coppinger,		CHARLES I.
5	J. Gallevan,	5	R. Gough,
6	N. Gallevan,	6	J. Coppinger,
7	J. Gough,	7	E. Stout,
8	J. Kerny.	8	J. Coppinger,
9	J. Every,	9	T. Roynane,
1610	N. Gallevan,	1630	P. Meagh,
1	J. Coppinger,	1	D. Walsh,
2	R. Gough,	2	P. Collins,
3	T. Roynane,	3	W. Walsh,
4	J. Every,	4	F. Stout.
5	E. Coppinger,		

☞ This year Bailiffs were allowed as magistrates; J. Collins, and J. Kernie, first Bailiffs.

	MAYORS.	BAILIFFS.
5	W. Bluet,	J. Ronayne, E. Gibbon,
6	R. Gough,	M. Uniacke, J. Gallevan,
7	J. Ronayne,	J. Coppinger, N. Nagle,
8	W. Gough,	W. Gough, J. Gallevan,
9	M. Uniacke,	T. Bluet, J. Hazard,
1640	T. Stout,	W. Coppinger, D. Bluet,
1	J. Gallevan,	W. Kerine, N. Bagbeare,
2	T. Stout,	D. Bluet, R. Mayers,
3	T. Stout,	J. Clove, J. Bucknerr,
4	J. Miller.	J. Vandelure, J. Taylor,
5	T. Stout,	T. Warren, R. Pratt,
6	A. Warren,	J. Britishford, T. Farmer.
7	R. Myers,	J. Britishford, T. Farmer,
8	T. Taylor,	A. Wandrick, T. Farmer,
		T. Warren.

EVENTS. 297

Year.	Mayors.	Bailiffs.
9	T. Warren,	H. Heard, G. Barnett,
1650	J. Langer,	T. Stephens, F. Baker,
1	A. Wandrick,	J. Cox, J. Mardock,
2	J. Britilhford,	J. Sims, J. Farthing,
3	J. Cox,	R. Gillet, T. Barker,
4	T. Farmer,	J. Nettles, T. Vaughan,
5	J. Morduck,	N. Stout, N. Stout.

PROTESTANT MAYORS and BAILIFFS.

KING CHARLES II.

6	J. Farthing,	J. Handcock, S. Clove,
7	J. Nettles,	H. Stout, P. Godwin,
8	T. Vaughan,	G. Davis, H. Davis,
9	T. Warren.	J. Luther, A. Vaughan,
1660	R. Mayers,	J. Stout, P. Hazard,
1	N. Stout,	A. Vaughan, H. Spencer,
2	J. Stout,	H. Deaton, W. Norman,
3	J. Langer,	N. Stout, J. Hazard,
4	R. Giles,	E. Percy, J. Pine.
5	T. Baker,	W. Sargent, R. Swimmer,
6	J. Luther,	S. Hayman, T. Hilgrove.
7	N. Deaton,	J. Merrick, G. Giles,
8	J. Hancock,	B. Morduck, W. Clove,
9	A. Farthing,	E. Lowndz, R. Waters,
1670	S. Hayman,	B. Bryan, R. Yeats,
1	E. Lowndz,	T. Cafoban, J. Gerald,
2	E. Lowndz,	T. Cafoban, J. Gerald,
3	M. Spencer,	A. Spencer, R. Lawndz,
4	E. Perry,	J. Atkins, R. Bevit,
5	D. Atkins,	R. Carcen, W. Palmer,
6	N. Lucas,	W. Hilbard, A. Hopkins,
7	J. Merrick,	E. Crockford, J. Clove,
8	J. Spencer,	J. Morduck, L. Dantner,
9	E. Lawndz,	R. Paradife, R. Ball,
1680	R. Yeats,	F. Baker, W. Sargent,
2	F. Luther,	J. Lucas, E. Nicholas,
3	J. Clove,	J. Scanaden, A. Vaughan,
4	R. Paradife,	D. Haliahan, R. Giles,

JAMES

REMARKABLE

JAMES II.

Year.	Mayors.	Bailiffs.
4	E. Crockford,	J. Cook, A. Luther,
5	J. Spencer,	J. Hayman, R. Walter,
6	O'Cook,	T. Vaughan, F. Farmer,
7	R. Giles,	H. Row, W. Turbit,

WILLIAM and MARY's REIGN.

8	N. Ronayne,	T. Walters, D. Roe,
9	A. Perry,	J. Scamaden, D. Lynch,
1690	R. Ball,	D. Seymour, D. Price,
1	F. Baker,	T. Seymour, D. Price,
2	R. Giles,	T. Croker, D. Donovan,
3	F. Walters,	S. Paradife, L. Knight,
4	J. Lucas,	G. Blackwell, D. Quade,
5	E. Nicholas,	R. Farthing, T. Coulins,
6	T. Croker,	S. Green, D. Bodwin,
7	J. Cook,	E. Landz, T. Taylor,
8	J. Scamaden,	W. Cooke, J. Salter,
9	J. Cook,	G. Salter, T. Elliot,
1700	J. Price.	S. Hayman, F. Murdock.

QUEEN ANN's REIGN.

1	J. Lucas,	D. Luther, D. Murdock,
2	T. Croker,	F. Mills, T. Buckner,
3	D. Luther,	T. Baker, E. Landz,
4	S. Hayman,	W. Knight, T. Carr,
5	T. Hayman,	F. Seymour, D. Farmer.
6	E. Landz,	C. Rea, F. Geazely,
7	J. Mills,	A. Ryland, T. Seymour,
8	W. Cook,	F. Oliver, T. Roper,
9	J. Luther,*	J. Freeman, S. Gardener,
1710	B. Murdock,	T. Farmer, S. Knight,
1	F. Baker,	J. Perry, J. Merrick,
2	T. Croker,	G. Giles, H. Ball,
3	R. Giles,	J. Lucas, R. Walters.

* *J. Luther died in office, and was succeeded by M. Lucas, who also died, and was succeeded by R. Giles.*

GEORGE

EVENTS.

GEORGE I.

Year.	Mayors.	Bailiffs.
4	J. Knight,	O. Nicholfon, — Champion,
5	G. Salter,	— Green, E. Giles,
6	J. Ryland,	T. Cook, T. Farmer,
7	C. Rea,	R. Taylor, G. Mannix,
8	R. Walters,	— Pratt, — Giles,
9	M. Lucas,	S. Green, T. Croker,
1720	T. Croker,	T. Buckner, G. Mernyne,
1	E. Gillet,	— Farmer, — Cahill
2	H. Ball,	T. Uniacke, J. Parker,
3	T. Uniacke,	— Vaughan, — Emington,
4	G. Giles,	A. Taylor, C. Elmore,
5	T. Knight,	R. Giles, C. Nixon,
6	G. Salter,	B. Croker, P. Mills.

GEORGE II.

7	G. Giles,	E. Jones, W. Coghlan,
8	E. Jones,	R. Cozens, S. Gardner,
9	H. Ball,	W. Emington, — Rogers,
1730	W. Emington,	T. Fudge, J. Nealon,
1	R. Giles,	J. Green, T. Cozens.
2	J. Parker,	W. Coleman, E. Gillet,
3	J. Parker,	H. Ruthven, — Freeman,
4	W. Coghlan,	T. Green, — Mannix,
5	L. Freeman,	H. Rogers, F. Browne,
6	H. Ruthven,	E. Uniacke, S. Luther,
7	T. Fudge,	B. Green, N. Rogers,
8	N. Rogers,	— Uniacke, T. Fifher,
9	S. Luther,	S. Hayman, T. French,
1740	G. Giles,	J. Price, R. Day,
1	B. Green,	T. Taylor, B. Merrick,
2	S. Hayman,	E. Green, J. Nixon,
3	J. Freeman,	S. Pratt, J. Merrick,
4	B. Croker,	T. Cook, J. Knight,
5	B. Croker,	J. Day, J. Lander,
6	T. Cook,	W. Taylor, T. Child,
7	T. Cook,	E. Green, E. Dartnell,
8	G. Mannix,	J. Hayman, J. Pratt,
		H. Rogers,

Year.	Mayors.	Bailiffs.
9	H. Rogers,	N. Giles, R. Croker,
1750	J. Hayman,	J. Labatt, T. Gimlett,
1	J. Hayman,	C. Fisher, R. Gore,
2	J. Labatt,	S. Allen, W. Molton,
3	J. Labatt,	J. Cook, G. Giles,
4	J. Cook,	B. Taylor, J. Bryan,
5	J. Uniacke,	R. Green, R. Webb,
6	N. Giles,	R. Ball, H. Coghlan,
7	J. Uniacke,	R. Seymour, T. Day,
8	R. Webb,	P. Power, R. Taylor,
9	H. Coghlan,	J. Giles, W. Roche,
1760	J. Pratt,	G. Fudge, G. Fudge.

GEORGE III.

Year	Mayors	Bailiffs
1761	R. Green,	R. Smith, R. Douthat,
2	S. Allen,	T. Green, W. Jackson,
3	P. Power,	W. Merrick, E. Smith,
4	T. Green,	O. Greatrakes, T. Fudge,
5	R. Green,	W. Gardner, T. Webb,
6	P. Power,	M. Parker, W. Nealon,
7	M. Parker,	G. Nash, J. Seymour,
8	B. Taylor,	H. Swayne, J. Hobson,
9	R. Green,	T. Fudge, P. Ellis,
1770	H. Swayne,	N. Stout, R. Uniacke,
1	S. Allen,	W. Meade, W. Pearce,
2	T. Lander,	T. Fieldhouse, T. Stroud,
3	R. Green,	J. Swayne, J. Allen,
4	N. Norcott,	W. Hayman, W. Jackson,
5	W. Jackson,	R. Dartnel, J. Brian,
6	J. Swayne,	R. Green, J. Pratt,
7	R. Uniacke,	H. Swayne, J. Merrick,
8	R. Green,	J. Swayne, H. Browne,
9	H. Swayne,	N. Stout, E. Green,
1780	W. Jackson,	S. Freeman, J. Gimblet,
1	R. Uniacke,	J. Ellard, D. Freeman,
2	T. Green,	J. Reeves, J. Lombard,
3	W. Jackson,	J. Sedgwick, J. Smith,
4	D. Freeman,	B. M. Jackson, S. Allen, J. Allen,

Year.	Mayors.	Bailiffs.
5	J. Allen,	T. Green, E. Green,
6	J. Sedgwicke,	W. Jackson, S. Nealon,
7	S. Allen,	B. M. Jackson, J. Green,
8	W. A. Haymay,	W. Merrick, J. Sedgwicke,
9	B. M. Jackson,	J. Green, R. Seymour,
1790	T. Green,	J. Hudson, T. John,
1	W. Jackson,	J. Scamaden, W. Huxtable.

RECORDERS of YOUGHALL.

1724 Henry Rugge,
1755 James Dennis, afterwards Lord Tracton.
1781 George Ponsonby.

TOWN-CLERKS.

1720 Charles Prince,
1758 William Coghlan,
1764 Thomas Cooke,
1773 Richard Martin,
1784 William Jenkin.

F I N I S.

The following Books, of established reputation, are to be had at EDWARDS's, *No. 6, Castle-street, opposite the Merchants New Coffee-House.*

            £. s. d.
Annual Register, from 1758 to 1778, 31 vols. 11 15 1
(Continued annually at 7s. 7d. per volume.)
Annual Register (new) or General Repository
 of History, Politics, and Literature; to
 which is prefixed, the History of Know-
 ledge, Learning, and Taste, in Great-
 Britain, 11 volumes neatly bound   5 0 0

CATALOGUE.

	£.	s.	d.

The same, elegantly bound and gilt 5 8 0
(Continued annually at 9s. 2d.h per vol.)
Any volume of the above work may be had at Edwards's.

Anderson's Observations on the means of exciting a Spirit of National Industry 2 vols. 0 10 10

Alison's Essays on the Nature and Principles of Taste, 0 6 6

Abelard's Letters to Heloisa, with the Answers; to which is prefixed, an account of their Amours and Misfortunes; together with the Poem of Eloisa to Abelard, by Mr. Pope, 0 2 8h

Bell's beautiful Edition of the Poets of Great-Britian, from Chaucer to Churchill, embellished with near 200 cuts; 109 vols. elegantly bound, gilt, and registered, 18 4 0

Bruce's Travels to discover the Source of the Nile, 6 vols. 2 5 6

—— (Peter-Henry) Memoirs of a Military Officer in the service of Prussia, Russia, and Great-Britain, 0 6 6

Beauties selected from the Works of Shakespare, 0 3 3

Beauties selected from M. Genlis, for the use of Children, 0 3 3

British Album, containing the Poems of Della Crusca, Anna Matilda, Abley, Benedict, the Bard, &c. &c. 0 4 4

Chambers's Dictionary of Arts and Sciences, 4 vols. 13 13 0

Coke on Lyttleton, with Notes by Hargrave and Butler, 2 16 10h

Cook's last Voyage Round the World, 3 v. 8vo. 1 2 9

Cherington's Memoirs; containing a description of the present Portuguese, 0 2 8h

Citizen of the World, 2 vols. 0 6 6

Companion to the Fire Side, 0 3 3

Chrysal; or the Adventures of a Guinea, 2 v. 0 7 7

Doddington's (George Bub) Diary, 0 3 3

Don

CATALOGUE.

	£.	s.	d.
Don Quixotte, by Smollet, *last edition*, 4 vols.	0	13	0
Evening Amusements for the Ladies,	0	2	8h
Enfield's Speaker; or Miscellaneous Pieces; selected from the best English writers, and disposed under proper heads, with a view to facilitate the improvement of Youth; to which is added (not in any other edition) the Elements of Gesture, by John Walker,	0	3	3
Enfield's Speaker, vol. 2d.	0	3	3
——— Biographical Sermons,	0	4	4
Elegiac Sonnets, by Charlotte Smith; with additional Sonnets,	0	2	2
Elegiac Lyre; a collection of Original Poetry, by Mark Charters,	0	2	2
Guthrie's General Gazetteer, a new edition,	0	8	8
——— Geography; *London edition*,	0	9	9
Goulard, on the Virtues of the Extract of Lead	0	2	8h
Glass's Complete Confectionary, made plain and easy,	0	2	8h
Gray's Abridgment of the History of England for Children,	0	2	2
Gibbon's Decline and Fall of the Roman Empire complete, 6 vols.	2	12	0

Those who has the *first* part of the above *Work, which ends with the Fall of the Roman empire in the West, may be supplied with the latter part, by applying to* A. Edwards.

Harris on the Use of the Globes,	0	4	10h
Historical, Political, and Literary Register, for 1769,	0	6	6
Holt's Characters of the Kings and Queens of England, intended for the Instruction of Youth,	0	6	6
Hoyle on Games; improved by Beaufort and Jones; epitomized to a convenient size for the pocket,	0	1	7h
Hooper's Memoirs of the year 2500, 2 vols.	0	5	5
Hume's History of England, *last edition*, 8 v.	2	12	0

Continu-

CATALOGUE.

	£.	s.	d.
Continuation of ditto, to the Death of George the Second, 5 vols.	1	12	6
Hervey's (Rev. James) Collection of Letters; to which is prefixed, an Account of his Life and Death, 2 vols.	0	6	6
Jackson's Instructions for Teaching Book-Keeping,	0	4	10h
Junius's Letters, *best edition*, 2 vols.	0	6	6
Letters from Edinburgh, describing the Manners and Customs of the People of that City, 2 vols.	0	6	6
Lounger (The) A periodical Paper, written at Edinburgh, by a Society of learned Men, 3 vols.	0	9	0
Labourer's Account-Book; by which an Account may be kept on one Page of forty different kinds of Workmen for a Week; the book will last a year,	0	2	0
Lodge's Peerage of England, Scotland, and Ireland, 7 vols.	3	8	3
Lady Mary Worthly Montague's Letters,	0	3	3
Mirror (The) A Periodical Paper, by the Author of the Lounger; containing the celebrated Story of Le Fleur, 2 vols.	0	6	6
Mason's celebrated English Garden,	0	3	3
Mrs. Teachum and her Nine Pupils,	0	1	7h
Mann's Catechism, *a new edition*, printed on good Paper, by A. Edwards; 1l. 4s. *per hundred,*—each	0	0	4
Prayer-Books of all Sizes and Bindings, from 1s. 6d. to	2	5	6
Pope's Homer's Illiad, *a new edition*, adapted for schools, 4 vols.	0	13	0
Renal's History of the European Settlements in the East and West-Indies, 6 vols.	2	5	6
The same in French, 7 vols. 8vo.	2	5	6
Reeve's History of the English law,—a necessary Book for all Gentlemen, 4 vols.	1	8	0
Rollin's Ancient History, 10 vols.	1	12	6
Rambles of Philo and his Man Sturdy,	0	3	3

Smollet's

CATALOGUE.

	£.	s.	d.
Smollet's Continuation of Hume's History of England, 5 vols.	1	12	6
Sheridan's Pronouncing Dictionary, *new edition*,	0	8	8
——— English Grammar,	0	2	8h
Shakespare's Dramatic and Poetic Works complete, with a Glossary, 3 vols.	2	0	0
Sterne's Works complete, 7 vols.	0	18	11h
——— Letters to his Friends,	0	2	8h
——— Sentimental Journey,	0	2	8h
——— Tristram Shandy, 3 vols.	0	8	1h
Scott's new Pronouncing Dictionary,	0	3	3
Spelling-Dictionary for the Pocket, *a beautiful edition by* Peacock,	0	4	4
The same by Entick,	0	5	5
The same, *a common edition*,	0	2	2
Tales of the Castle; or Stories of Instruction and Delight, by M. Genlis, 4 vols.	0	13	0
Theatre de Education, 4 tome.	0	10	10
Thickness's Travels in Spain, 2 vols.	0	5	5
The World Displayed; being a Collection of Voyages and Travels; in all 21 vols.	2	5	6
Yorrick's Letters to Eliza,	0	0	6h

Italian, Spanish, and Portuguese Dictionaries and Grammars,

Greek, Latin, French, English, and Irish Dictionaries and Grammars, of all kinds; with every kind of Book used in Classical and other Schools.

Religious Books of all Descriptions.

Newberry and Burton Books, for the Amusement of Children.

Walker's, Exshaw's, and the Universal Magazines and Reviews, arrive regularly to *Edwards*.

Almanacks, Registries, Directories, Pocket-Ledgers and Memorandum-Books, for Gentlemen and Ladies.

All the Public Acts of Parliament, as soon as printed.

Tragedies, Comedies, Operas, and Farces, &c. &c.

MUSICAL ARTICLES.

Instructions for for the Harpsichord, Violoncello, Tenor, Violin, Flute, Guitar, and Singing.

CATALOGUE.

Ruled Music Books and Paper, for all Inſtruments.
Violoncello, Harpſichord, Guitar, and Violin Strings, always to be had freſh

VARNISHING ARTICLES.

Paper, Prints, Borders, Feſtoons, Flowers, Sprigs, Corners and Bruſhes, for that agreeable employment for Females.

Lundy Foot's Snuff;—Straſburg, Rappee, and Carrot Pigtail, always to be had freſh.

EDWARDS is conſtantly ſupplied with the following Articles in the *Stationary Line*, at the cheapeſt Prices.

LETTER PAPERS.	PLAIN.				GILT.			
	p.	Q	p	R	p	Q	p	R.
Beſt Engliſh Demy Royal	1	1	19	0	2	2	34	1h
The ſame Extra Thick	1	3	22	9	2	6	45	6
Beſt Engliſh Thick Poſt	0	11	17	0	1	8	29	3
The ſame large, for Merchts. uſe	1	0	18	5	2	0	36	0
Beſt Engliſh Thin Poſt,	0	8	12	0	1	4	22	9
The ſame large, for Merchts. uſe	0	10	14	0	1	8	28	0
Thick Poſt lined for Ladies writing	1	1	19	0	2	2	34	1h
Pankers very thin Poſt	1	0	16	0	2	0	32	0
Baſkerville's ſingle glazed Poſt	1	6	26	0	3	0	52	0
—— double ditto	2	2	38	0	4	4	68	3

☞ Folio Papers double the price of Letter; Mourning Papers ſame Price as Gilt

Edwards has a curious ſort of Wove Letter Paper, which is getting very much into uſe.

Drawing Papers, from 2d to 1s 1d per Sheet

Vellum Paper for Varniſh Work, from 6d h to 1s 7d h per Sheet.

India Paper, for Artificial Flowers.

Tiſſue Paper, for Gold and Silver Lace

Blue Paper for hanging Rooms, equal only to 6d p doz.

Copy Paper from 4d to 1s 4d per Quire, and from 6s. to 1l 2s 9d per Ream

All kinds of Account Books, engaged to bear Ink.

Curious Ruled Paper, for Account Books.

Superfine

CATALOGUE.

Superfine Red and Black Sealing-Wax.
Red, Black, and variegated Wafers
The whitest Wax-Candles, 2, 3, 4, or 6 to the pound.
Wax-Candles for Carriages and Lanthorns.
Wax Taper in bits at 4d 6d 10d 20d or 3s. 3d per lb.
Best Dutch'd and Clarify'd Quills and Pens, from 2s 2d.
to 4s 4d per hundred
Sliding and plain Black and Red Lead Pencils.
Black Shining and White Sand, and Pounce.
Stewart's Dublin Ink-Powder.
Best Black and Red Ink, Penknives and Ink-Stands.

ARMY STATIONARY.

Muster Rolls; Monthly, Half-Monthly, and Review Returns, for Horse and Foot; Affirmations, Passes, Discharges, Furloughs, Morning Reports, Orderly and Memorandum Books, with every Article in the *Stationary Line* made use of by the Army, which he has had the honour of serving these *nine years*.

PATENT MEDICINES.

A. Edwards is appointed, by the Proprietors of the following valuable Medicines, agent for the sale of them in the City and County of Cork; from whom he receives a fresh supply every month, and will take any of them back, that may be returned unopened.

	£.	s.	d.
Anderson's Pills—per box	0	1	7h
Adam's Solvent for the Stone and Gravel, bottle 1 3s.—large	0	1	2 9
Antiacid Lozenges, for the Heart-burn	0	1	1
Bennett's most efficacious Worm-Powder—bot.	0	2	8h
Bateman's Pectoral Drops—per bottle	0	1	4
British Oil—bottle	0	1	1
Blown Smelling-Bottles, newly invented	0	1	1
Cephalic Snuff	0	1	1
Duffy's genuine London Elixer	0	2	2
Dalby's Carminative—bottle	0	2	2
Eau de Luce in cut bottles, 2s. 2d. and	0	3	3
Essence of Coltsfoot, for Coughs	0	4	4

Essence

CATALOGUE.

	£.	s.	d.
Essence of Peppermint—bottle 1s. 7d. h. and	0	3	3
Essence of Spruce—pot will make 20 gallons	0	4	4
Godbold's Vegetable Balsam, an effectual Cure for Consumptions and Asthmas—bottle	1	2	9
Goulard's genuine Extract Saturn—bottle	0	1	1
Greenough's Tincture for the Teeth	0	1	4
Glass's genuine Magnessa—box	0	4	4
Hemet's Essence of Pearl—bottle	0	3	3
Hemet's Tooth-Powder—box	0	3	3
Hill's (Sir John) Balsam of Honey	0	4	4
Hill's (Ormskirk) Medicine, for the bite of a Mad Dog—packet	0	6	6
Hooper's Female Pills—box	0	1	7h
Huxam's Tincture of Bark—bottle	0	3	3
James's genuine Fever Powders	0	3	3
James's Analeptic Pills	0	5	5
Jesuits Drops (real London) observe each bottle signed *T. Ravenscroft*	0	2	8h
Issue Plasters, engaged to stick without filleting box	0	1	7h
Kennedy's effectual Corn Plaster—box	0	1	4
Pectoral Lozenges of Tolu, for Coughs	0	1	1
Peppermint Lozenges—box	0	1	1
Ruspini's Tooth-Powder	0	1	1
Salt of Lemon, for taking out Ink-spots and Iron-molds	0	1	1
Spilsbury's Antiscorbutic Drops—bottle	0	5	5
Steers's Opodeldoc—bottle	0	2	8h
Stoughton's great Stomach Cordial	0	1	4
Turlington's Balsam of Life—bottle	0	2	2
Velno's Vegetable Sirrup—bottle	0	13	6

PRINTING-WORK.

Books; Pamphlets; Shop-Bills; Hand-Bills; Leafes; Brewers Permits; Landlords Receipts; Tithe Notes; Manor-Court Processes and Decrees; Free Masons Summonses; Magistrates Informations, Warrants, Rocognizances, Committals, and Supercedeses; Promissory Notes; Freemens Passes, &c *done in the neatest manner, and on the cheapest terms*, by A. Edwards.

www.ingramcontent.com/pod-product-compliance
Lightning Source LLC
Chambersburg PA
CBHW030746250426
43672CB00028B/1107